TASMANIA

» IN PHOTOS «

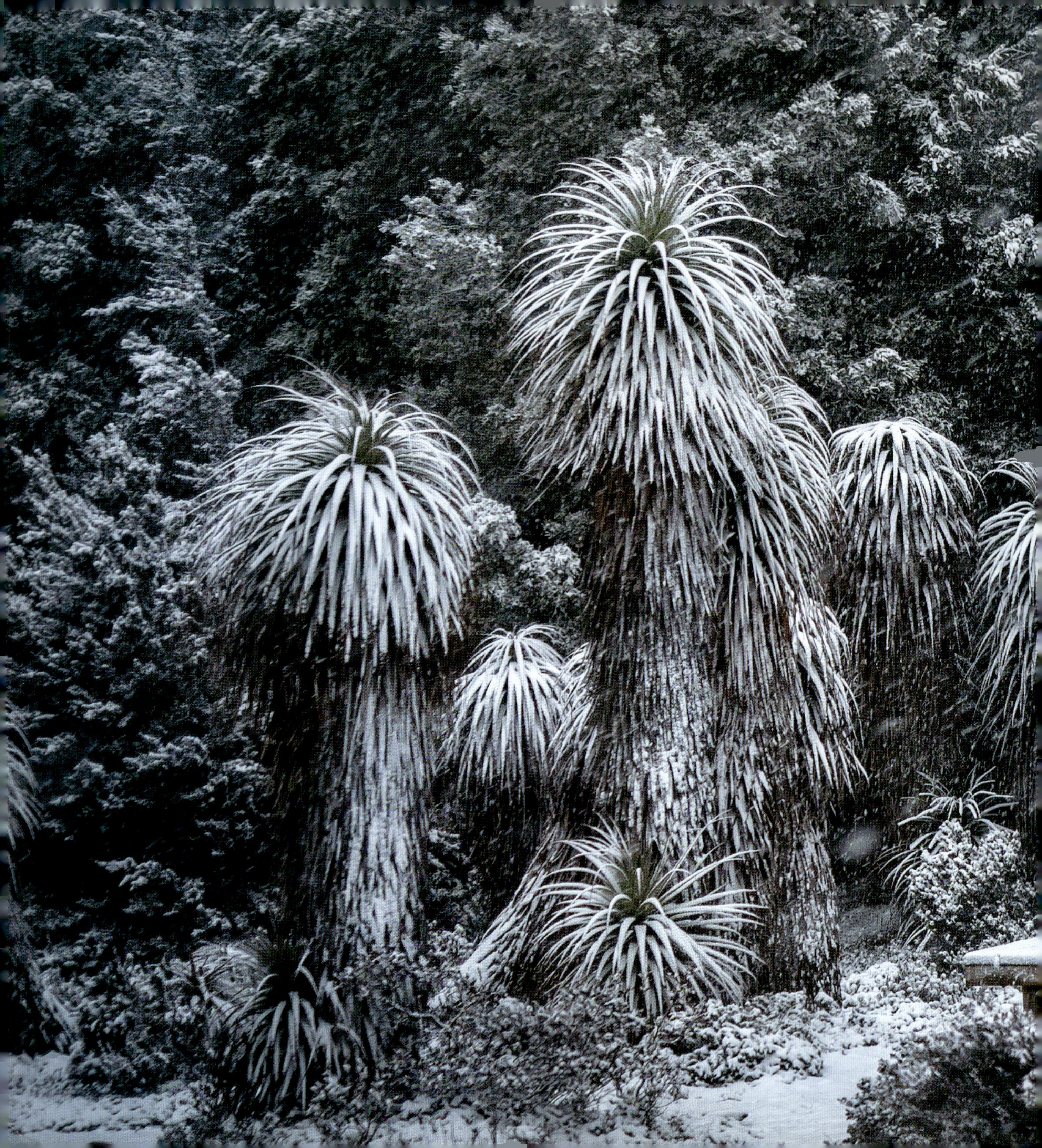

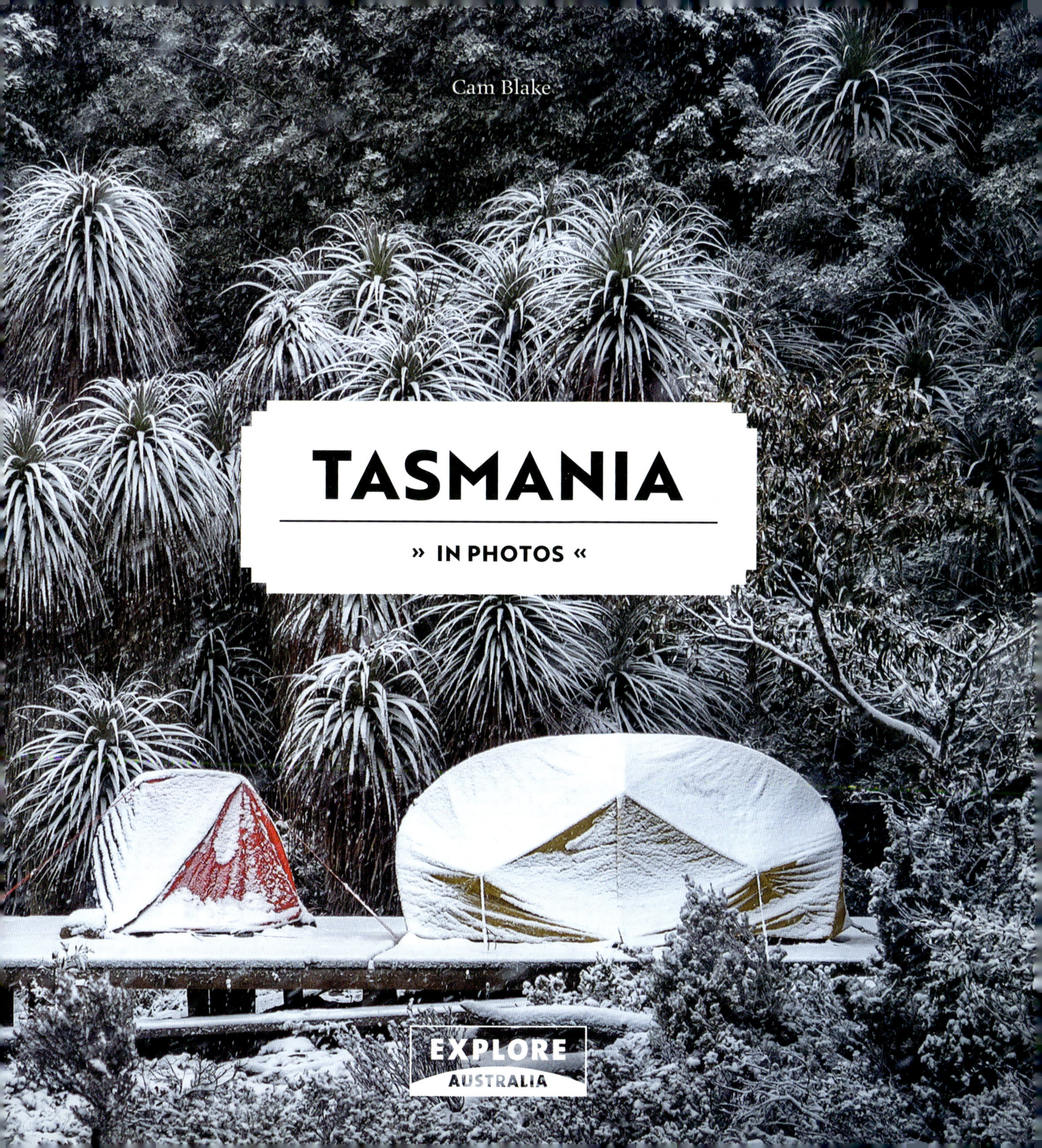

Cam Blake
TASMANIA
» IN PHOTOS «
EXPLORE
AUSTRALIA

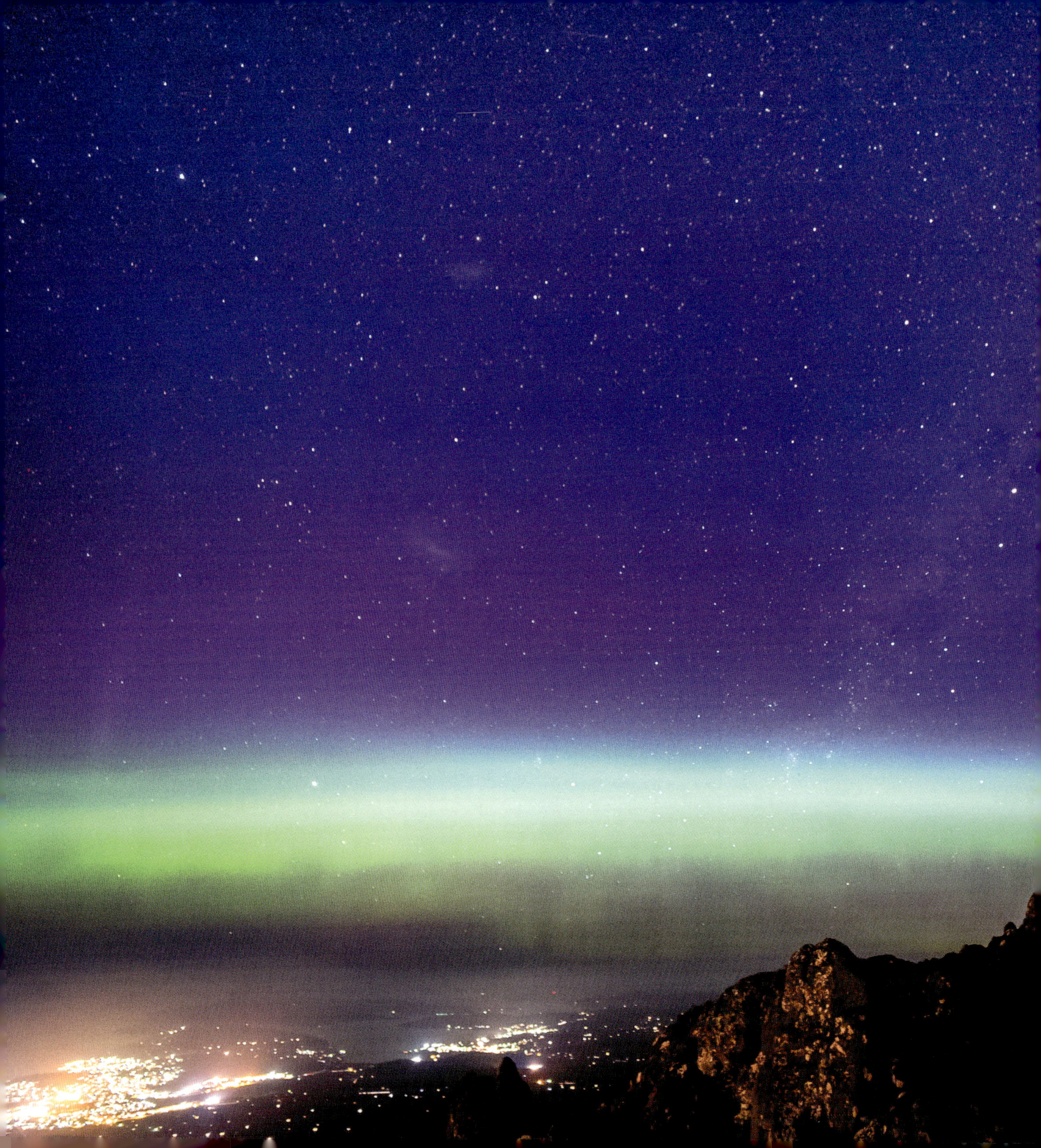

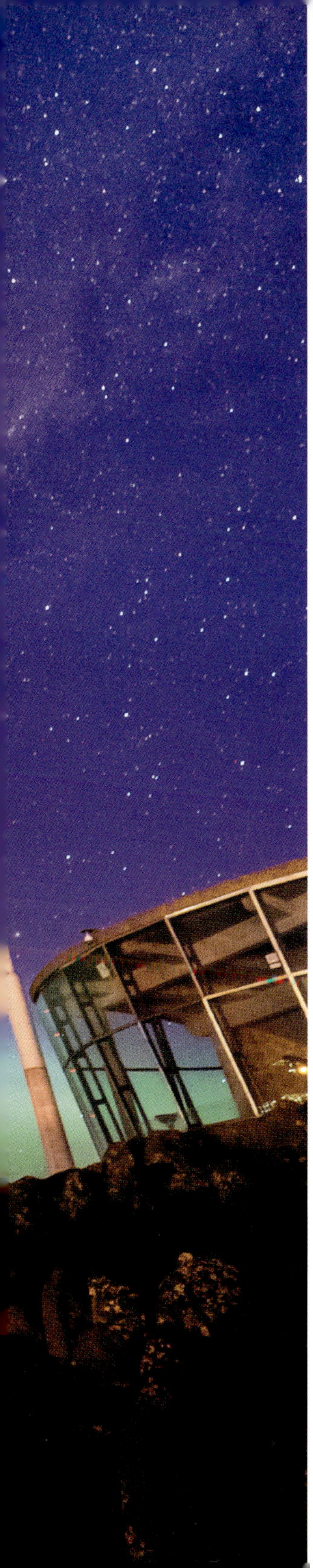

» INTRODUCTION

As a wilderness photographer living in Tasmania, I have the enviable privilege of exploring and capturing this beautiful island state. It has a knack for revealing something spectacular around every corner: whether you are sightseeing on the west coast, soaking up the sun on the east coast or dining in Hobart's buzzing waterfront region, Tasmania has it all.

Famously known for its natural beauty, Tasmania has come of age in the last decade and is now one of the world's travel hotspots. Here, you can experience all genres of travel – hike into nature and be isolated for days or live it up in luxury at the exquisite Saffire Freycinet Hotel surrounded by beautiful coastline. And our different seasons offer ever-changing attractions and natural encounters unique to Tasmania. Something for everyone.

Capturing images for *Tasmania in Photos* has resulted in me falling in love with Tasmania and its splendour all over again. I was confident that I had seen everything it had to offer but I was wrong. Visiting the spectacular northern Flinders and King islands was a highlight and revealed unrivalled natural beauty, all so close to Tasmania and mainland Australia.

I met many amazing people on my journey for this book. Locals are very proud of this state and their hospitality shines through from every corner of the island.

For photographers playing at home, images in this book were captured using Olympus camera bodies and lenses, surviving some of the harshest conditions Tasmania had to offer. I can only urge anyone that hasn't visited Tasmania to put this island paradise at the top of their travel list. And if you have visited before, do as I have; revisit and fall in love with it once again.

CAM BLAKE

» LEFT Lights, camera, action on top of Hobart's kunanyi/Mount Wellington

» PREVIOUS Winter camping on the Overland Track in Cradle Mountain–Lake St Clair National Park

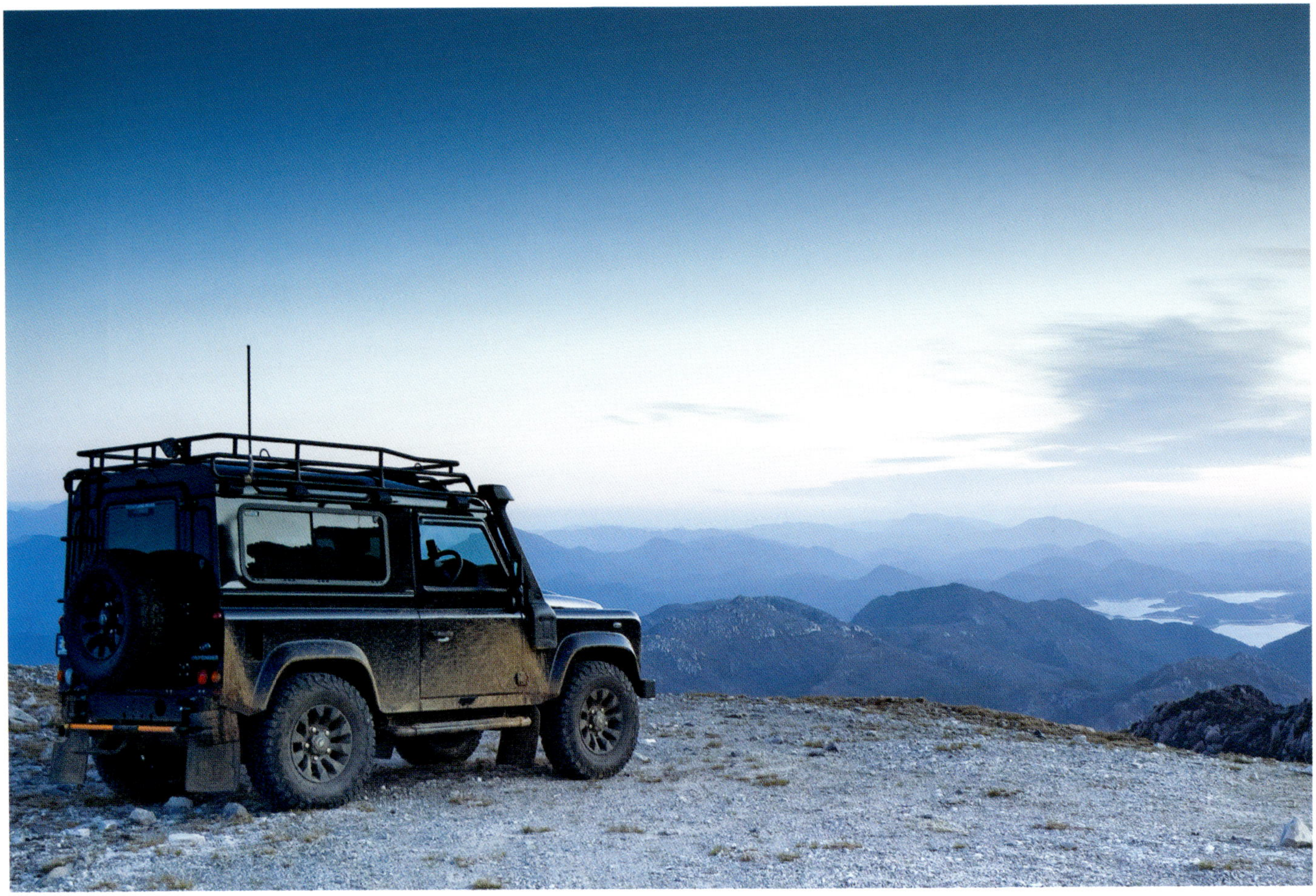

» **ABOVE** On top of Tasmania after a long day of exploring the western region of this wild island

» **OPPOSITE** Cradle Mountain in all its glory during the vibrant season of autumn

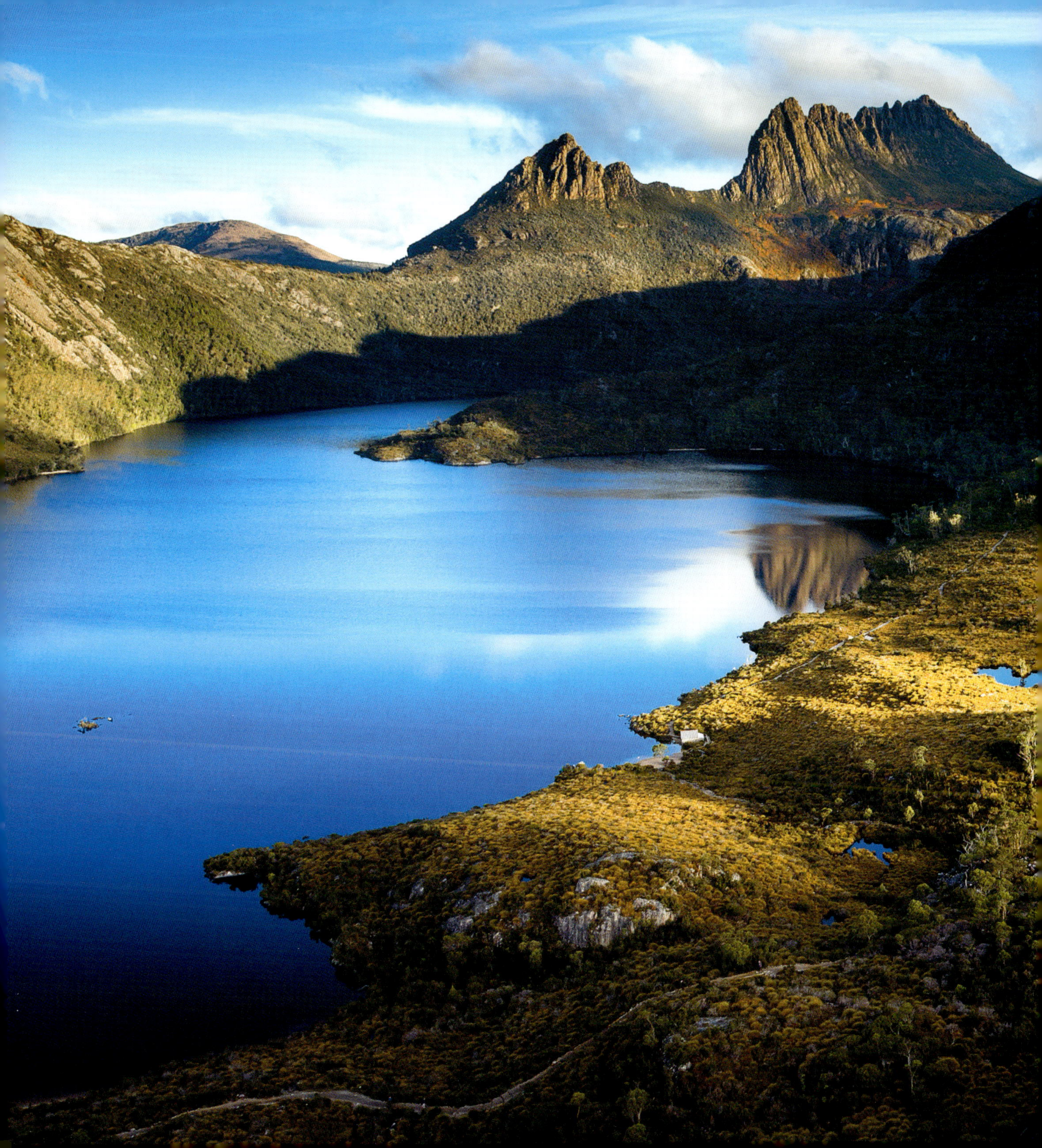

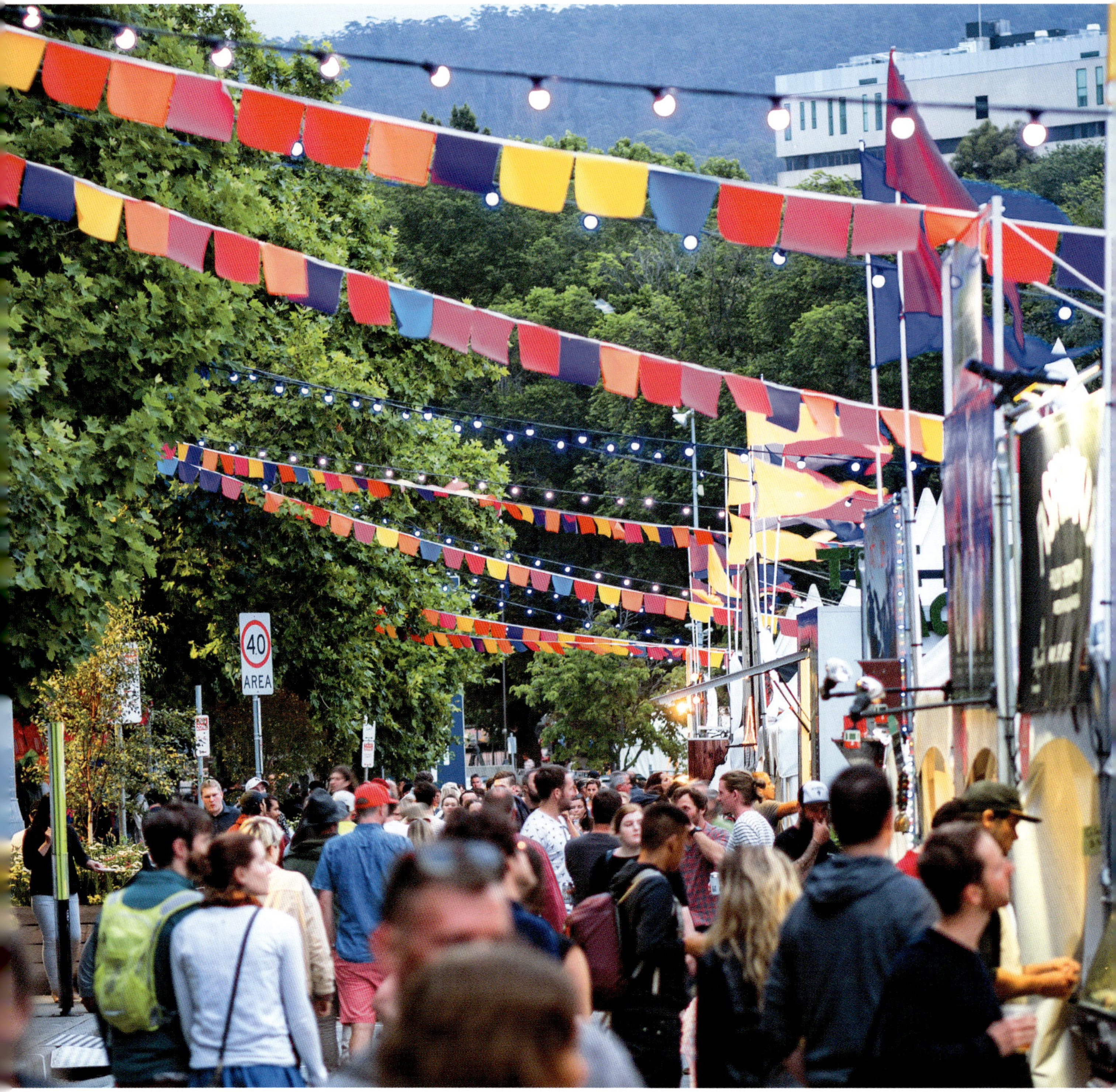
40
AREA

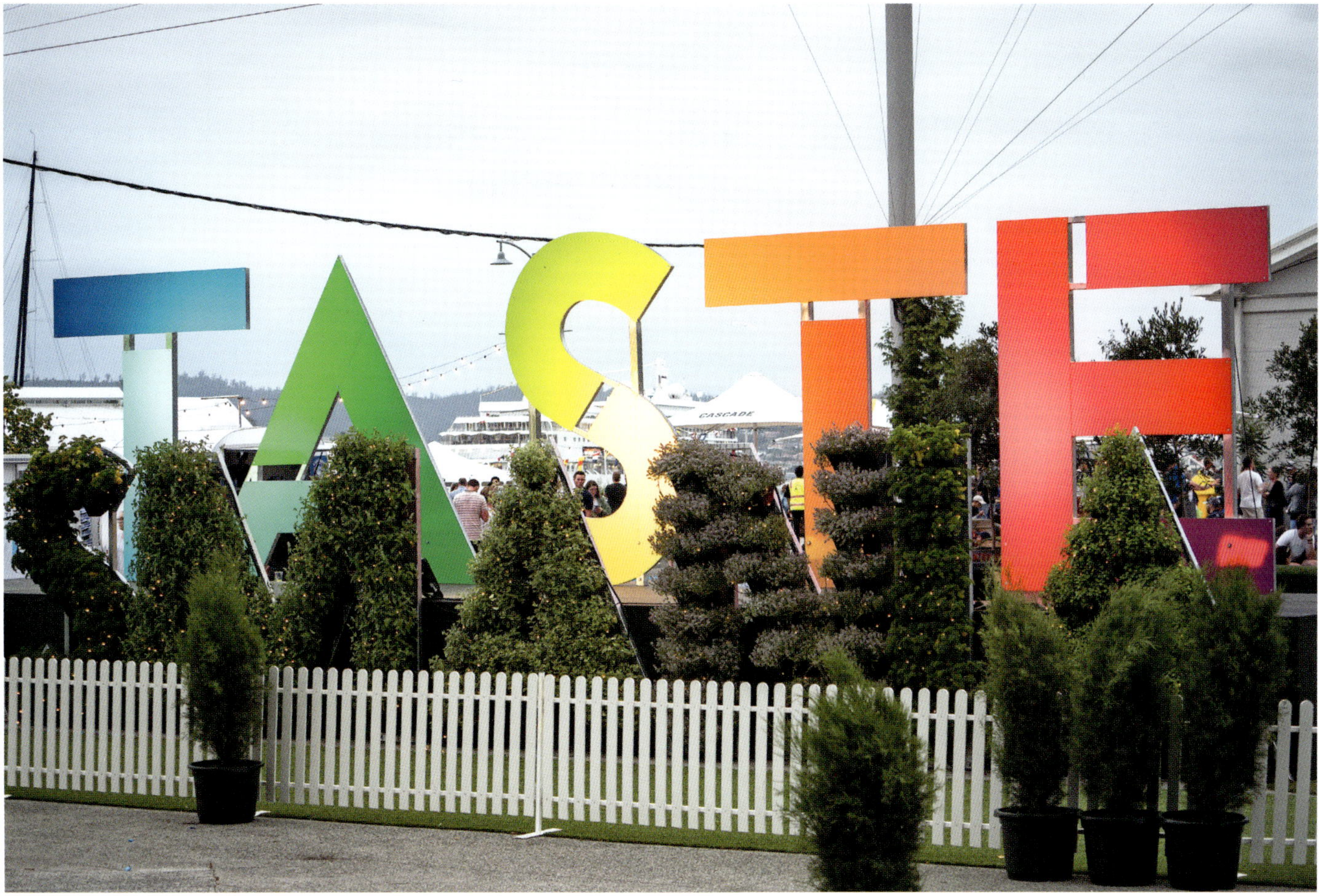

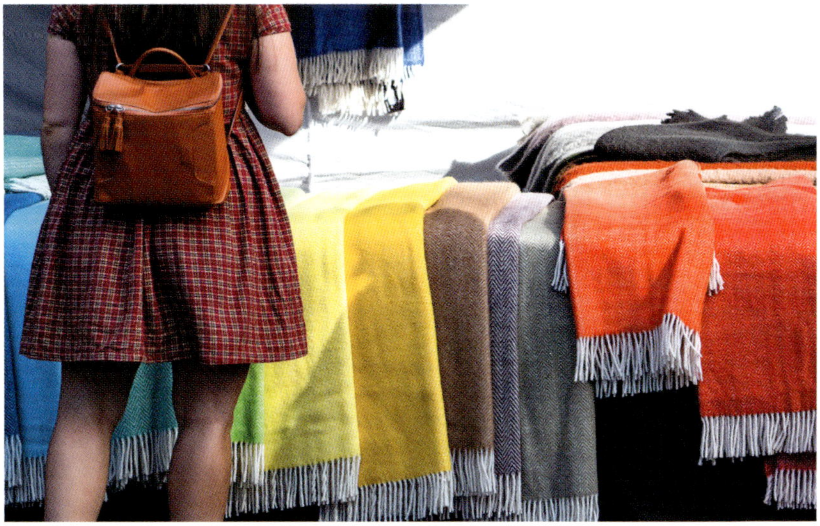

» **ABOVE** Hobart's Taste Festival is a special gastronomic experience in quality food and produce

» **LEFT** Colours and textures catch a keen shopper's eye at Salamanca Market

» **OPPOSITE** Food stalls lining the Salamanca area

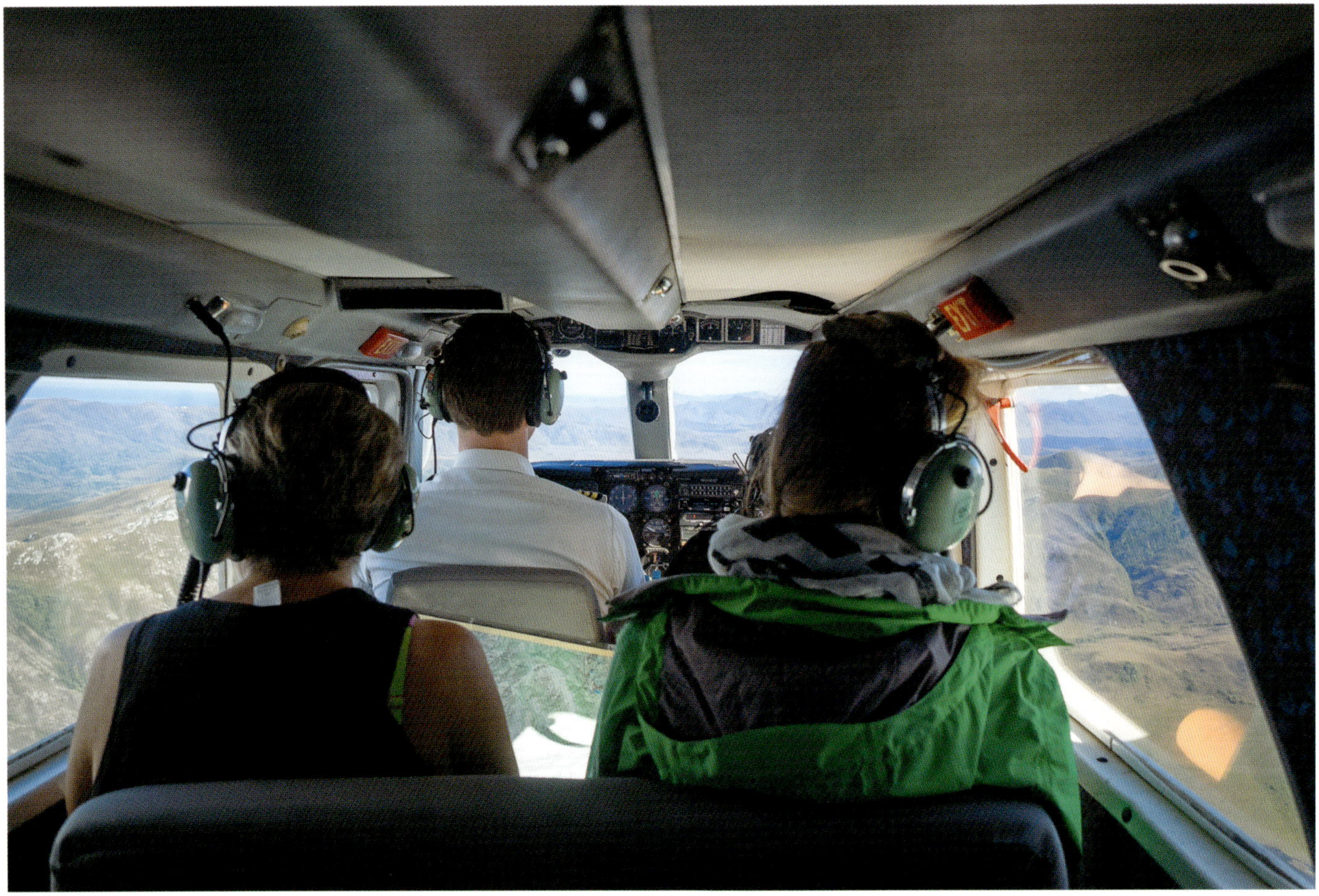

» **ABOVE** Approaching Melaleuca, deep in Tasmania's Southwest National Park

» **OPPOSITE** Look up! Tasmania's impressive rainforest canopies

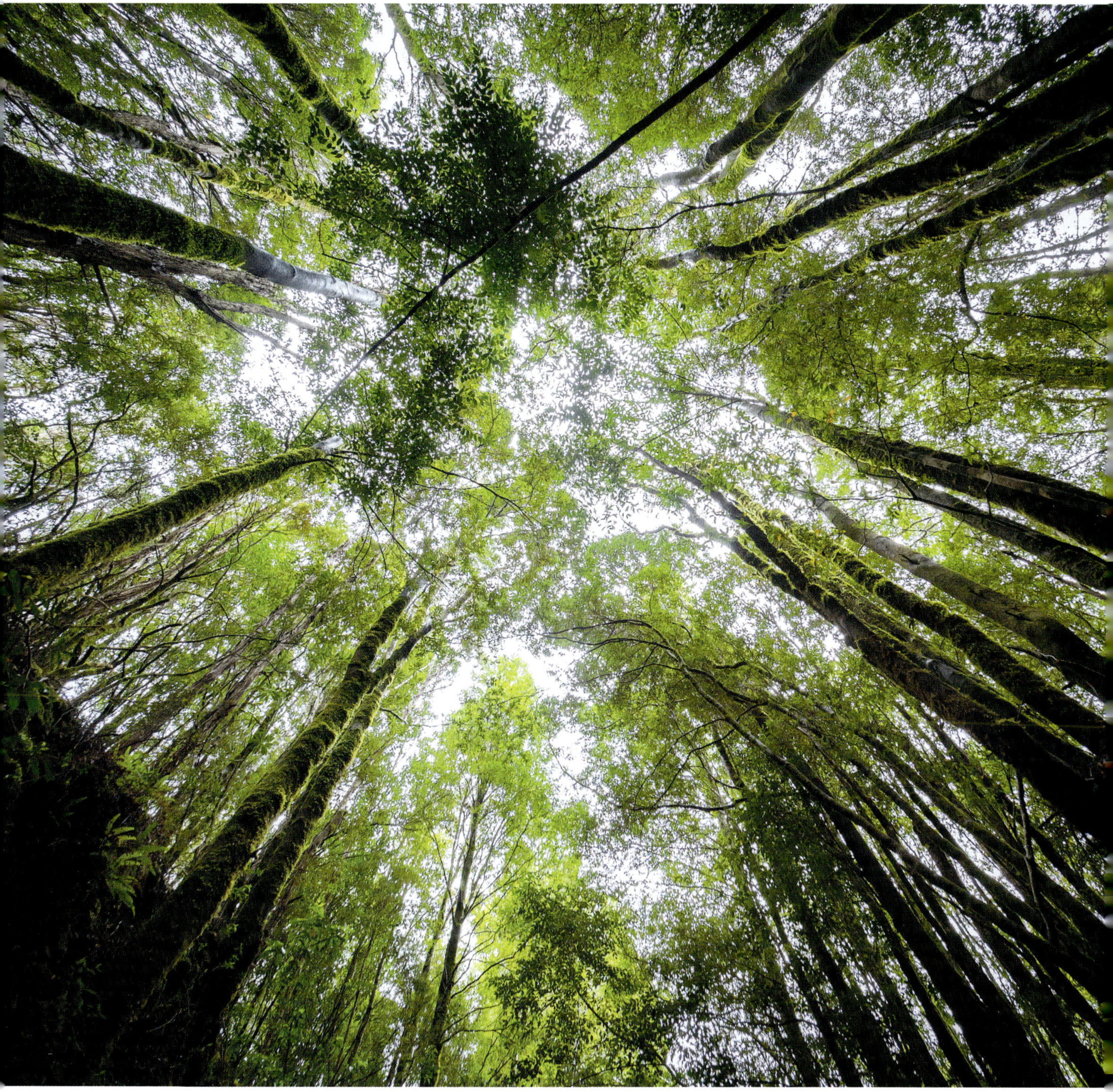

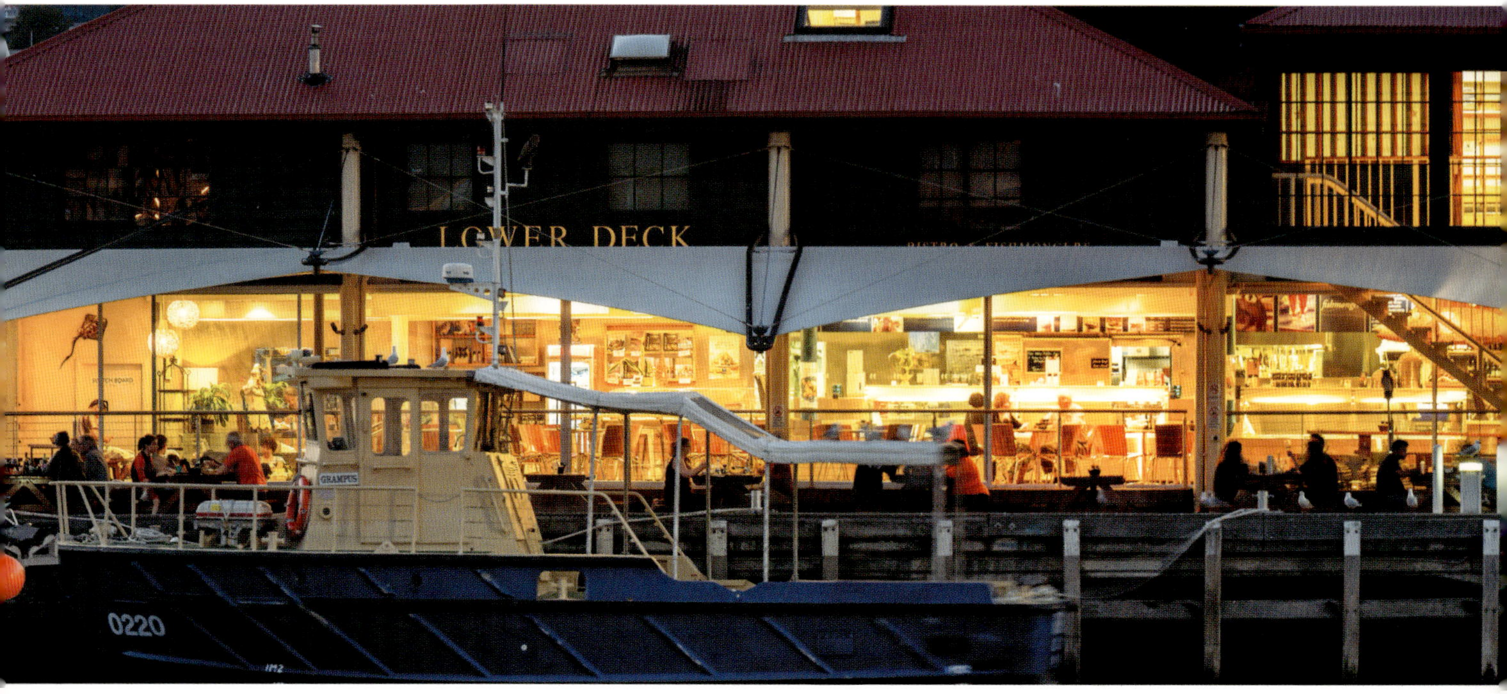

» **ABOVE** Dinnertime at Hobart's famous Mures restaurant

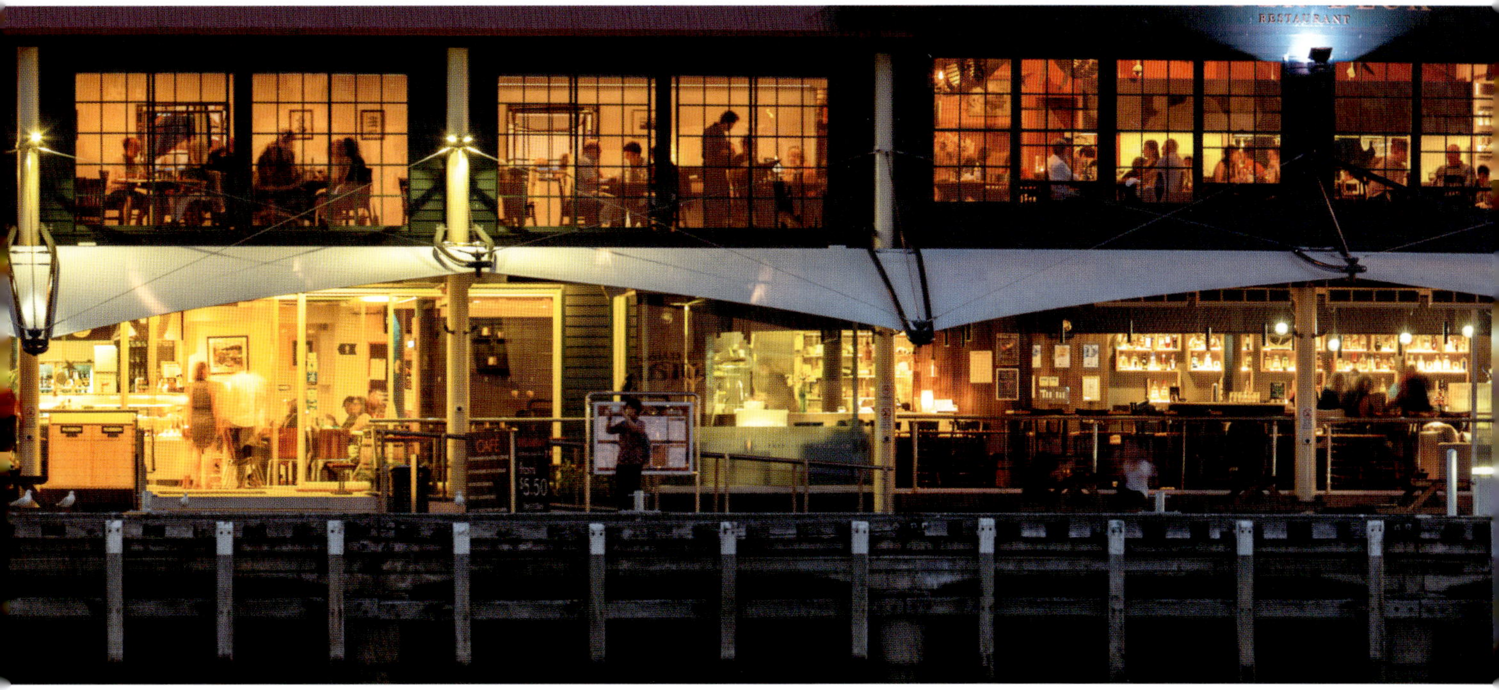
RESTAURANT
CAFÉ
from
$5.50

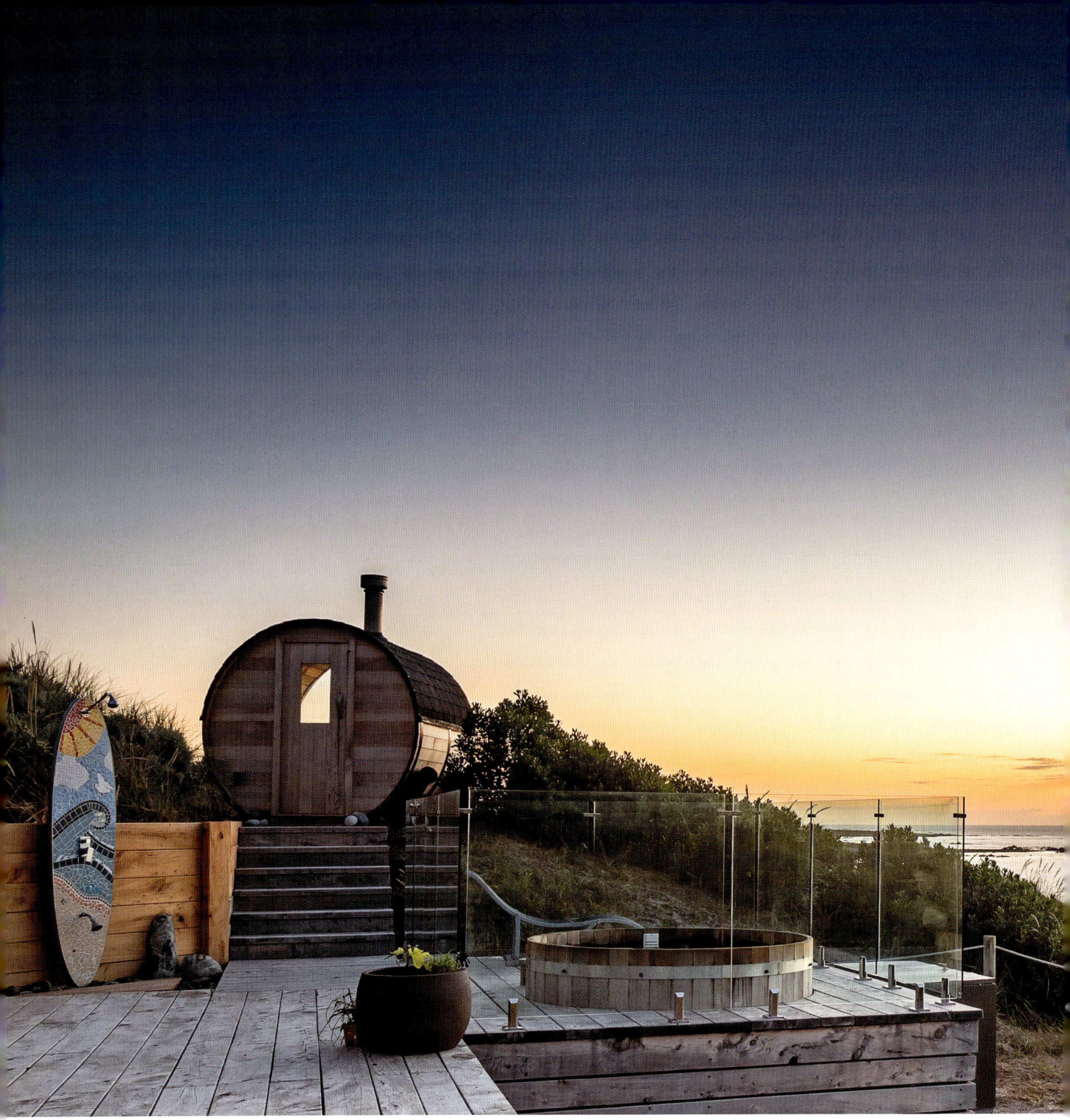

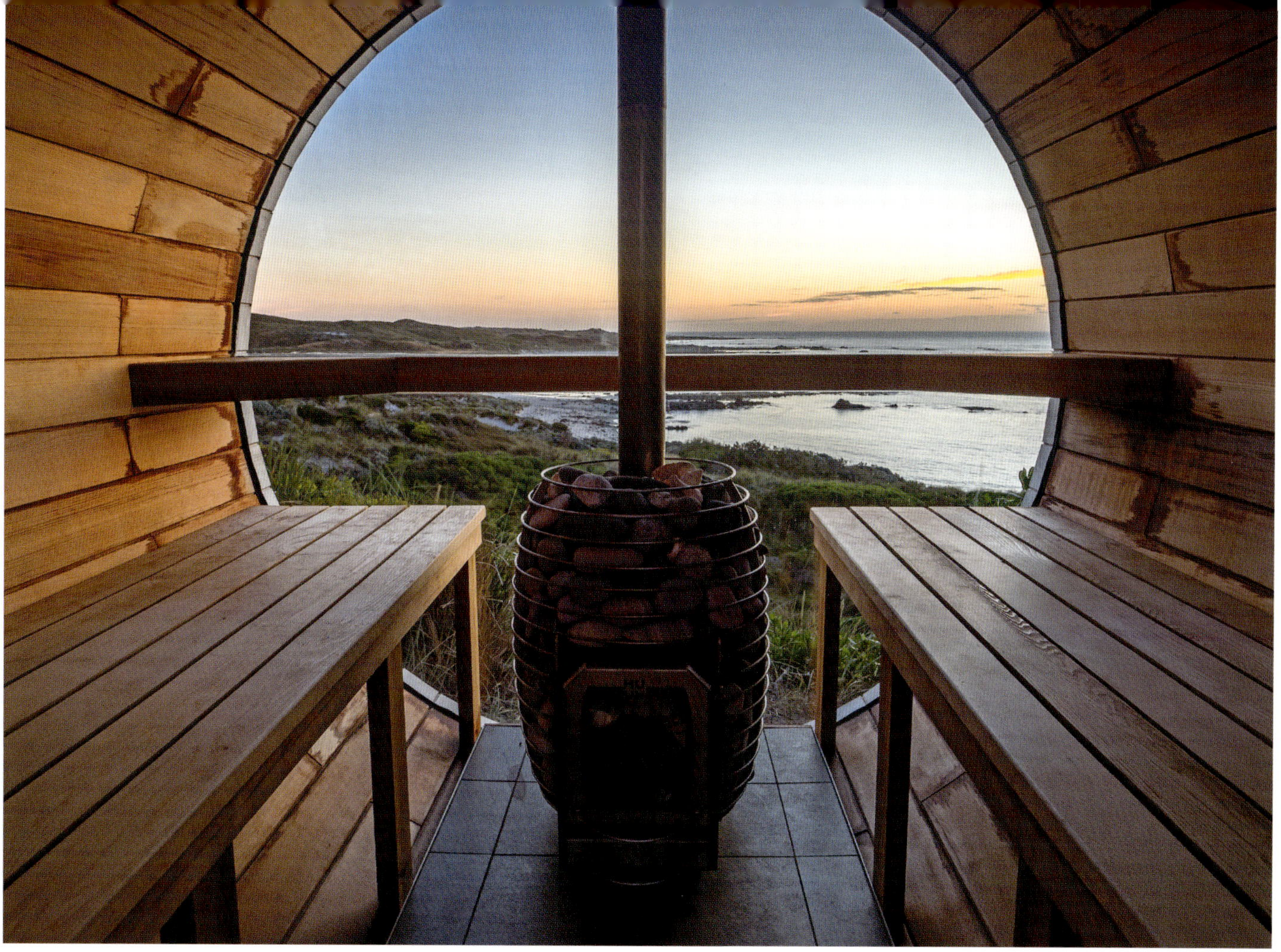

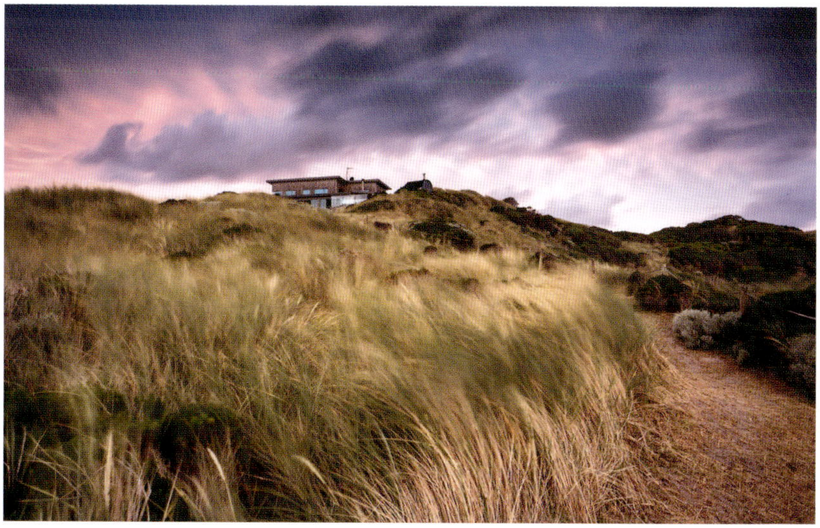

» **ABOVE** King Island Escape's Porky Beach House has a sauna with a view

» **LEFT** Windswept coastline of King Island

» **OPPOSITE** Taking it easy at a King Island escape

» **RIGHT** Wild coastlines and rugged landscapes welcome brave travellers in the takayna/Tarkine region

» **OPPOSITE** A winter storm passes over the Highland Lakes Road

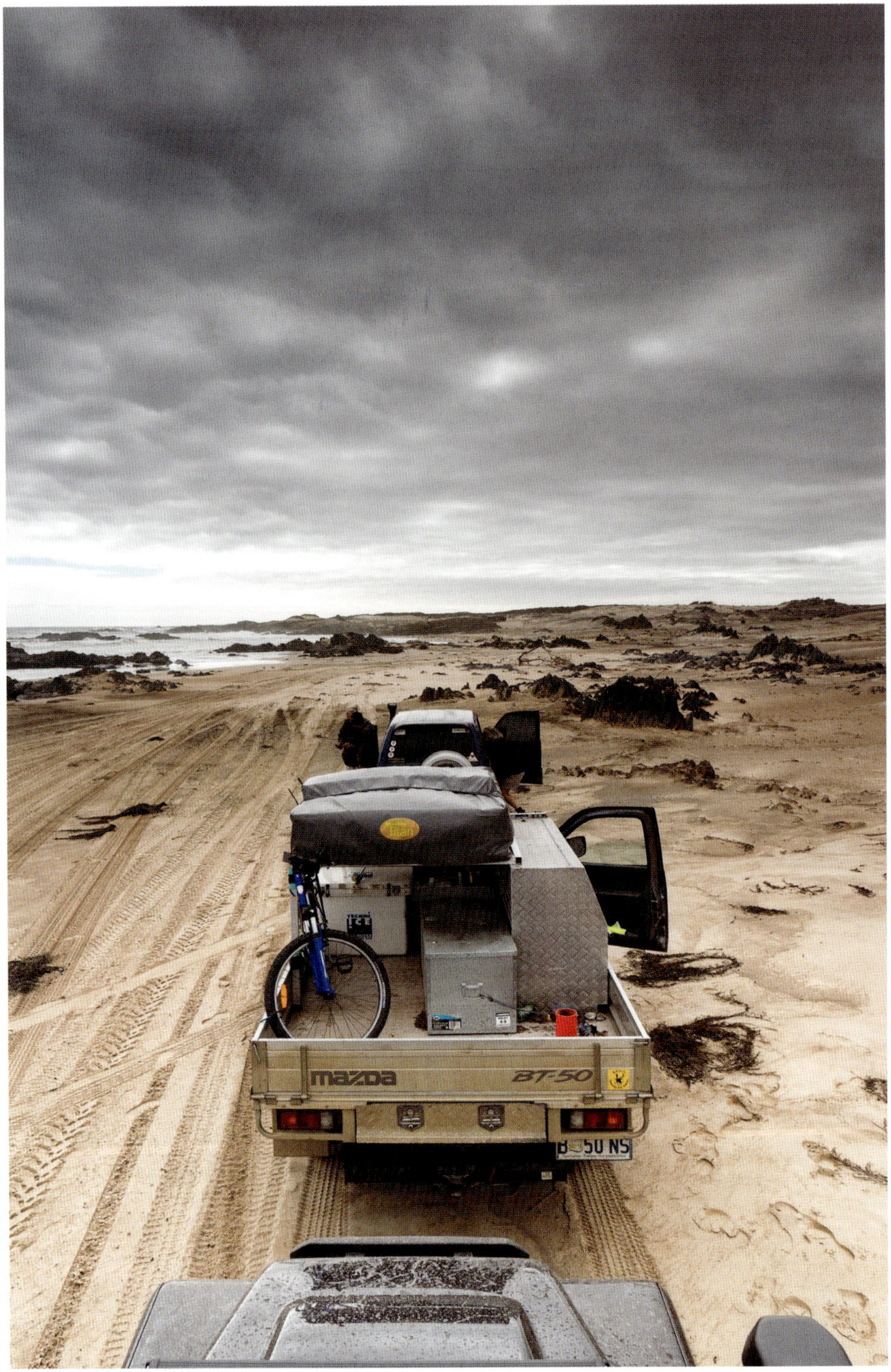

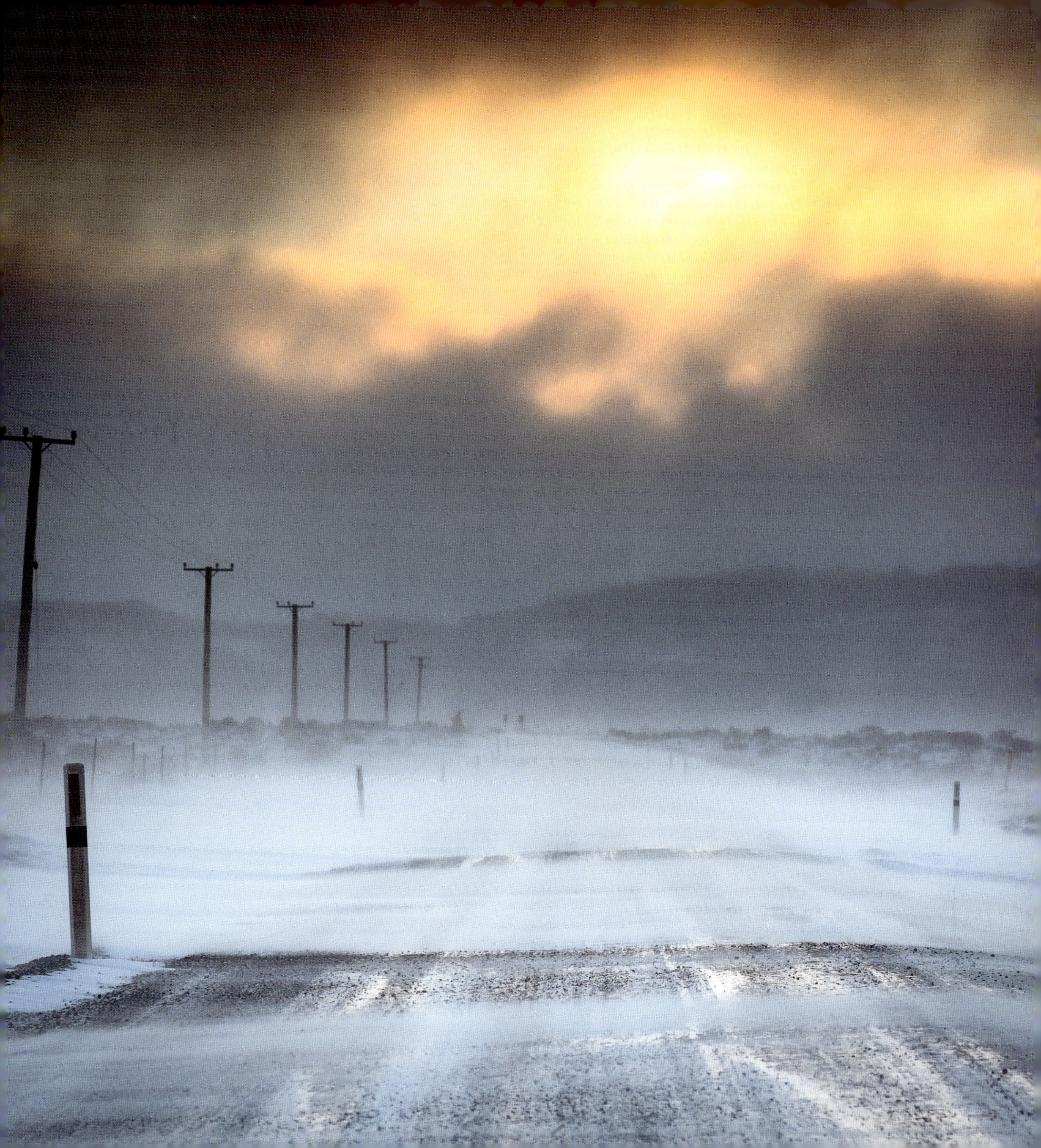

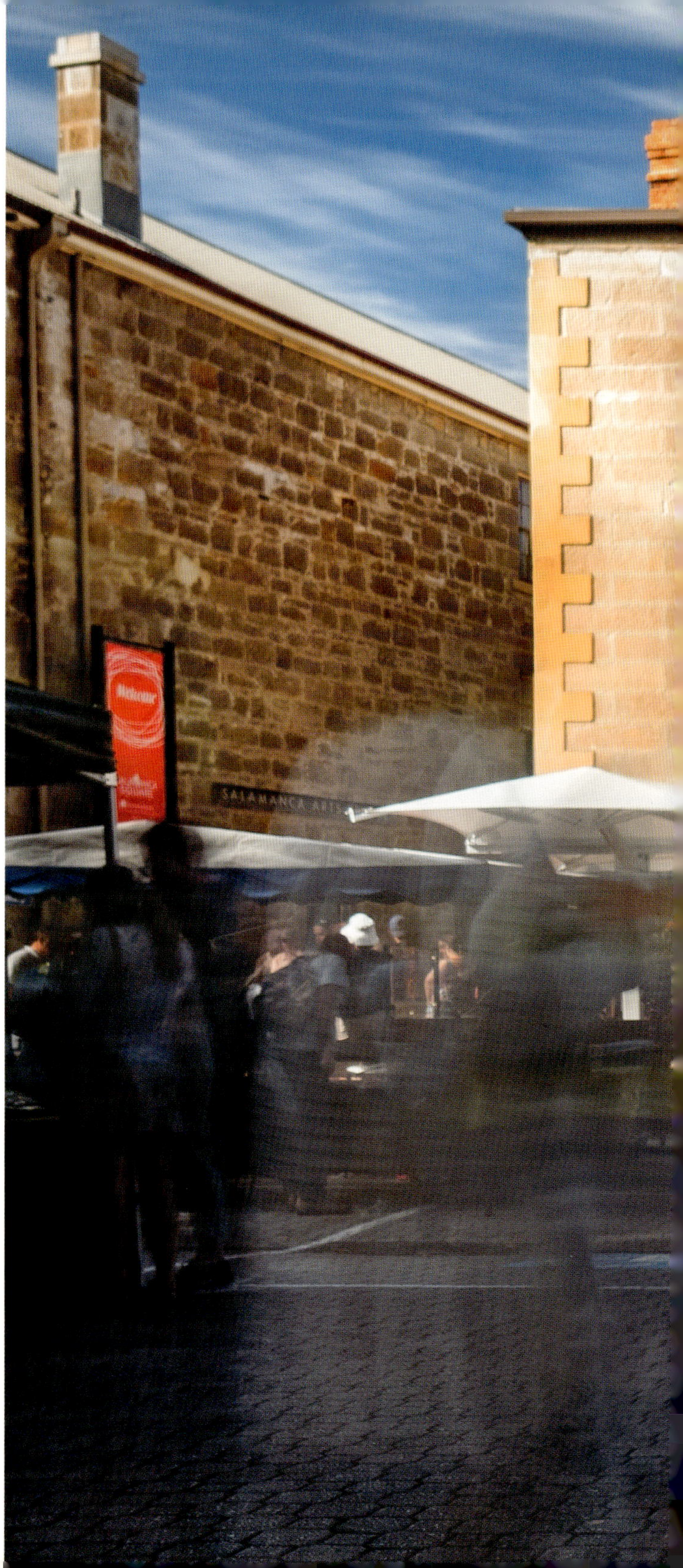

» RIGHT Time to eat. Salamanca Market sells Tasmania's best foods to satisfy the hungry traveller

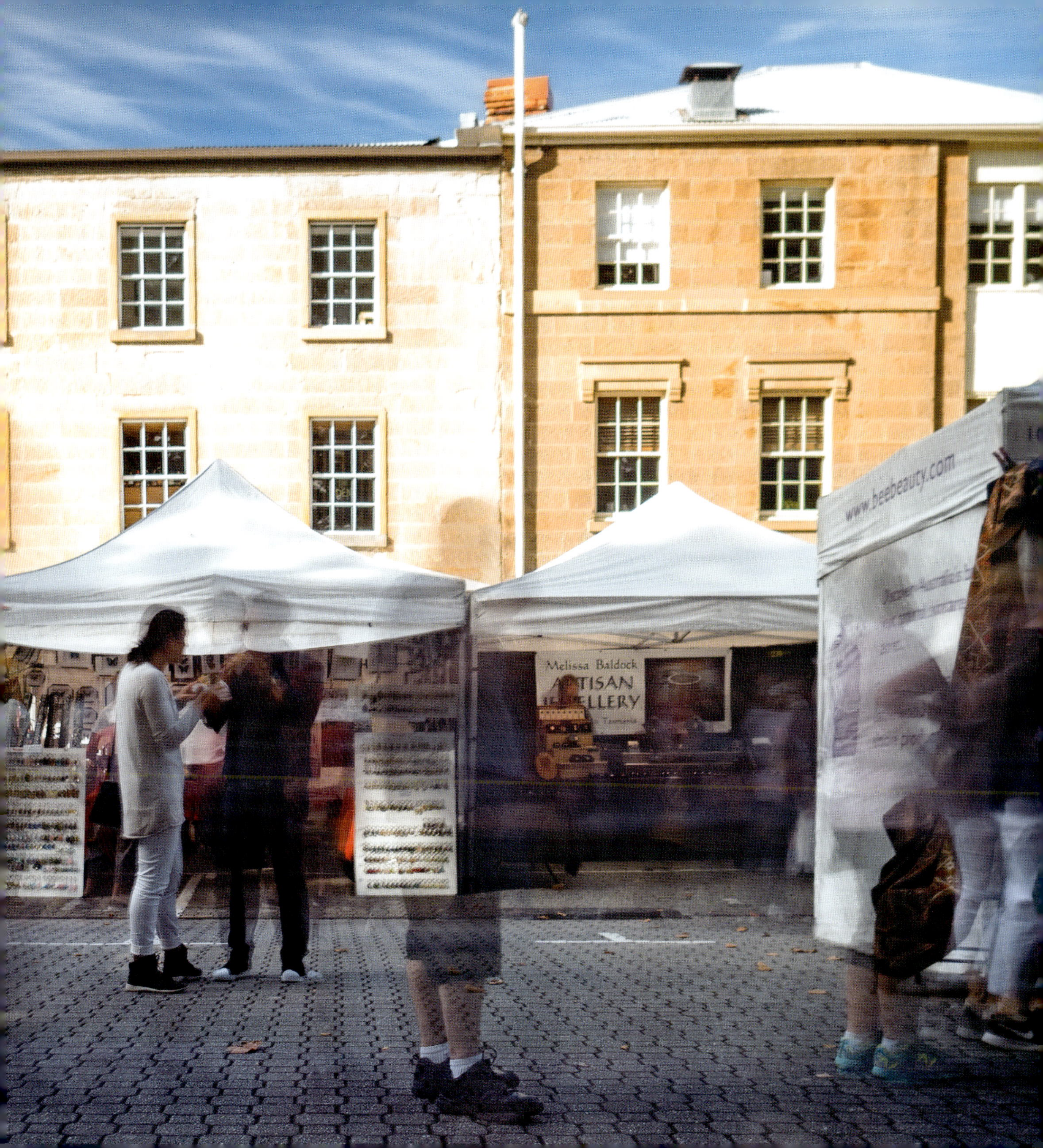
www.beebeauty.com
Melissa Baldock

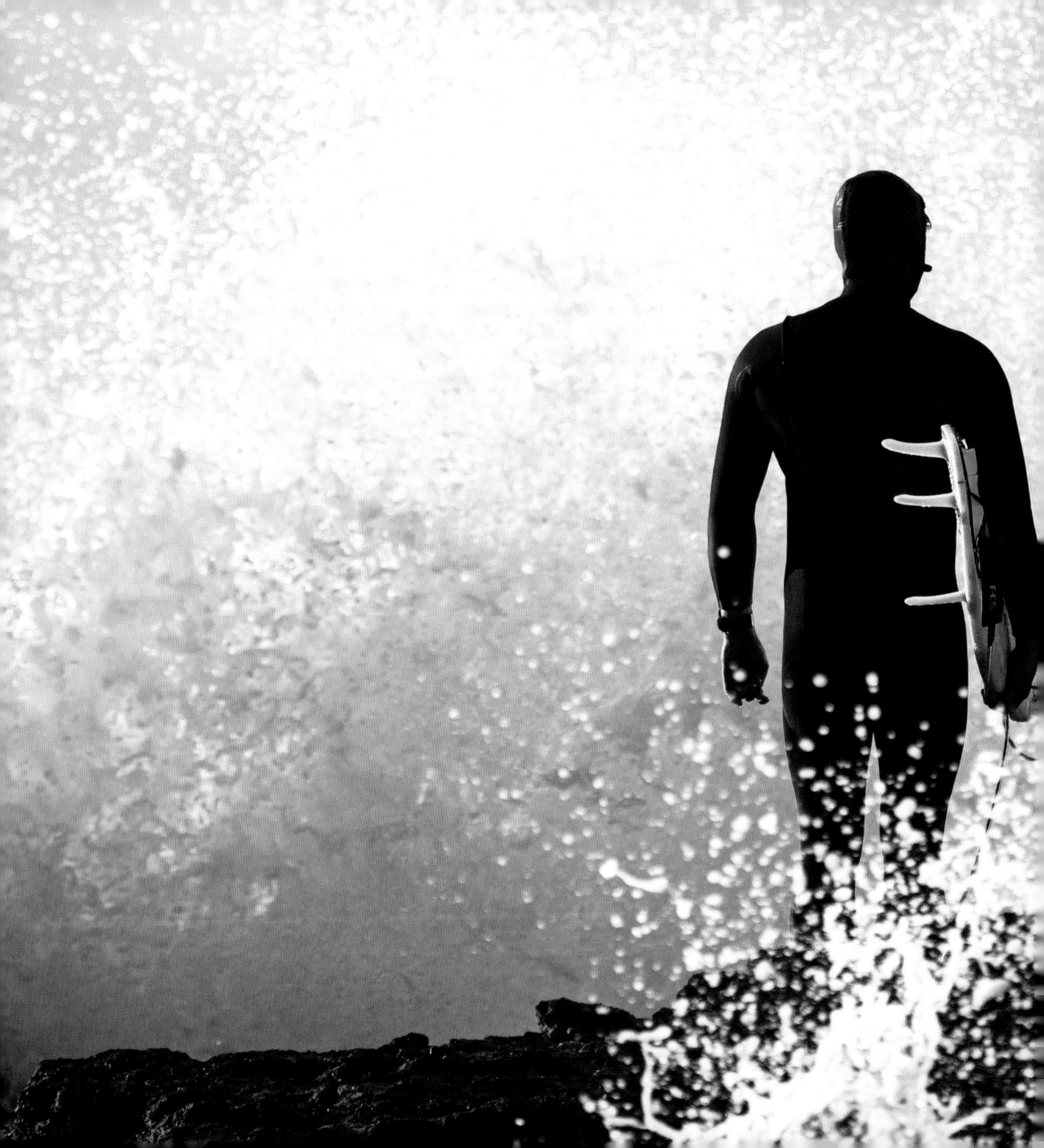

» **LEFT** Surf's up at Goat Bluff in Tasmania's south

» **OVERLEAF** Winter comes alive with the Dark Mofo festival in Hobart

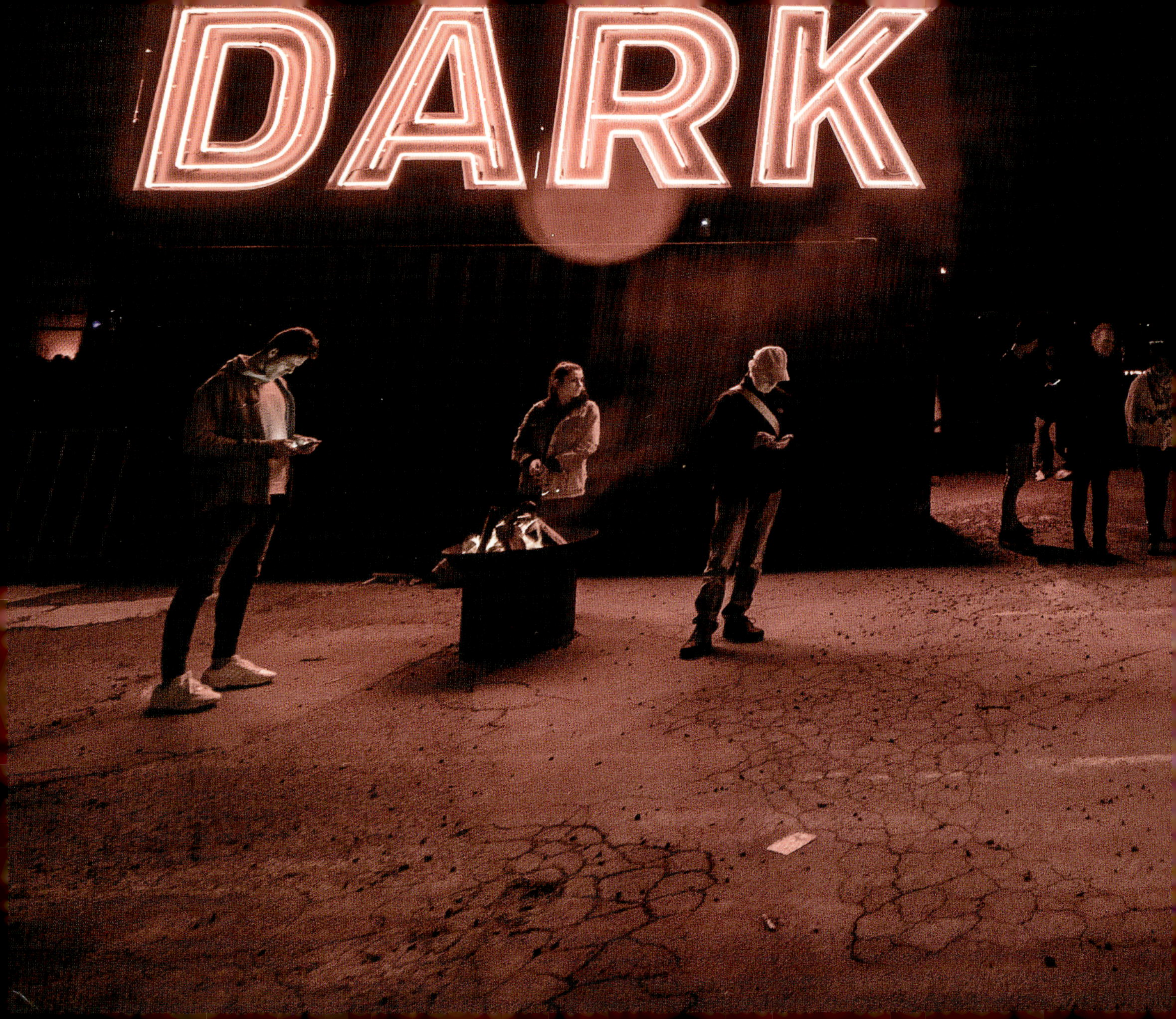
DARK

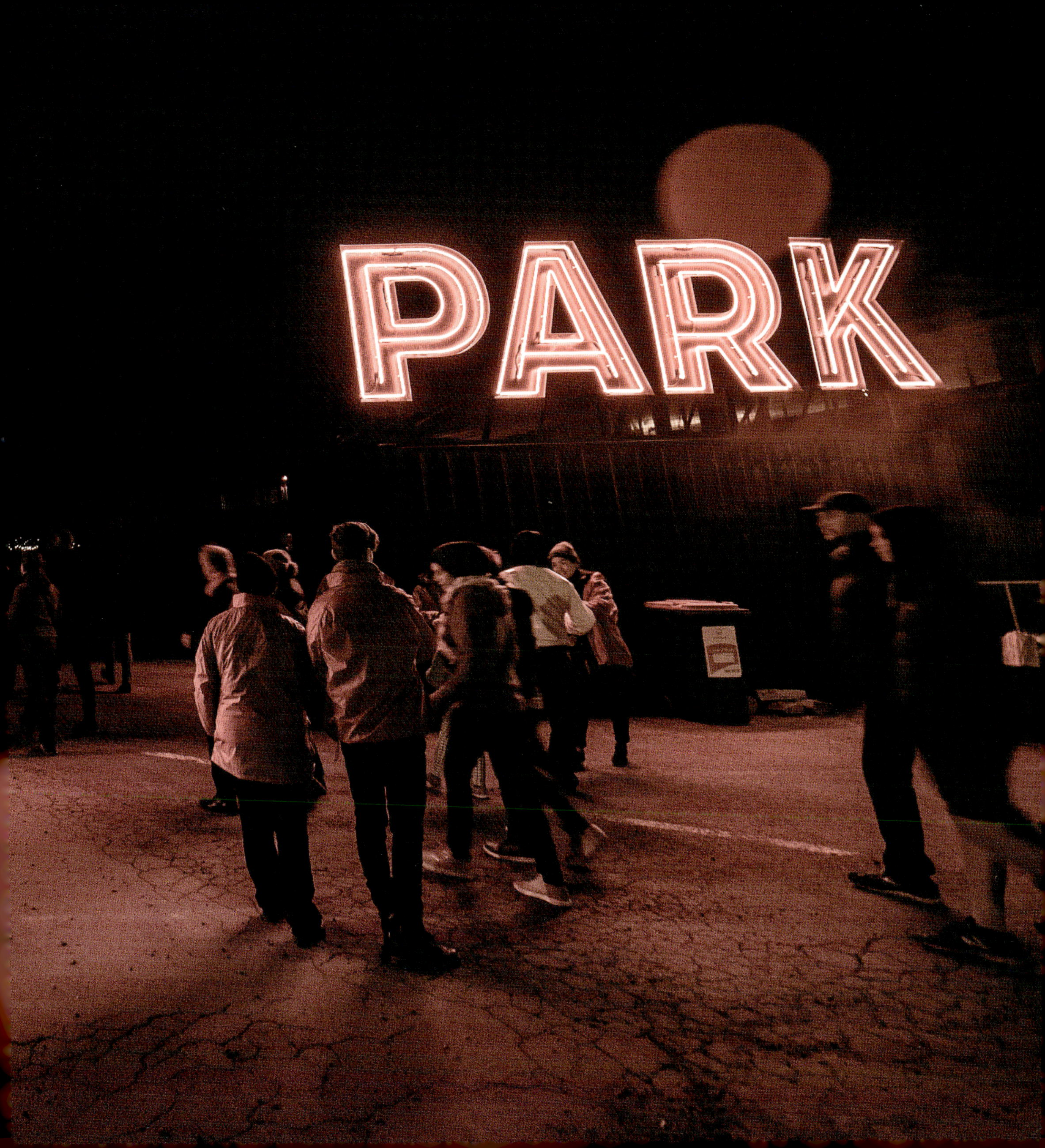
PARK

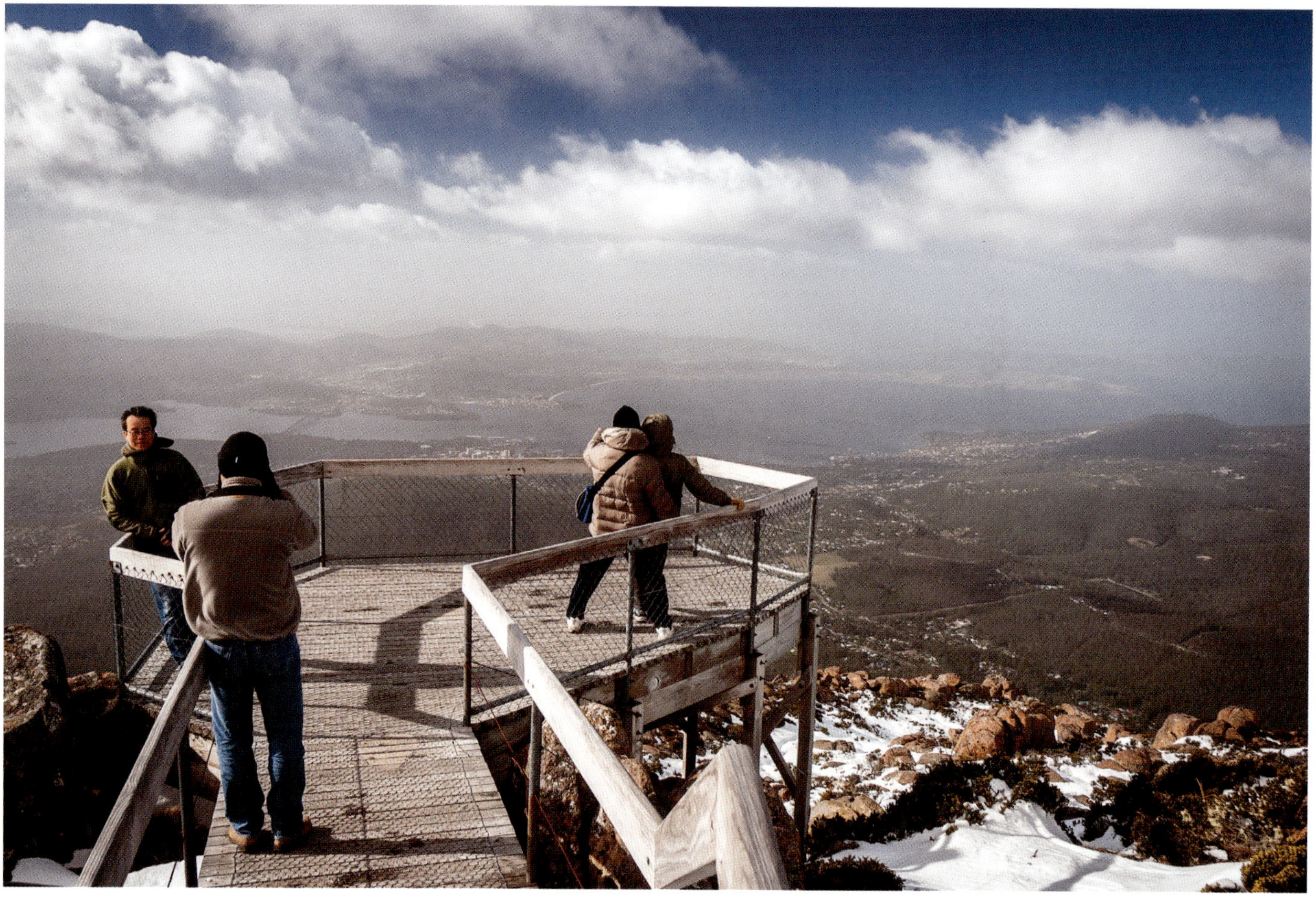

» **ABOVE** If the wind doesn't take your breath away, the view will!

» **RIGHT** A pademelon right at home in fresh snowfall at Cradle Mountain–Lake St Clair National Park

» **OPPOSITE** A cold snap transforms Tasmania's Central Highlands region

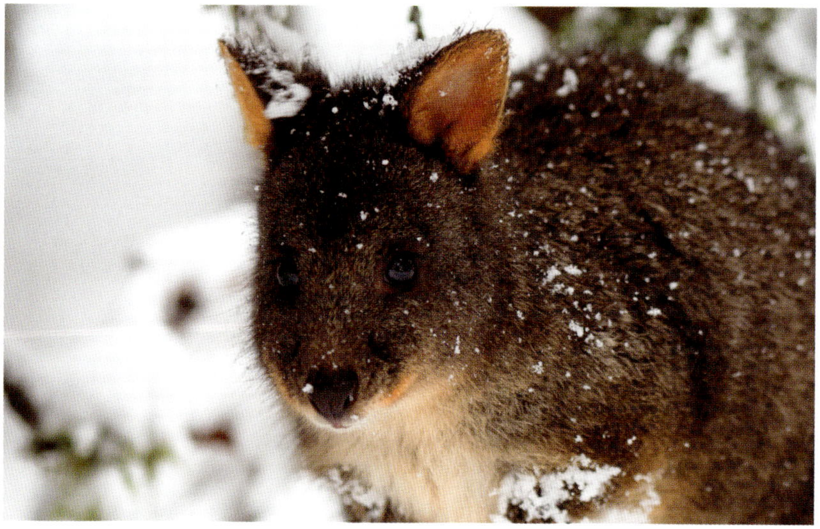

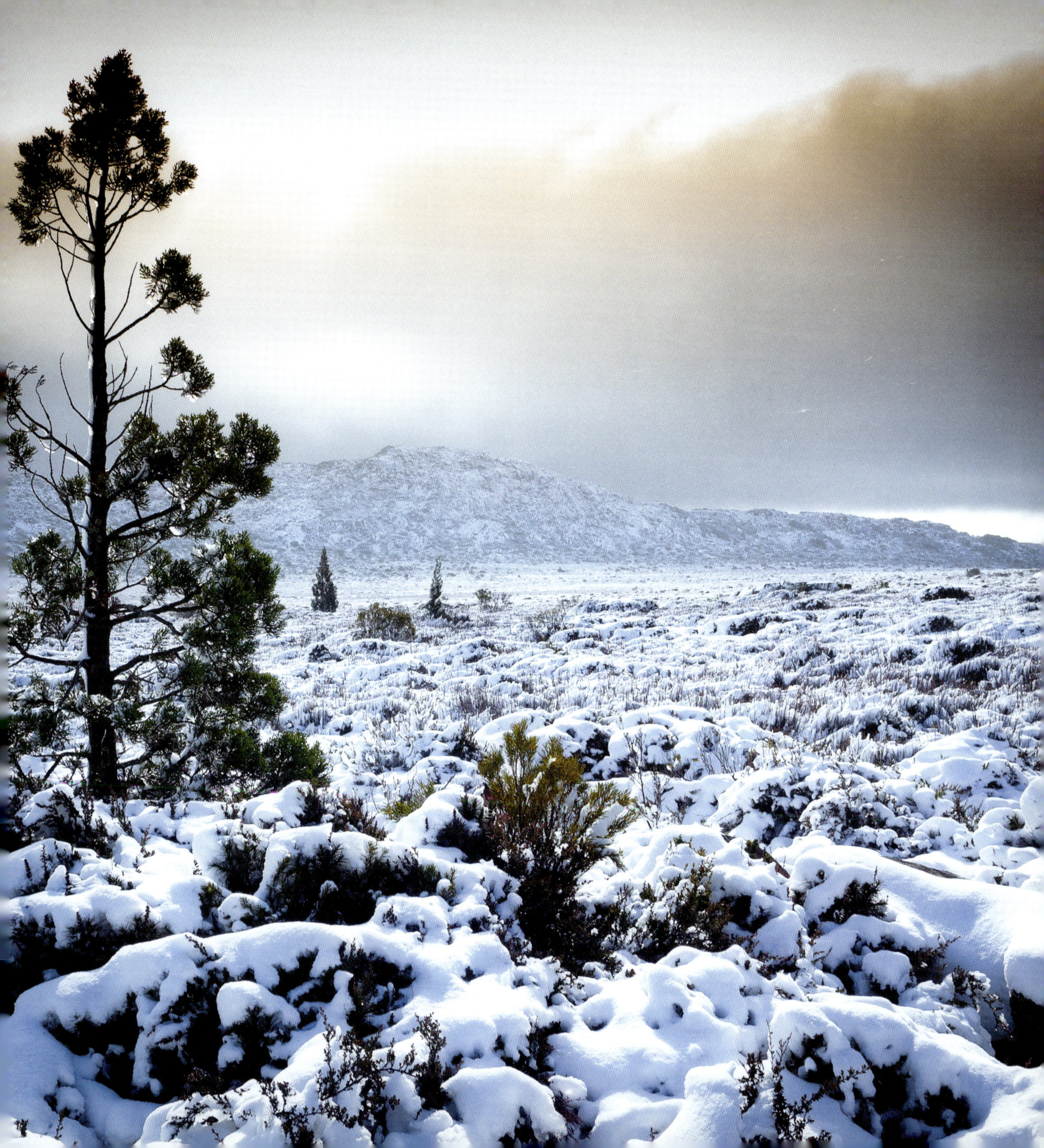

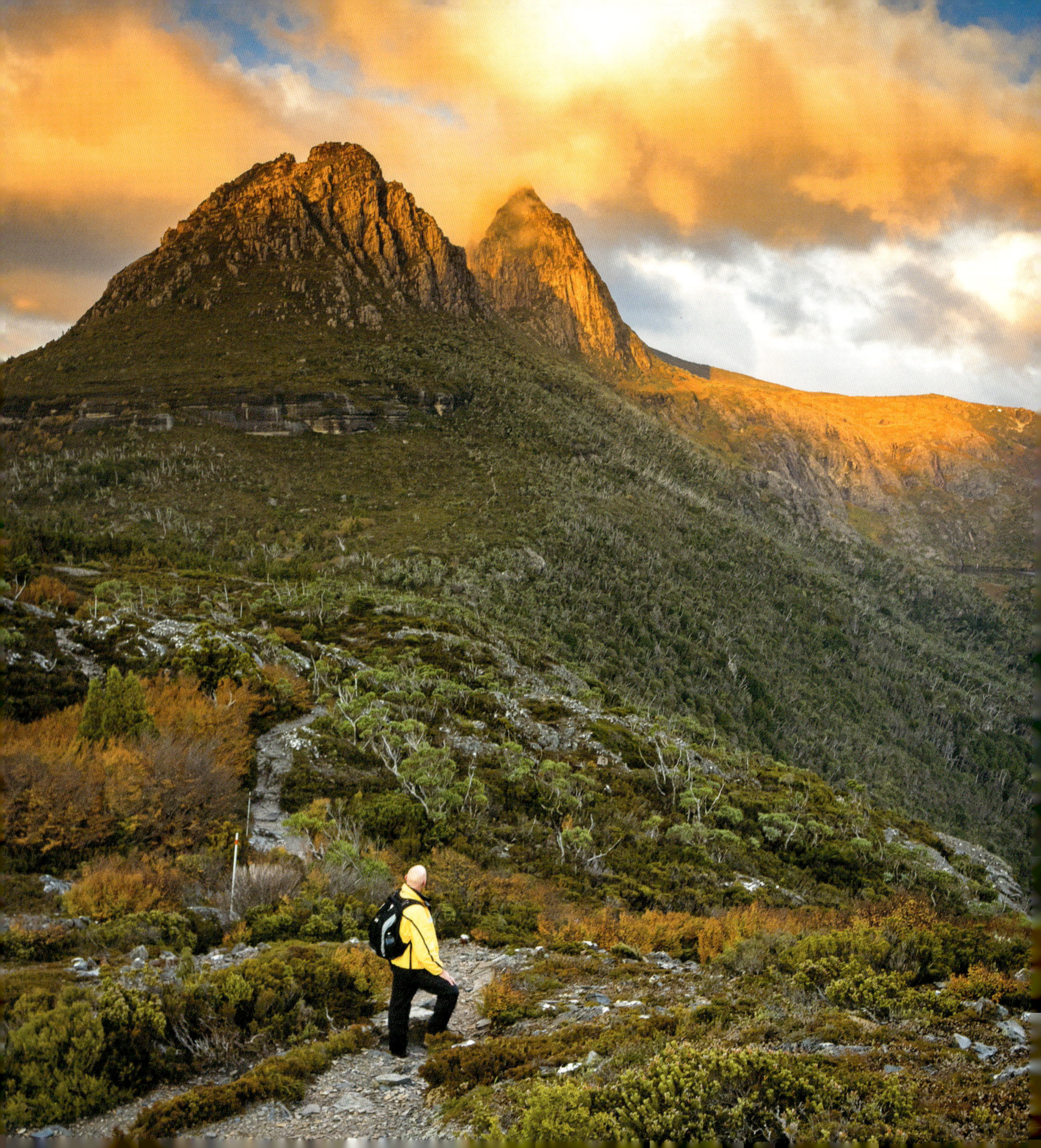

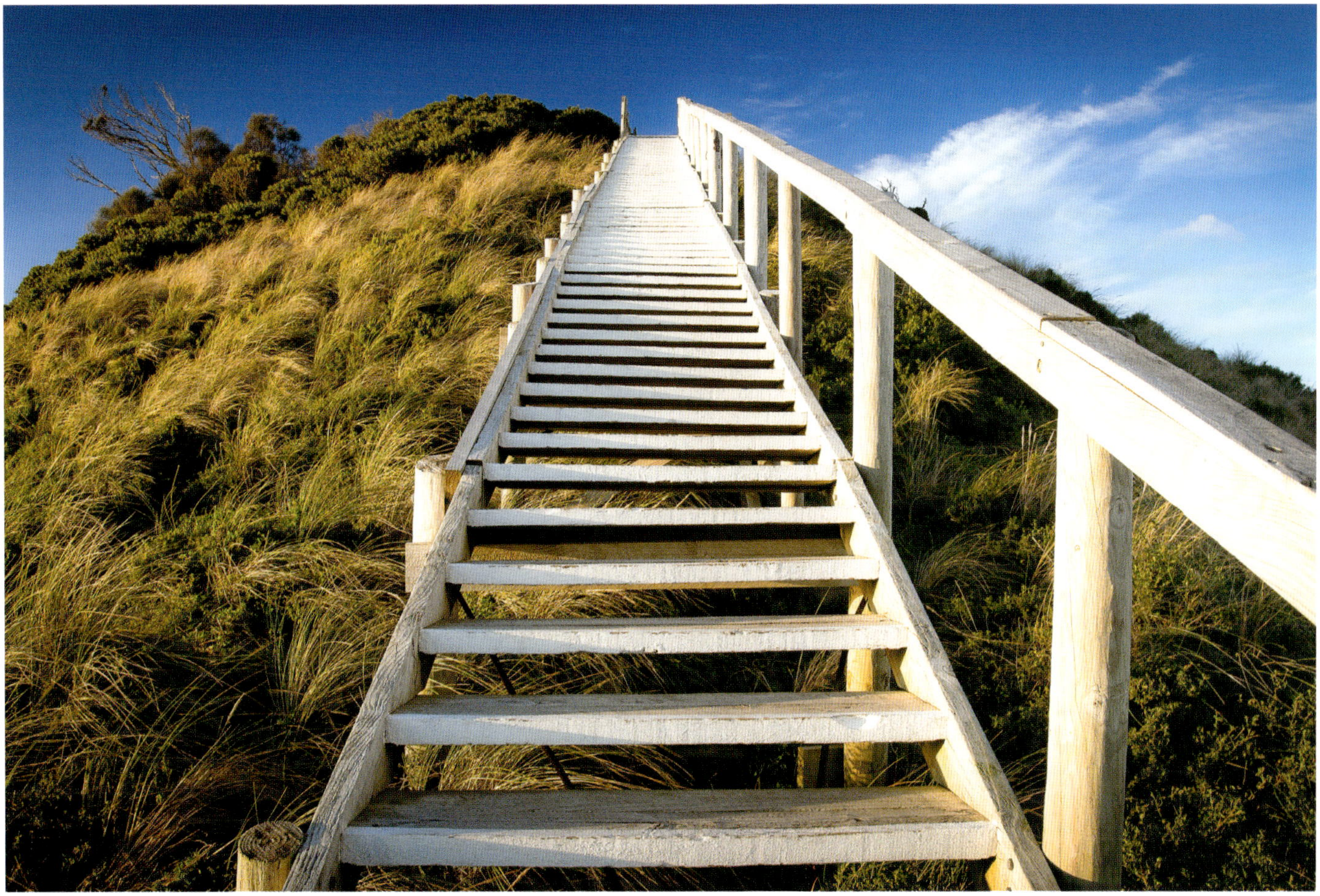

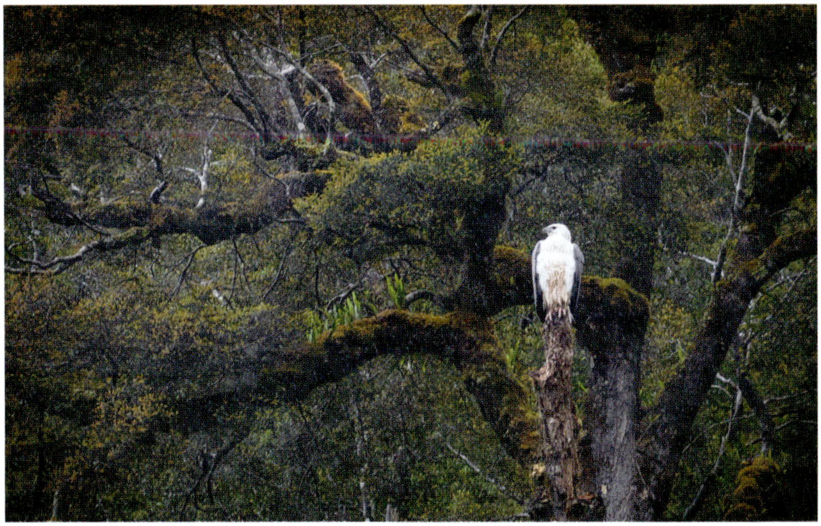

» **ABOVE** The climb to the lookout at Bruny Island Neck, where there are magnificent views across the whole south of the Island

» **LEFT** A Tasmanian sea eagle sits proudly with his eye on the wilderness

» **OPPOSITE** Early morning hike into Cradle Mountain–Lake St Clair National Park

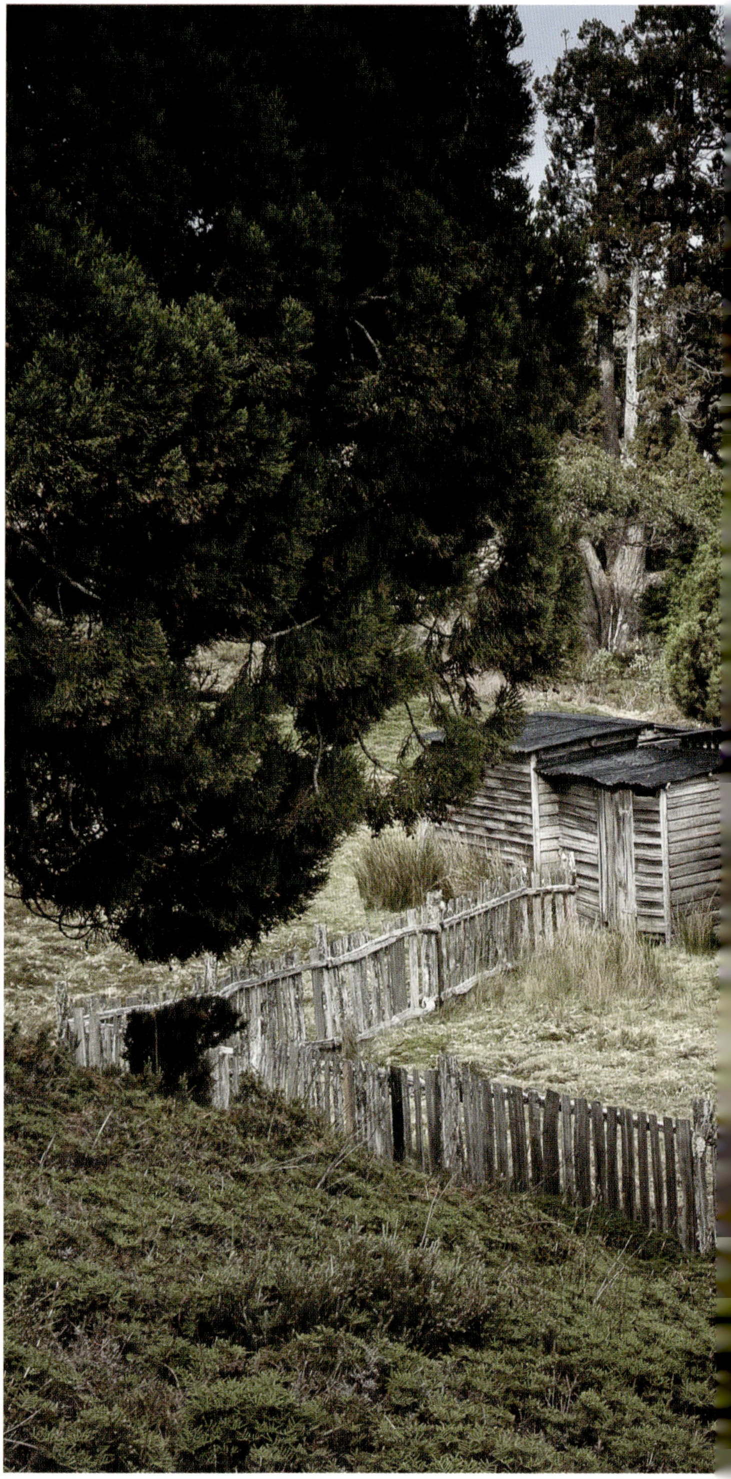

» **RIGHT** Rustic Mount Kate Hut within Cradle Mountain–Lake St Clair National Park

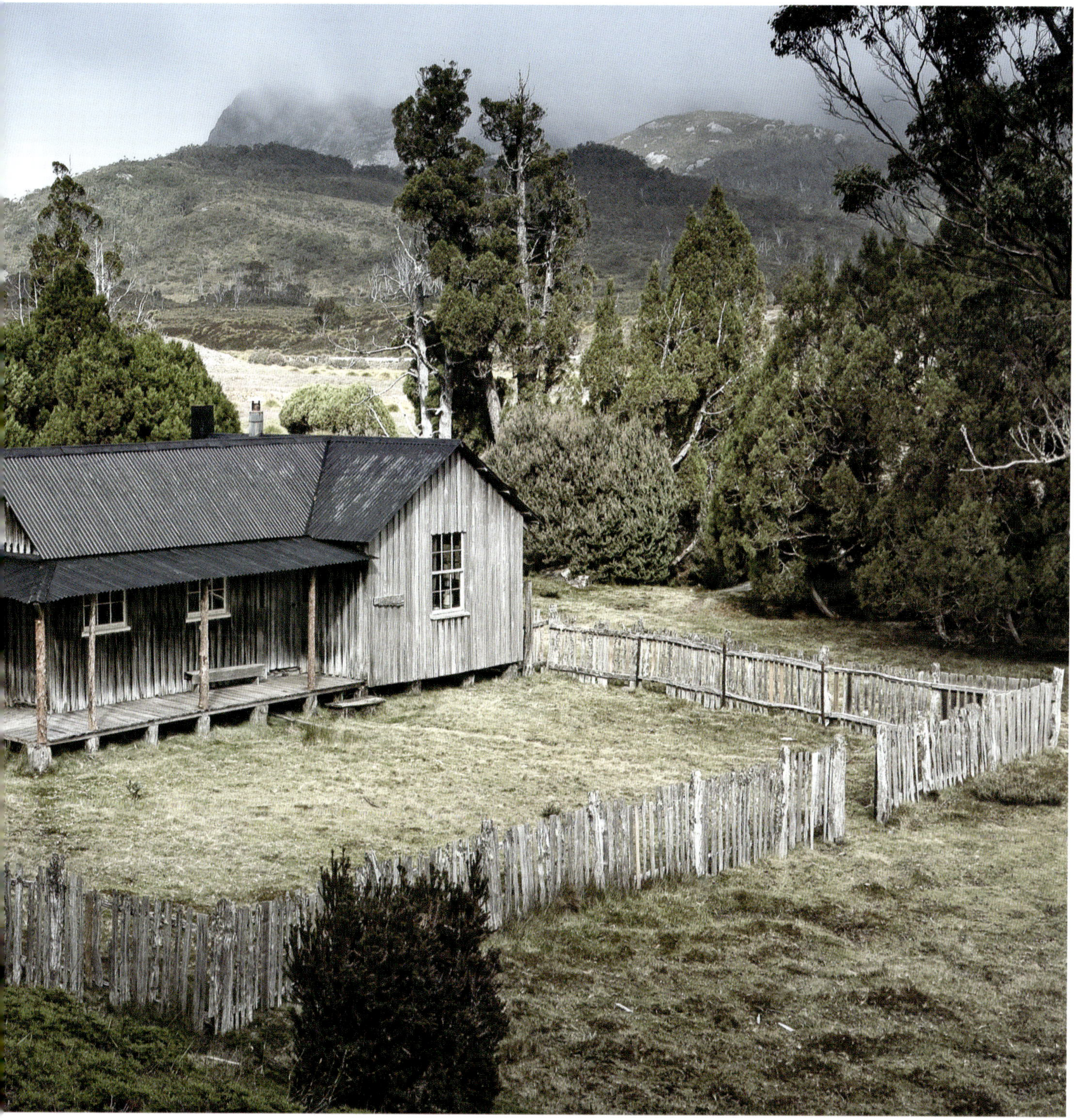

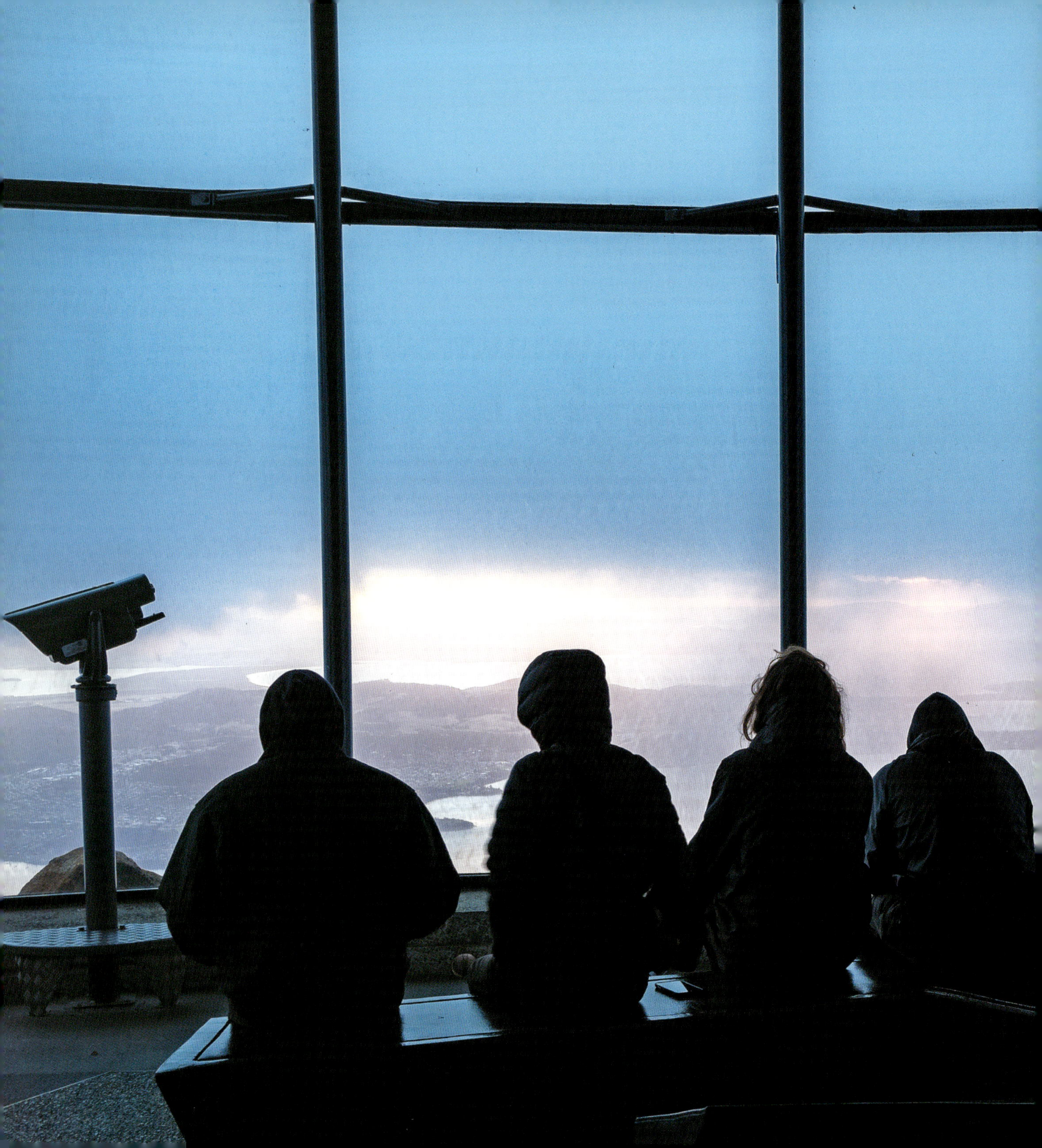

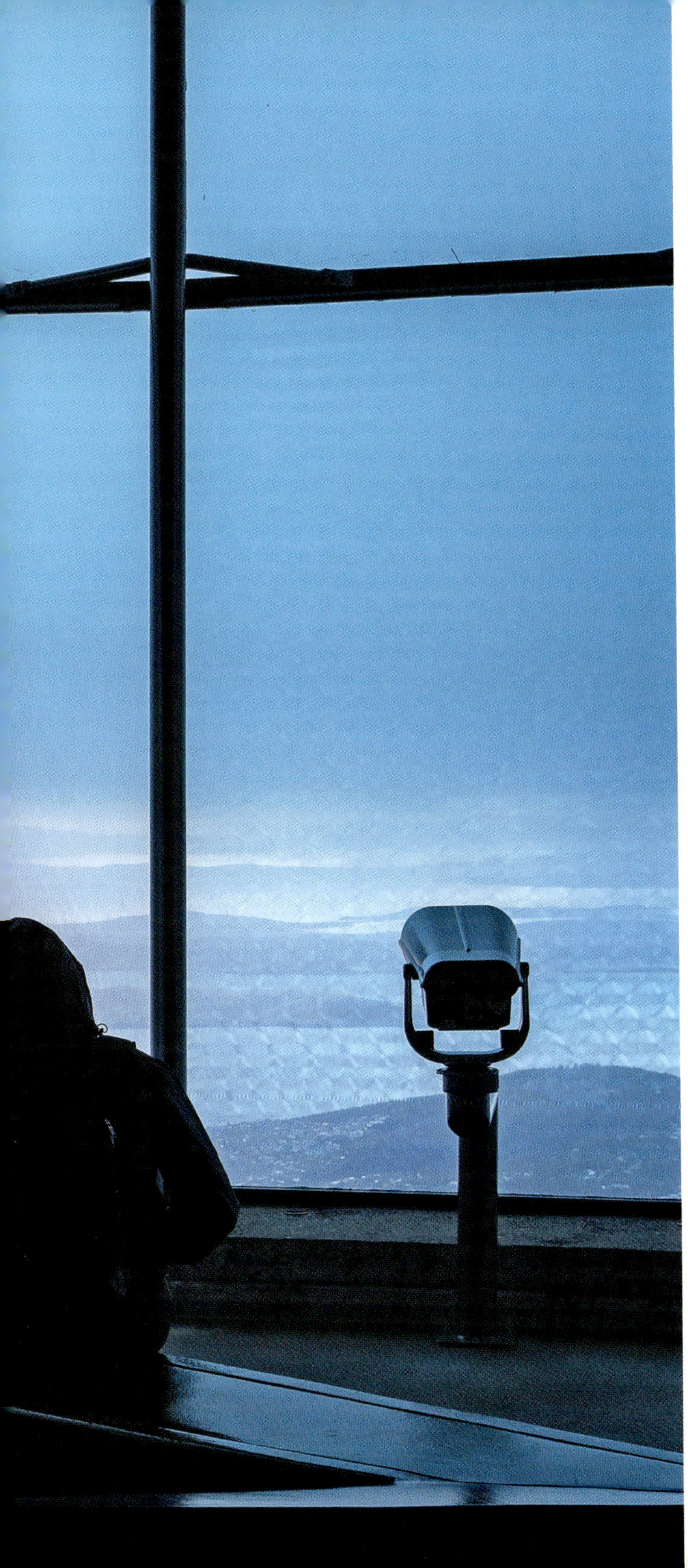

» **LEFT** An eager bunch of tourists atop kunanyi/Mount Wellington for sunrise

» **OVERLEAF** You are guaranteed to see these fellas relaxing on the rocks as you venture around the coast of Bruny Island

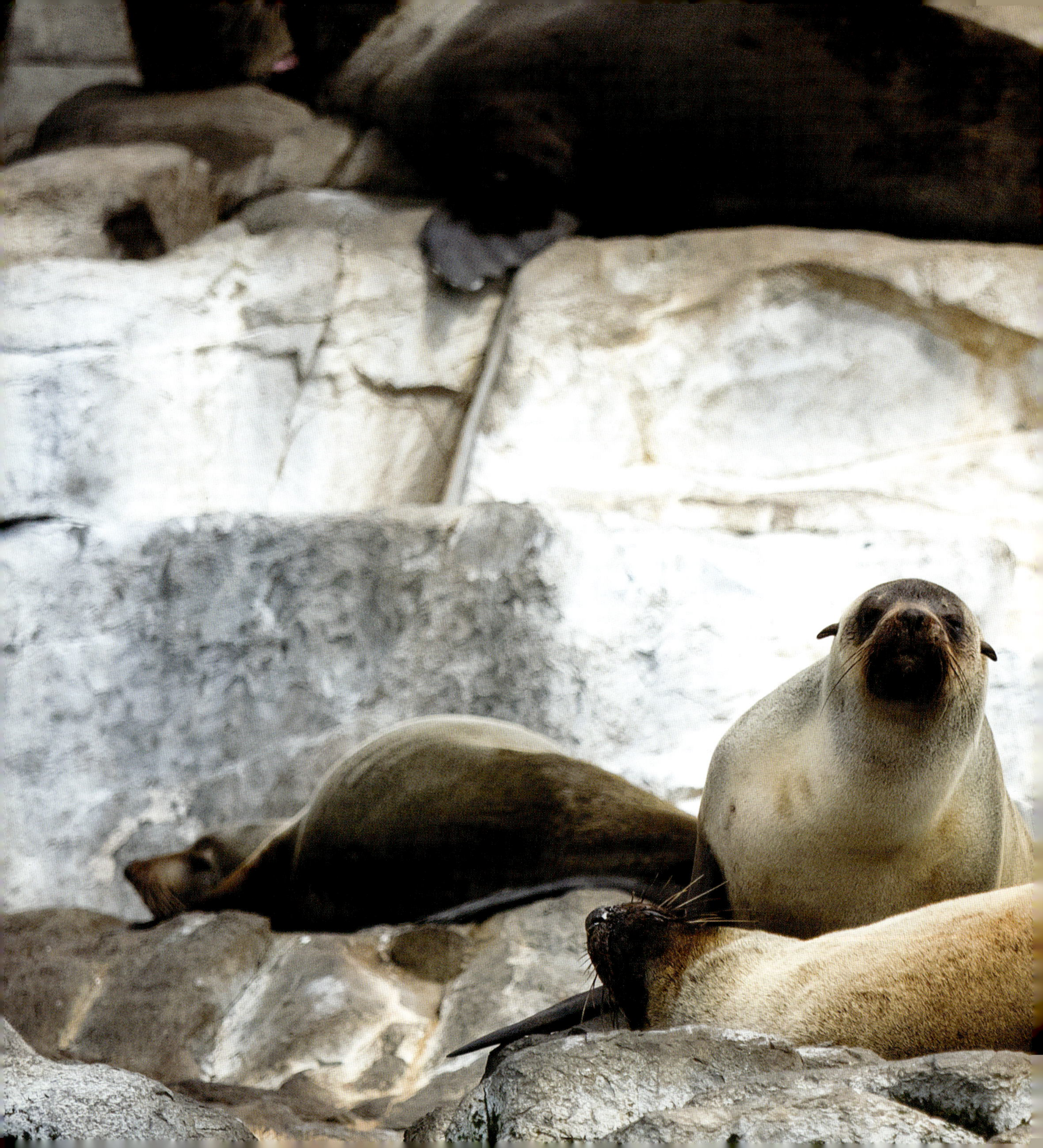

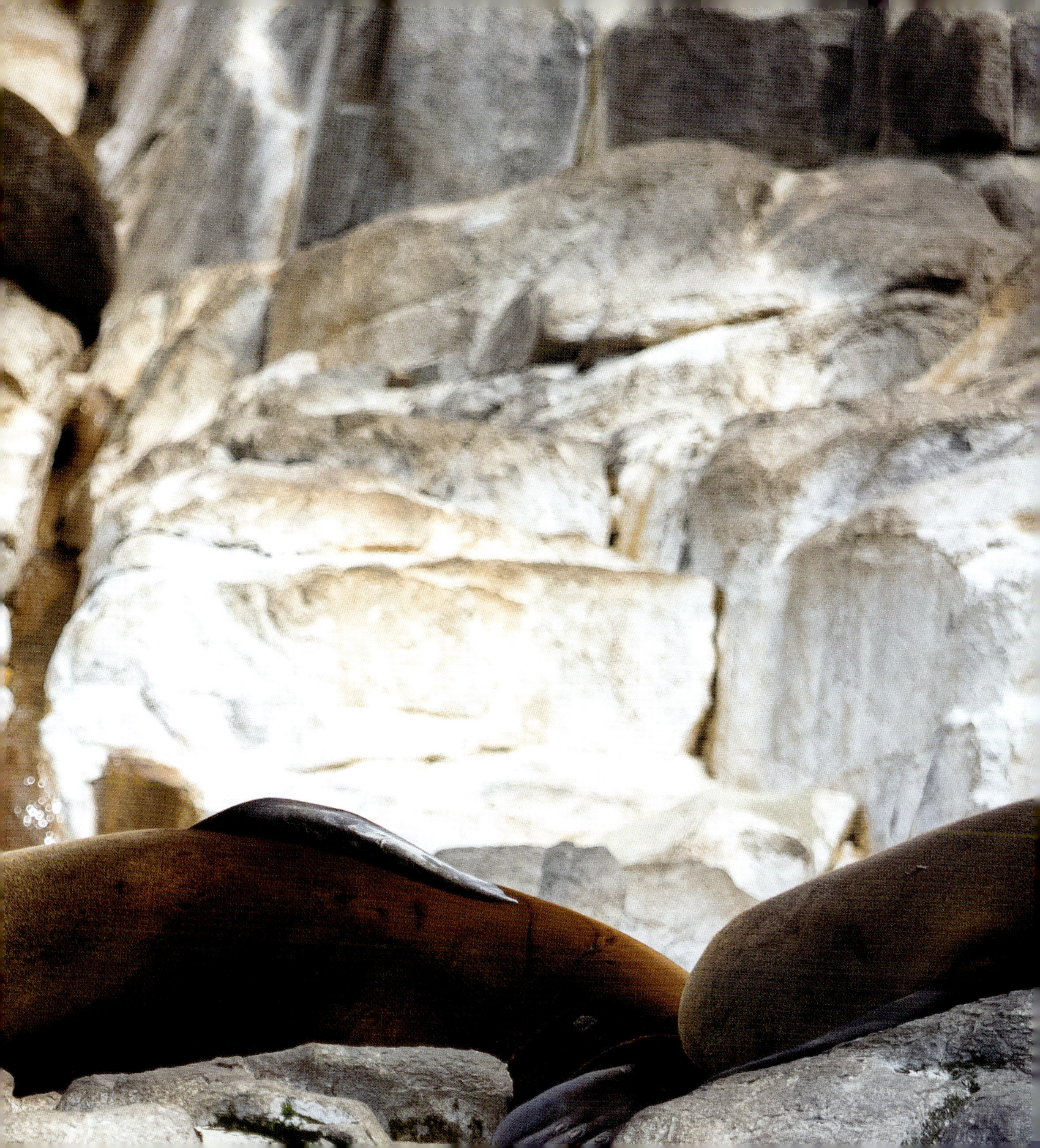

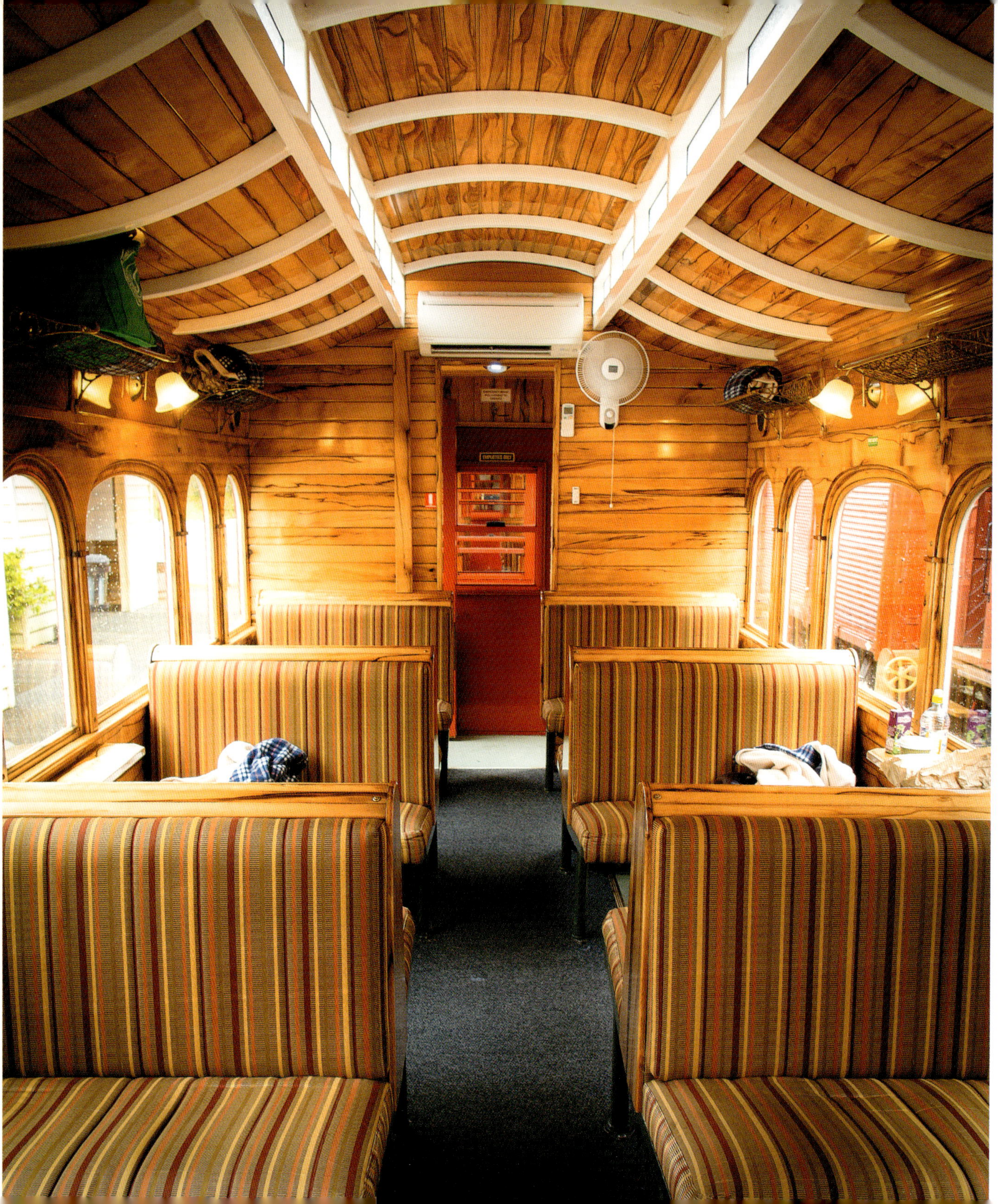

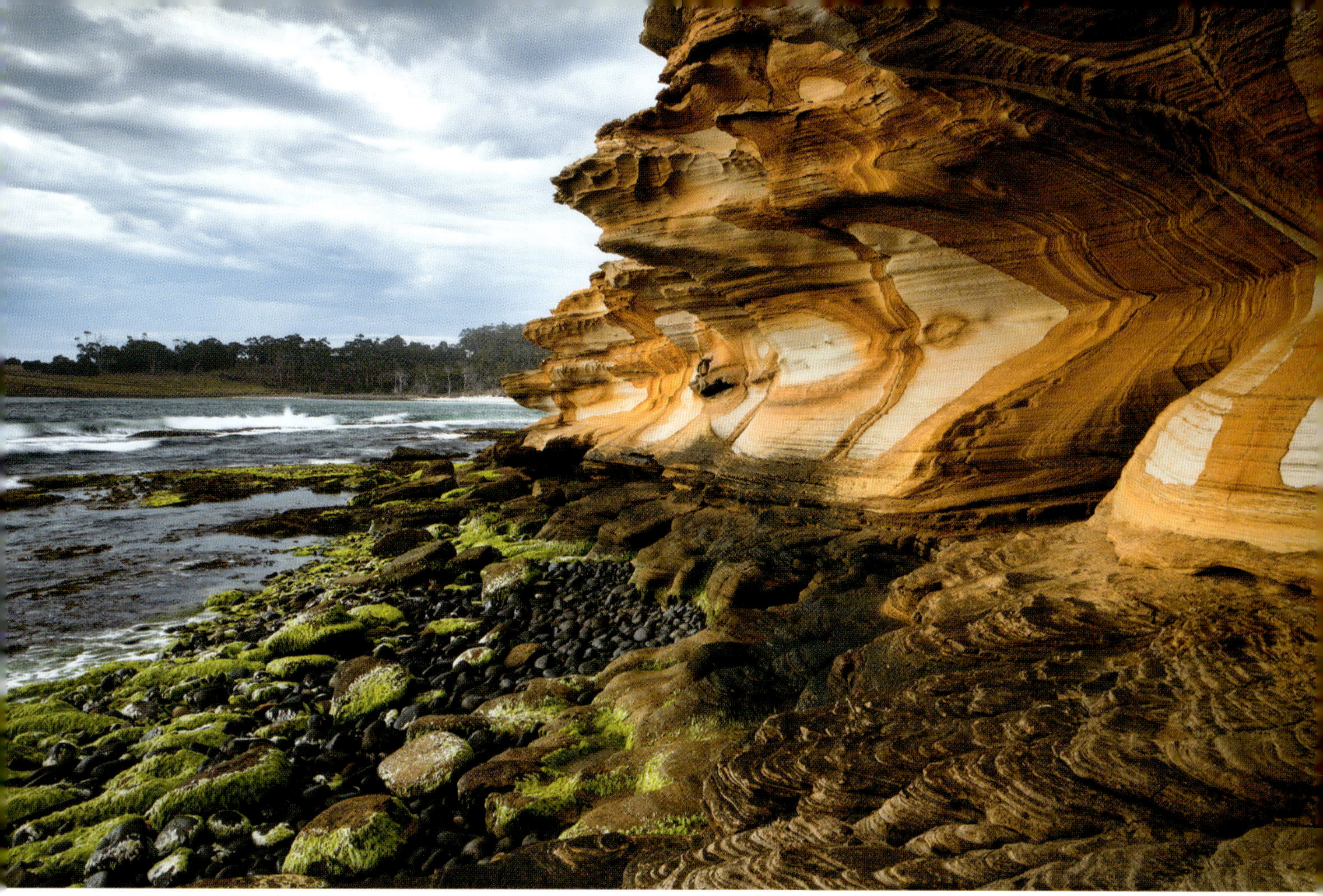

» **ABOVE** Weathered away over hundreds of years, these Maria Island sandstone cliffs are an incredible place to explore

» **OPPOSITE** Travel back in time along the West Coast Railway, departing from Queenstown and Strahan

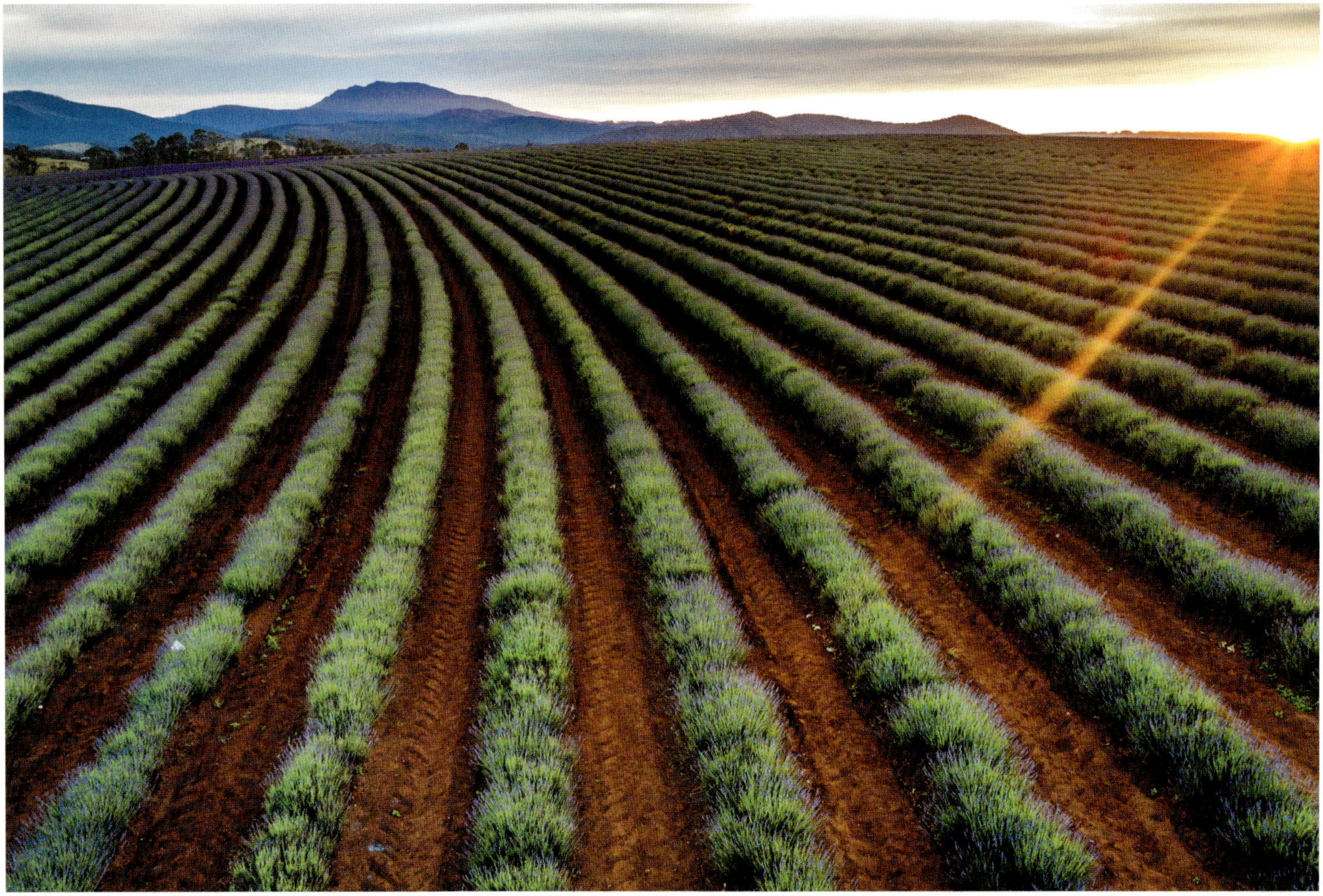

» **ABOVE** Late afternoon light bathes Bridestowe Lavender Estate

» **RIGHT** Gorgeous patterns inside Tasmanian abalone shells

» **OPPOSITE** A local peacock showing off at Cataract Gorge Reserve, Launceston

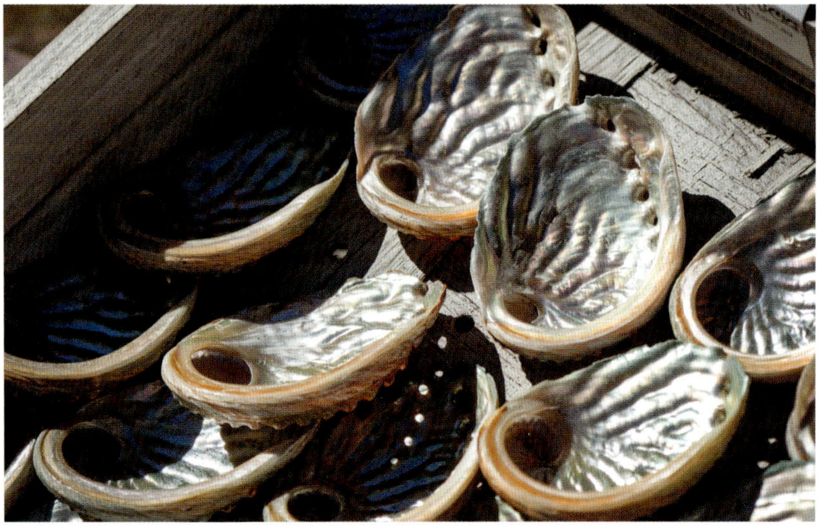

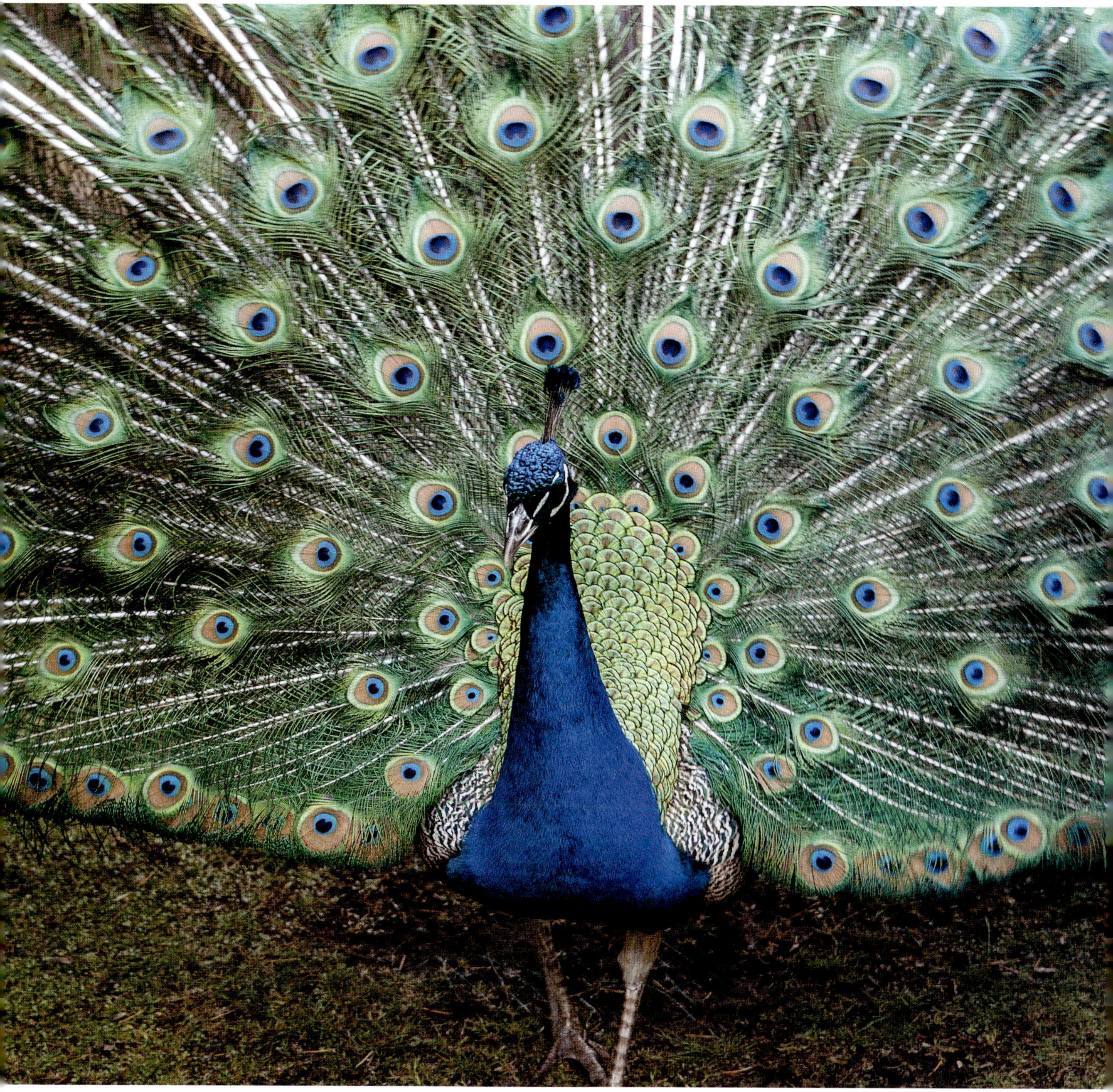

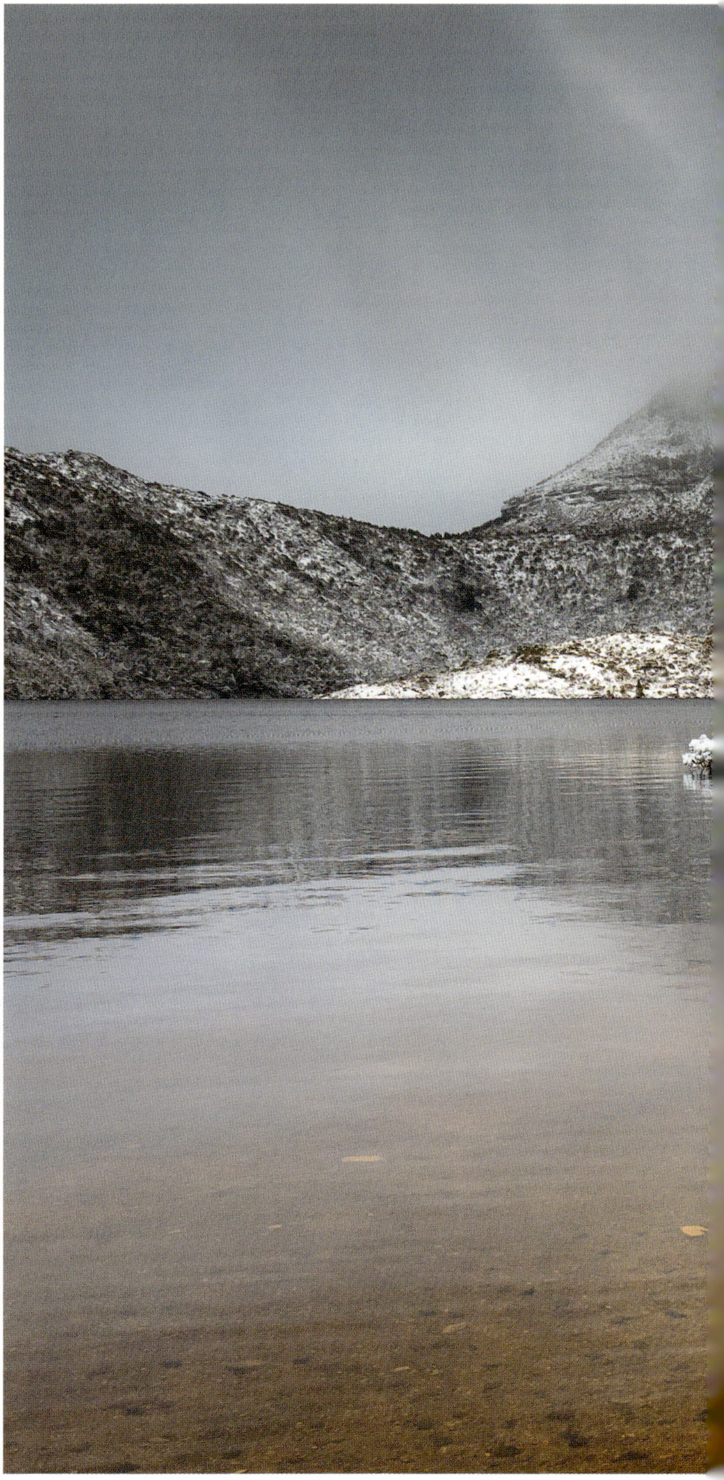

» **RIGHT** A light dusting of snow renders Cradle Mountain a winter wonderland

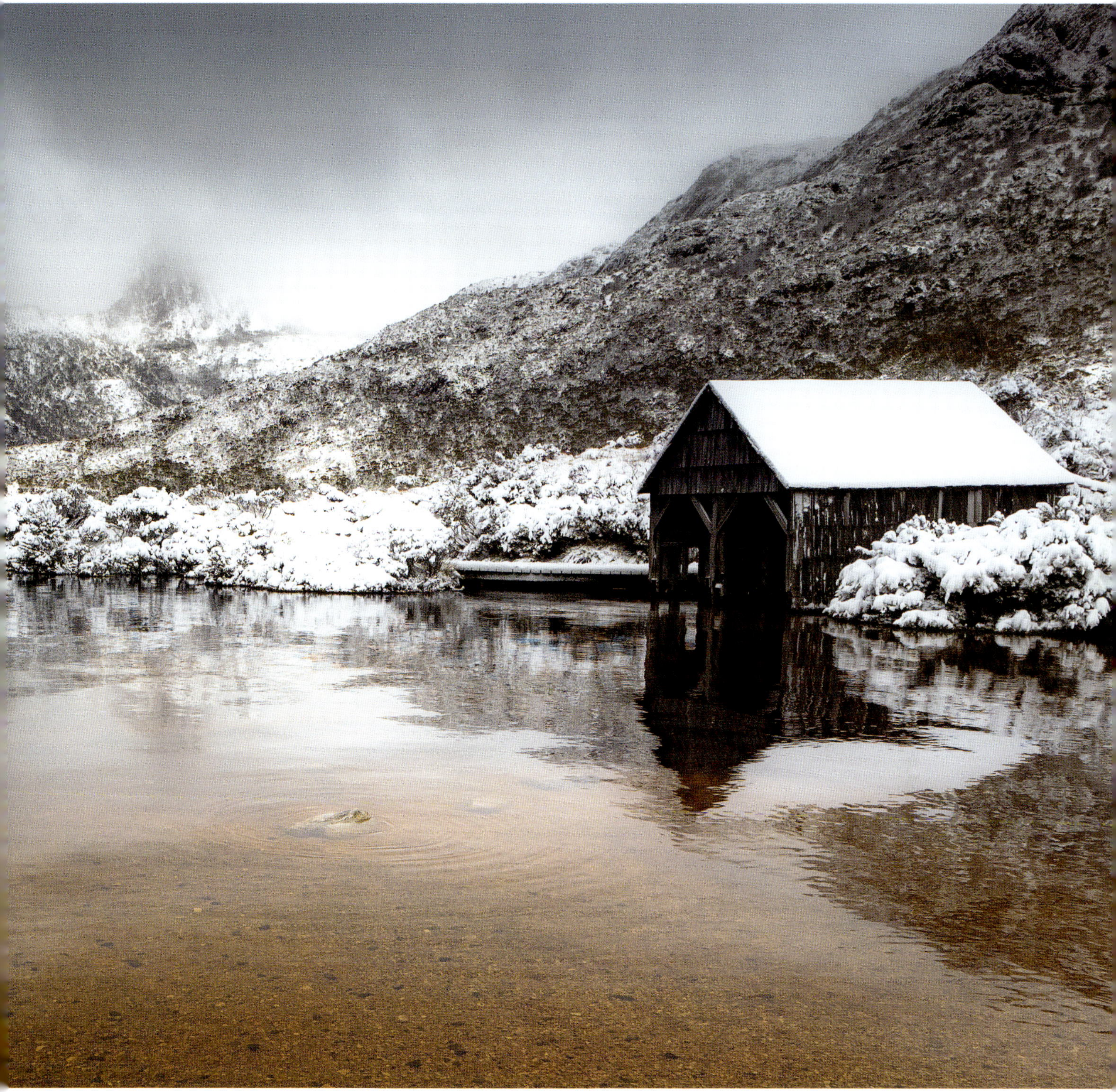

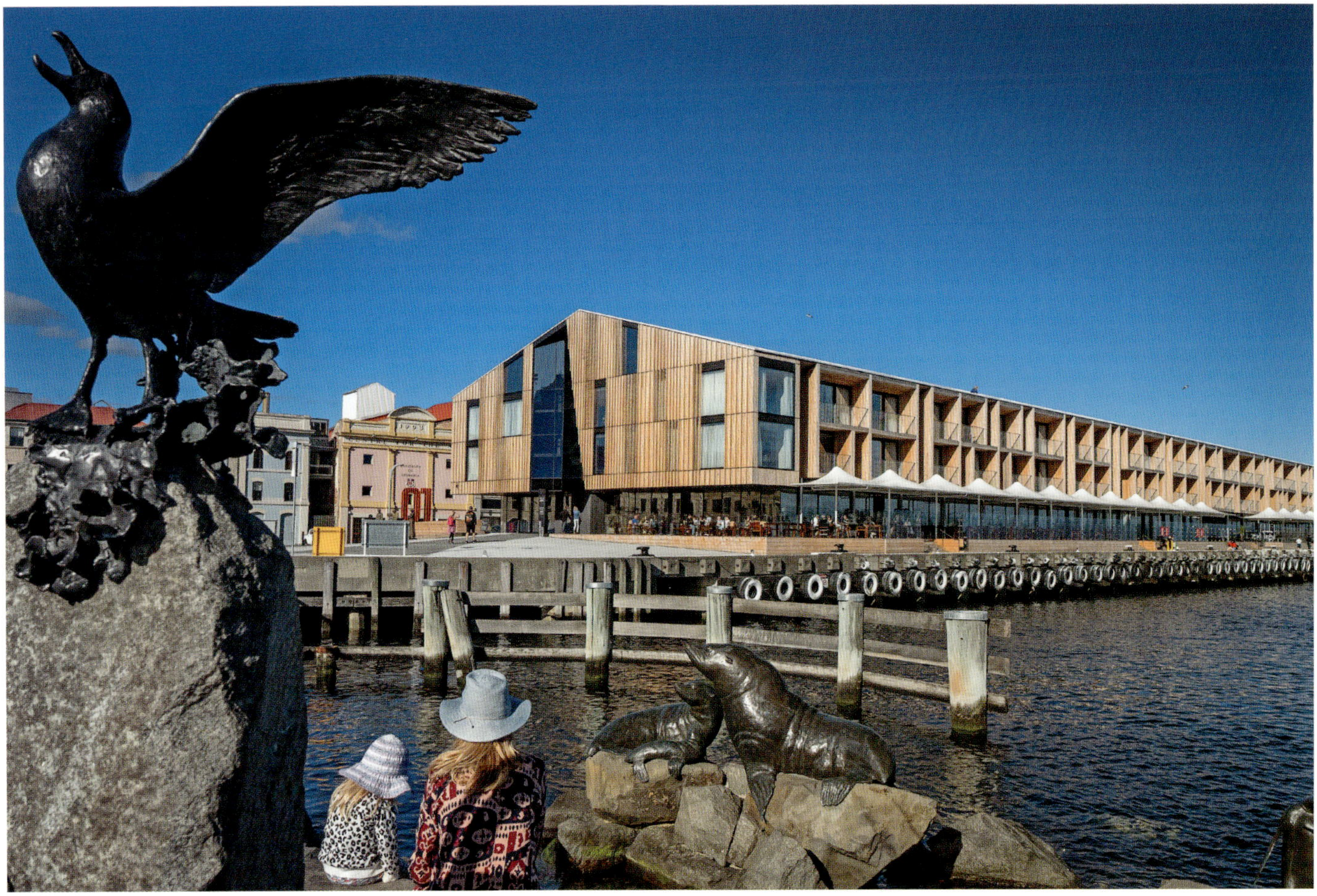

» **ABOVE** Looking out over the stunning MACq 01 Hotel along Hobart's waterfront

» **OPPOSITE** Seeing a cow on board the ferry to MONA art museum isn't out of the ordinary!

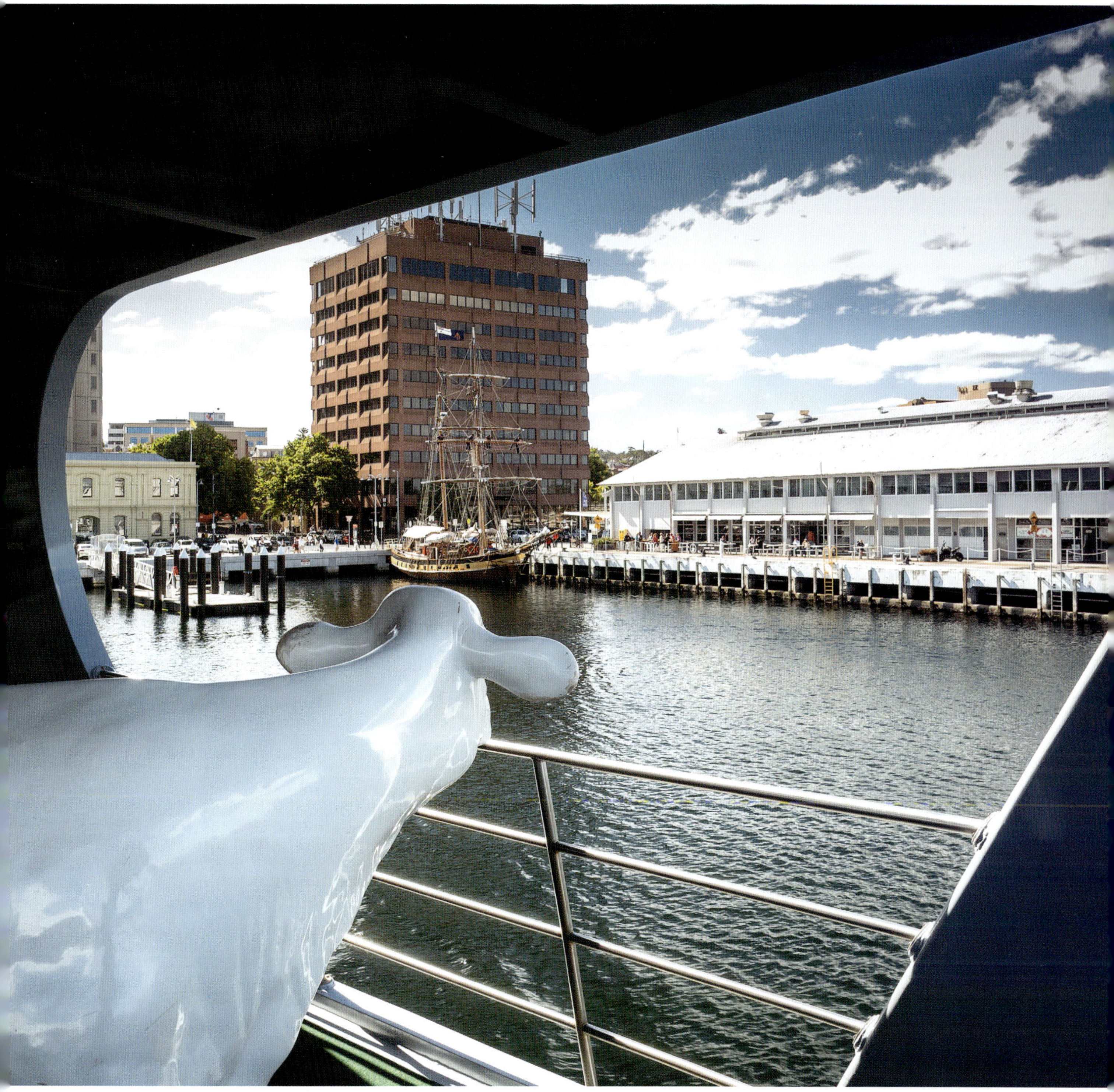

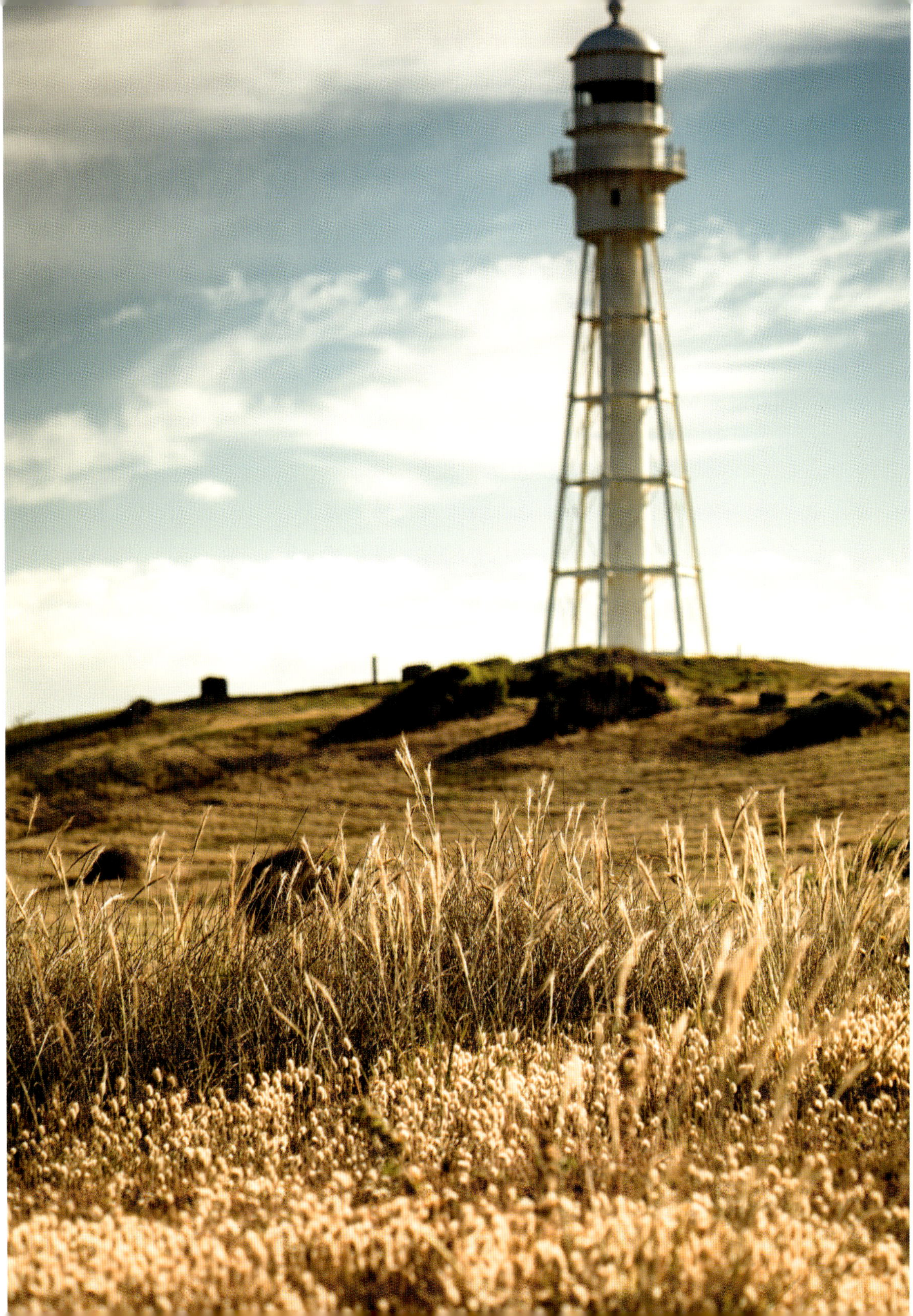

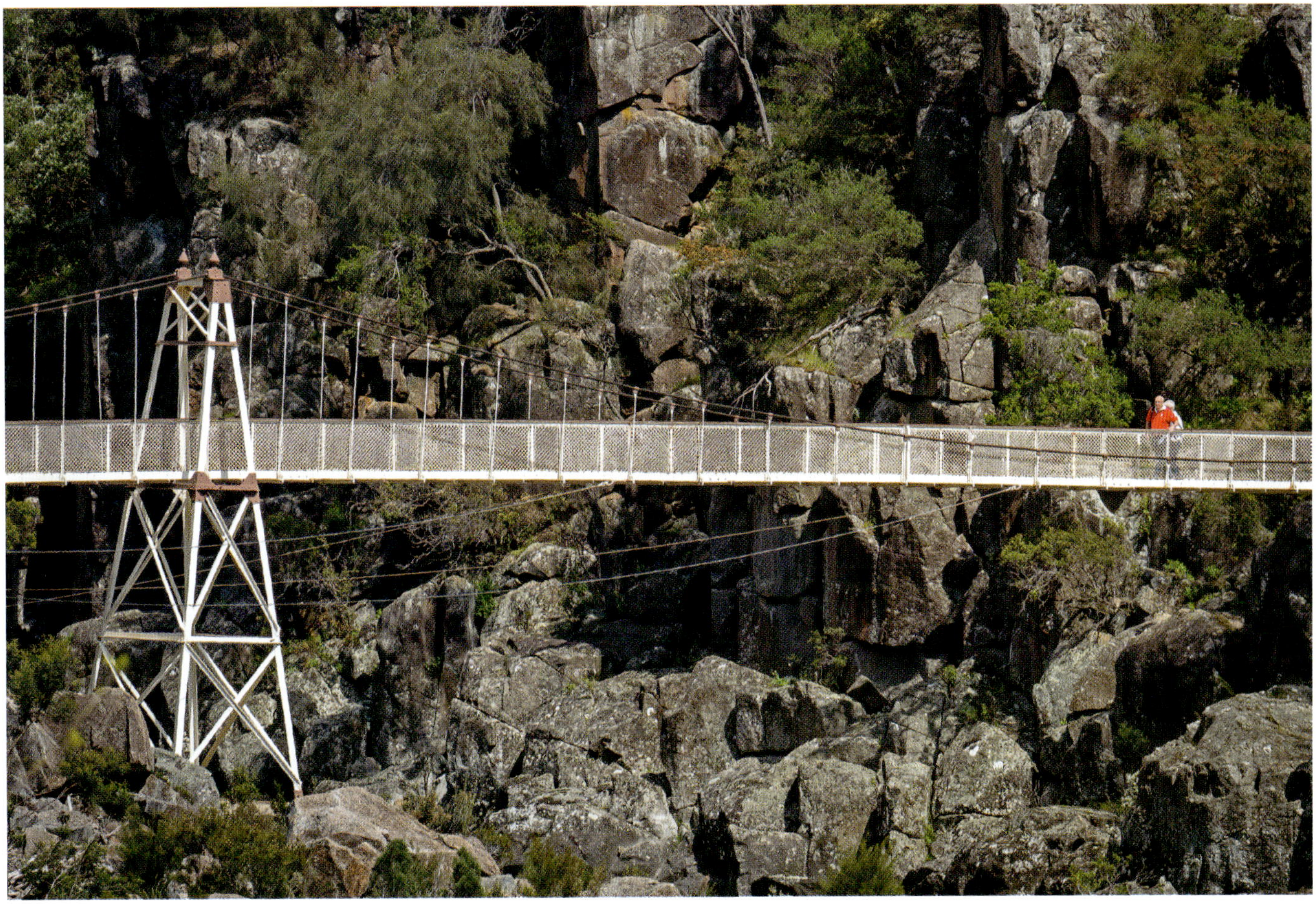

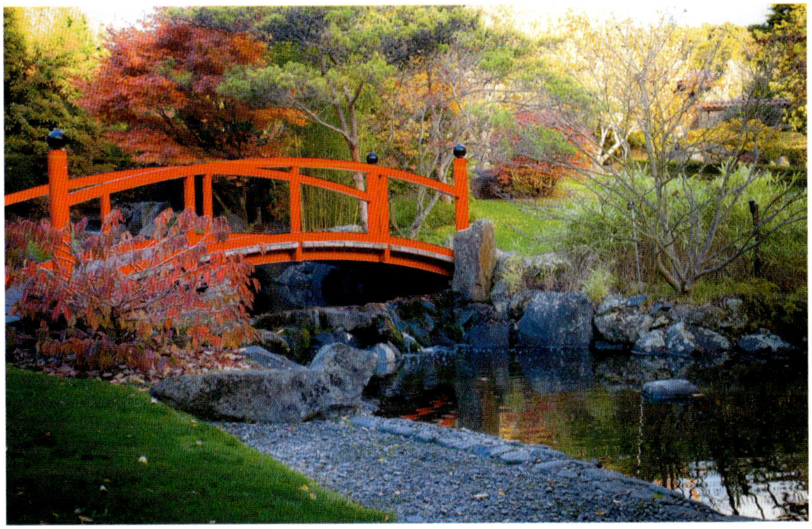

» **ABOVE** A stroll around the incredible Cataract Gorge is a must do for anyone visiting Launceston

» **LEFT** The stunning Japanese garden in Royal Tasmanian Botanical Gardens

» **OPPOSITE** The Currie Lighthouse overlooks the west coast of King Island. Australia's worst civil maritime disaster, the sinking of the Cararaqui, happened just a few kilometres from here

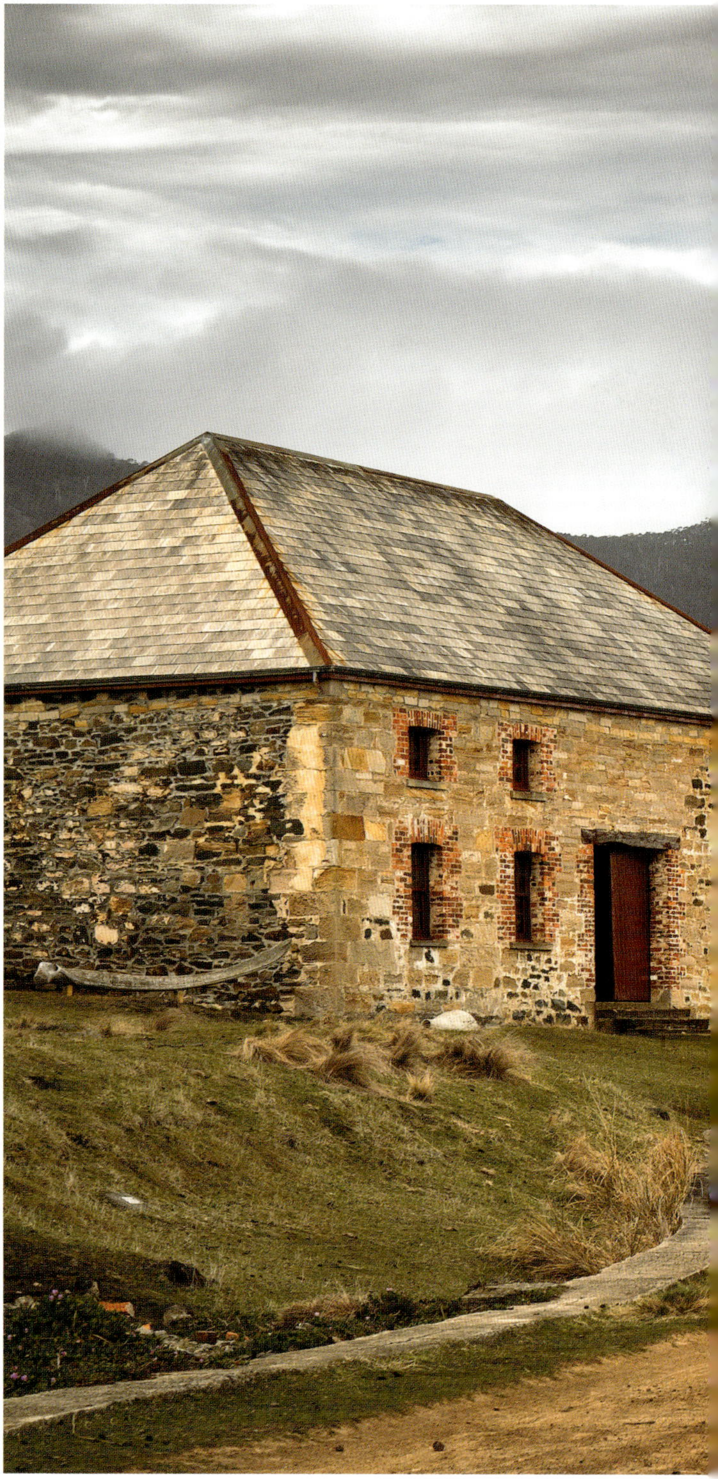

» **RIGHT** Maria Island is scattered with beautiful ruins from yesteryear, when it was bustling with activity

» **OVERLEAF** Horseshoe Falls is a serene place to gather your thoughts in Mount Field National Park

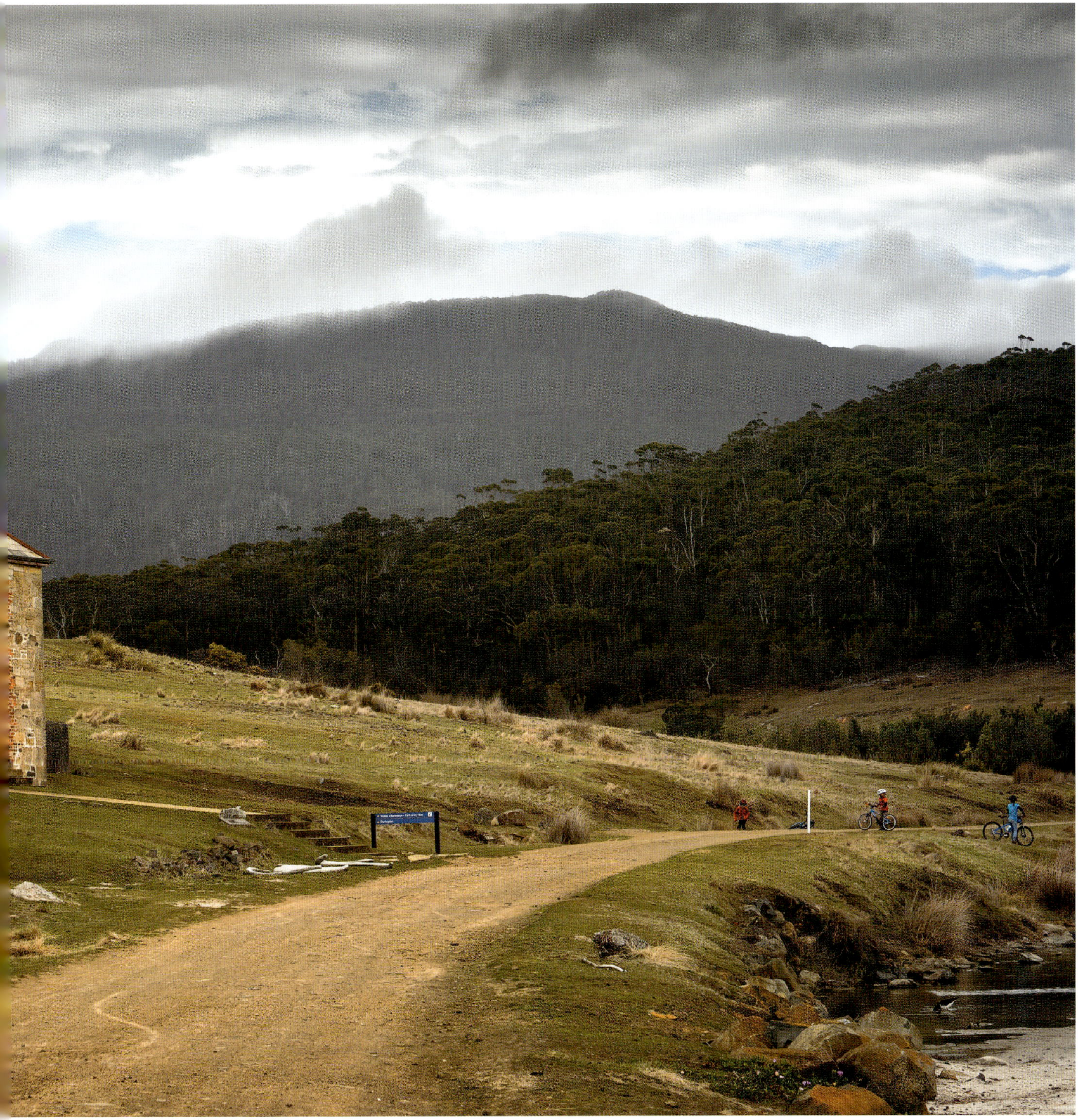

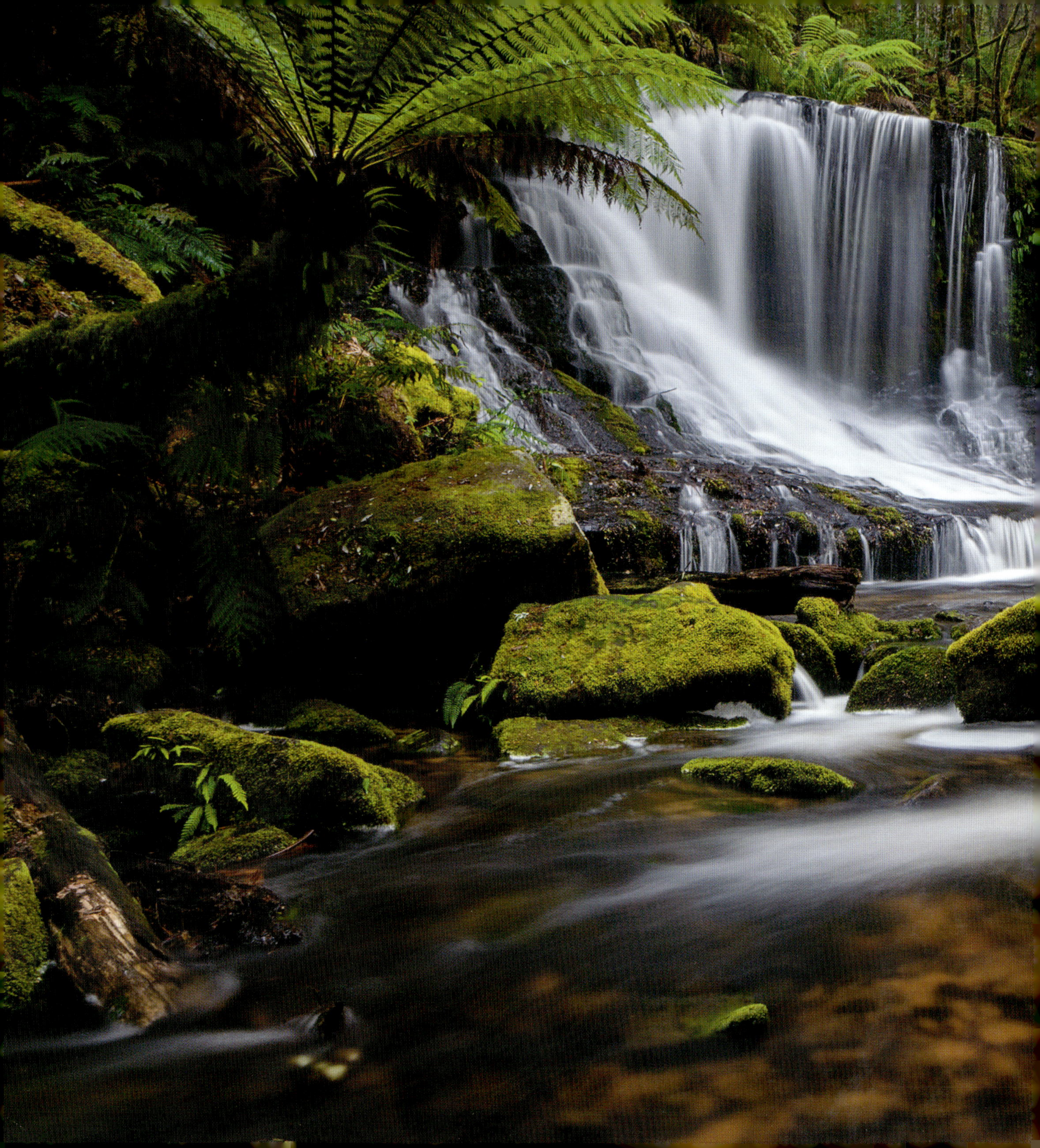

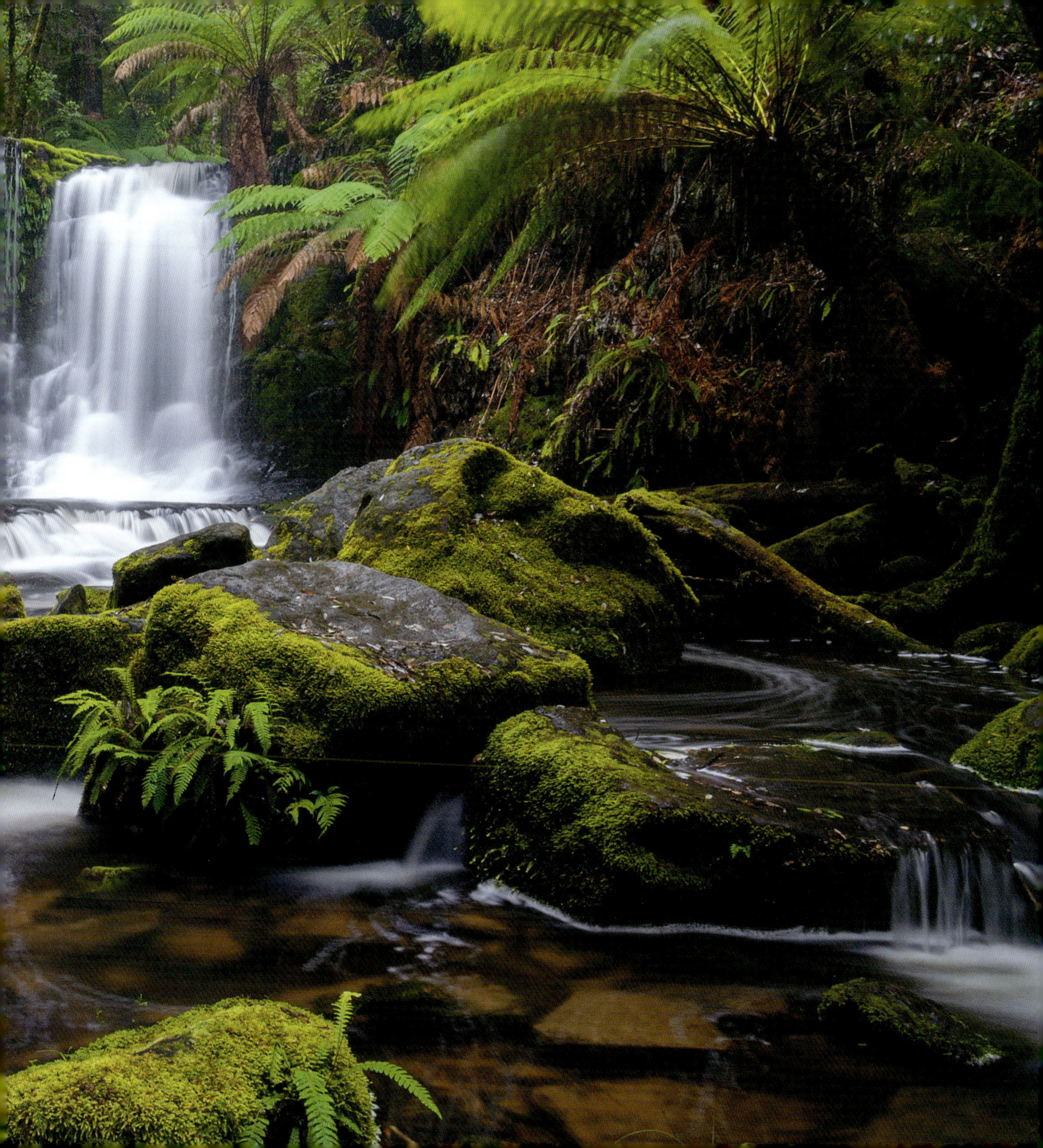

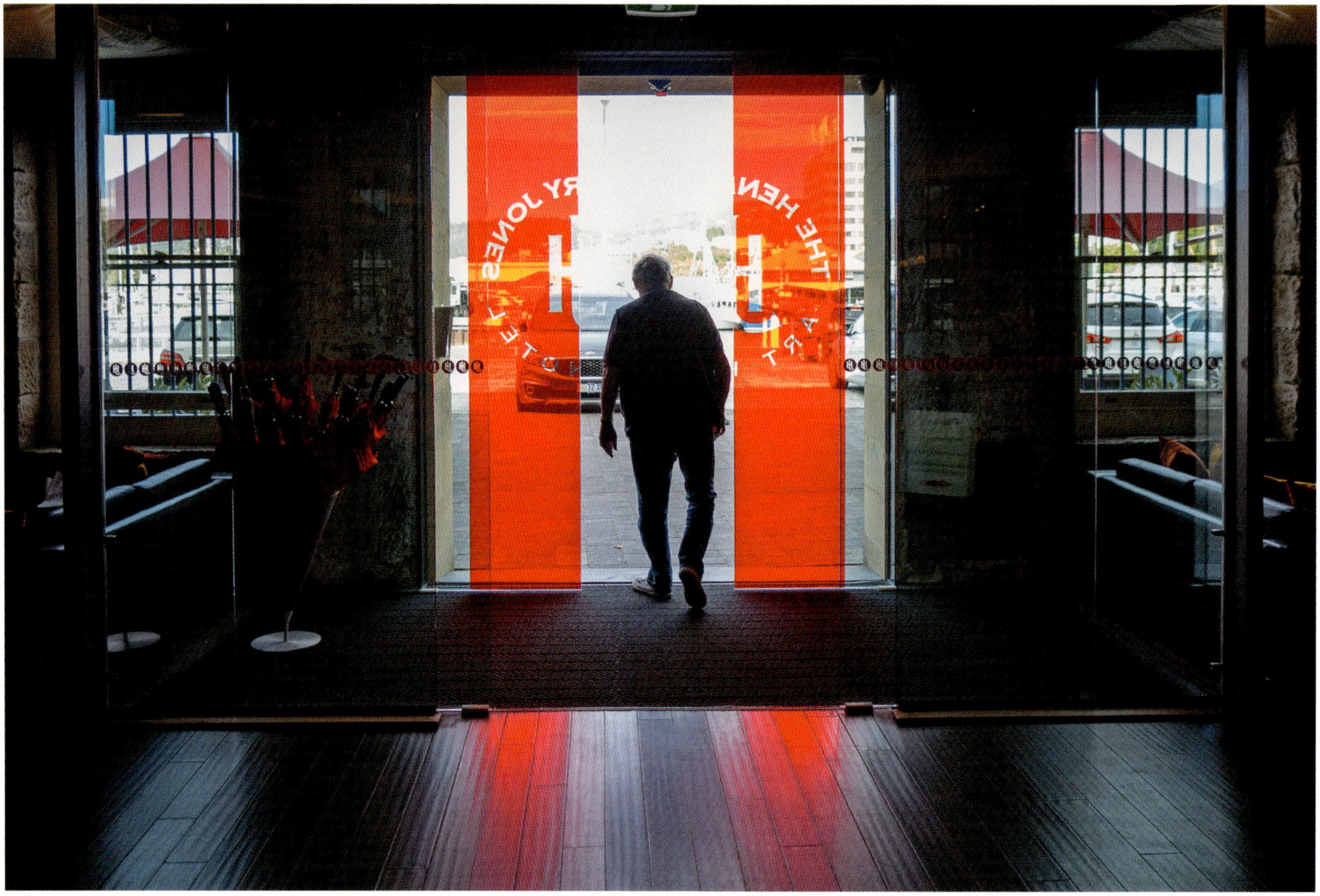

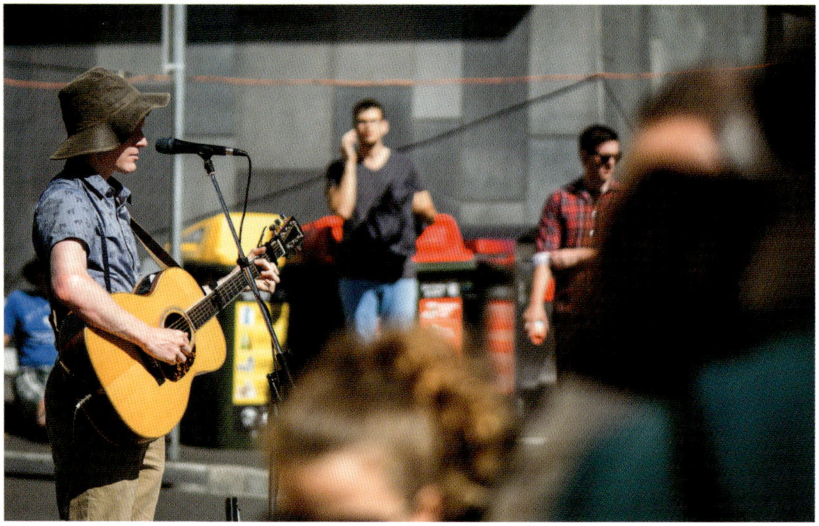

» **ABOVE** Checking out of the exquisite Henry Jones Art Hotel in Hobart

» **RIGHT** Street performers add lovely sounds to the hustle and bustle of Salamanca Market

» **OPPOSITE** Colourful characters and their cars from the Variety Bash charity event stop for refreshments in Bothwell

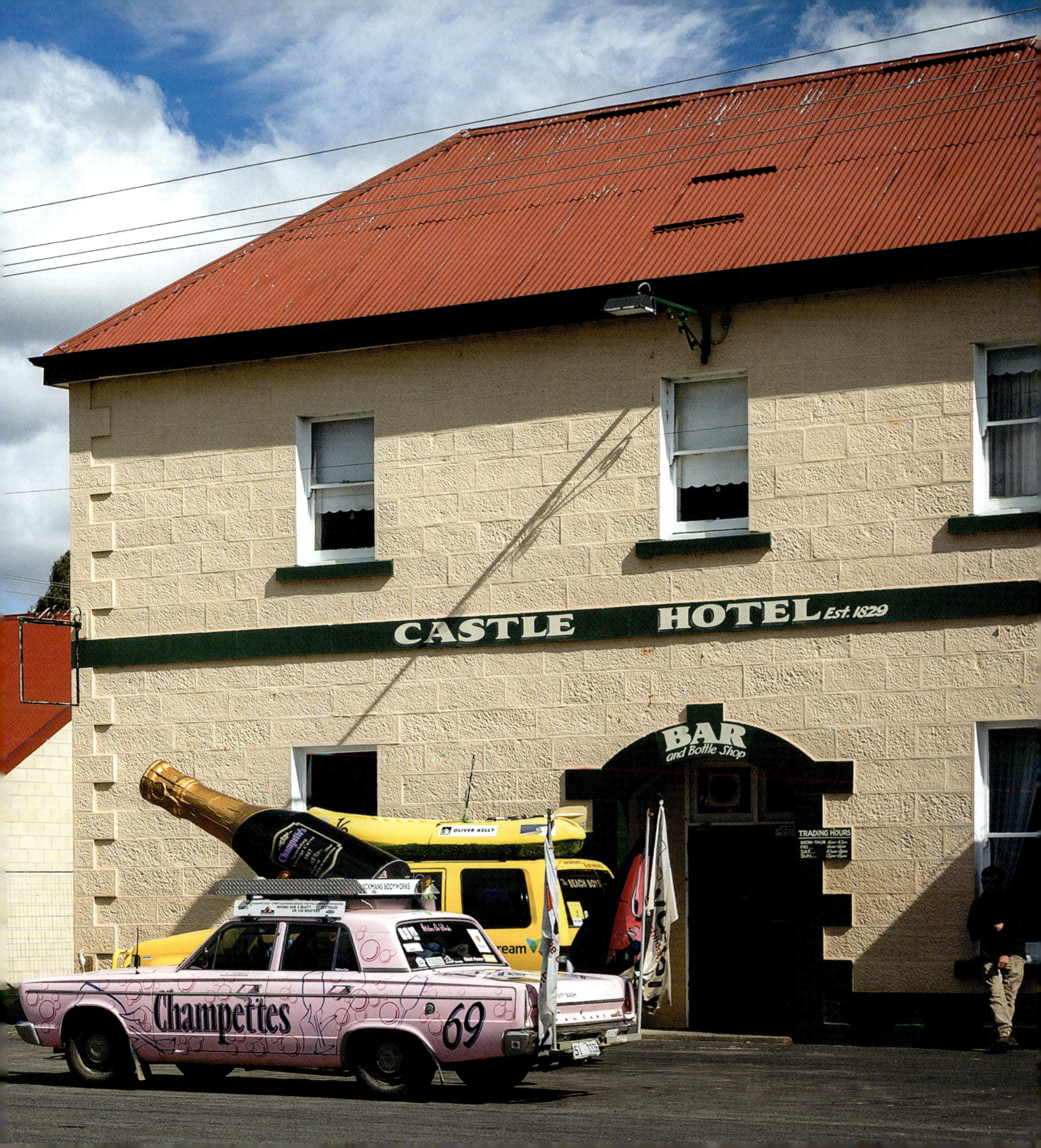
CASTLE HOTEL Est. 1829
BAR and Bottle Shop
TRADING HOURS
Champettes
69

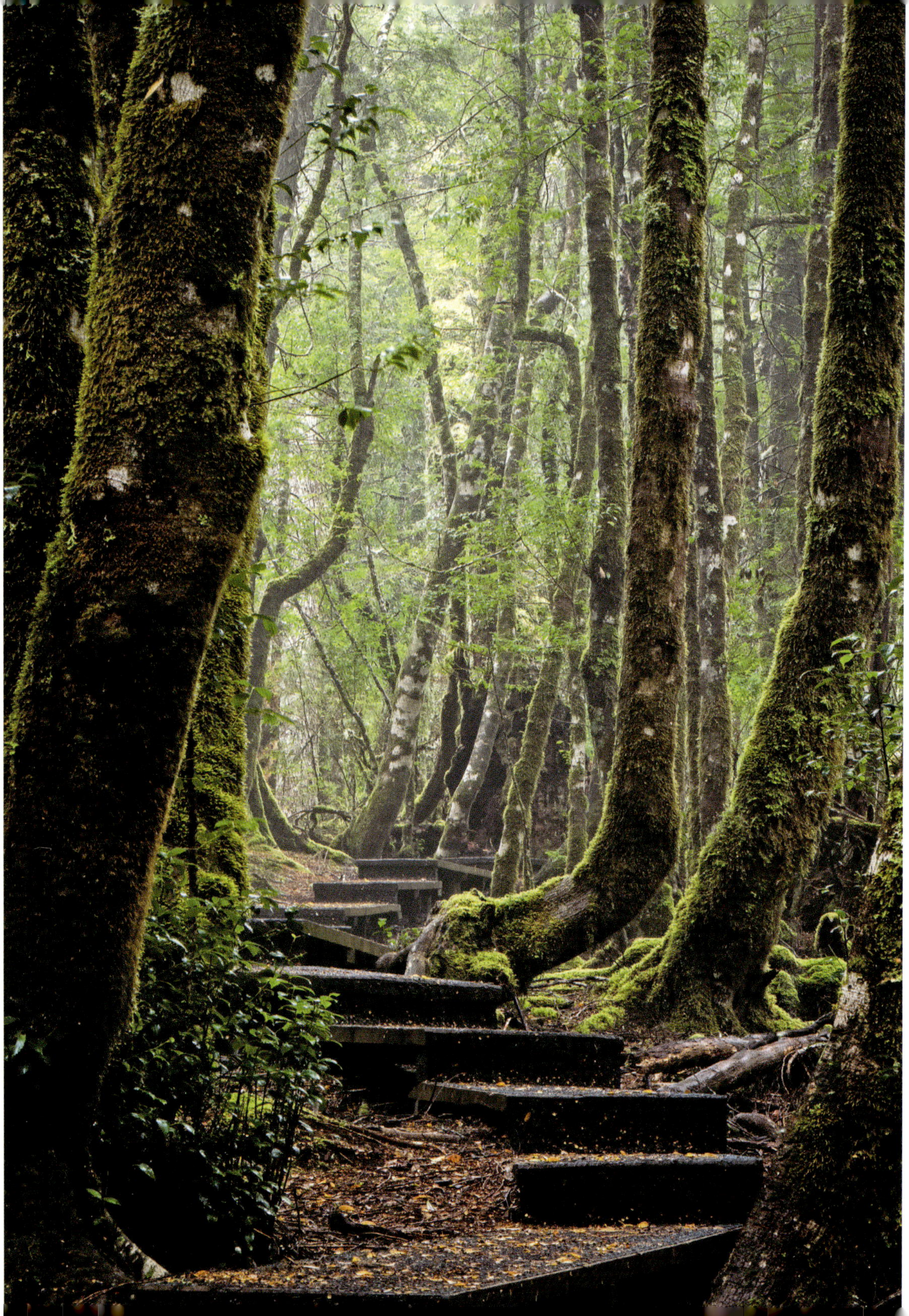

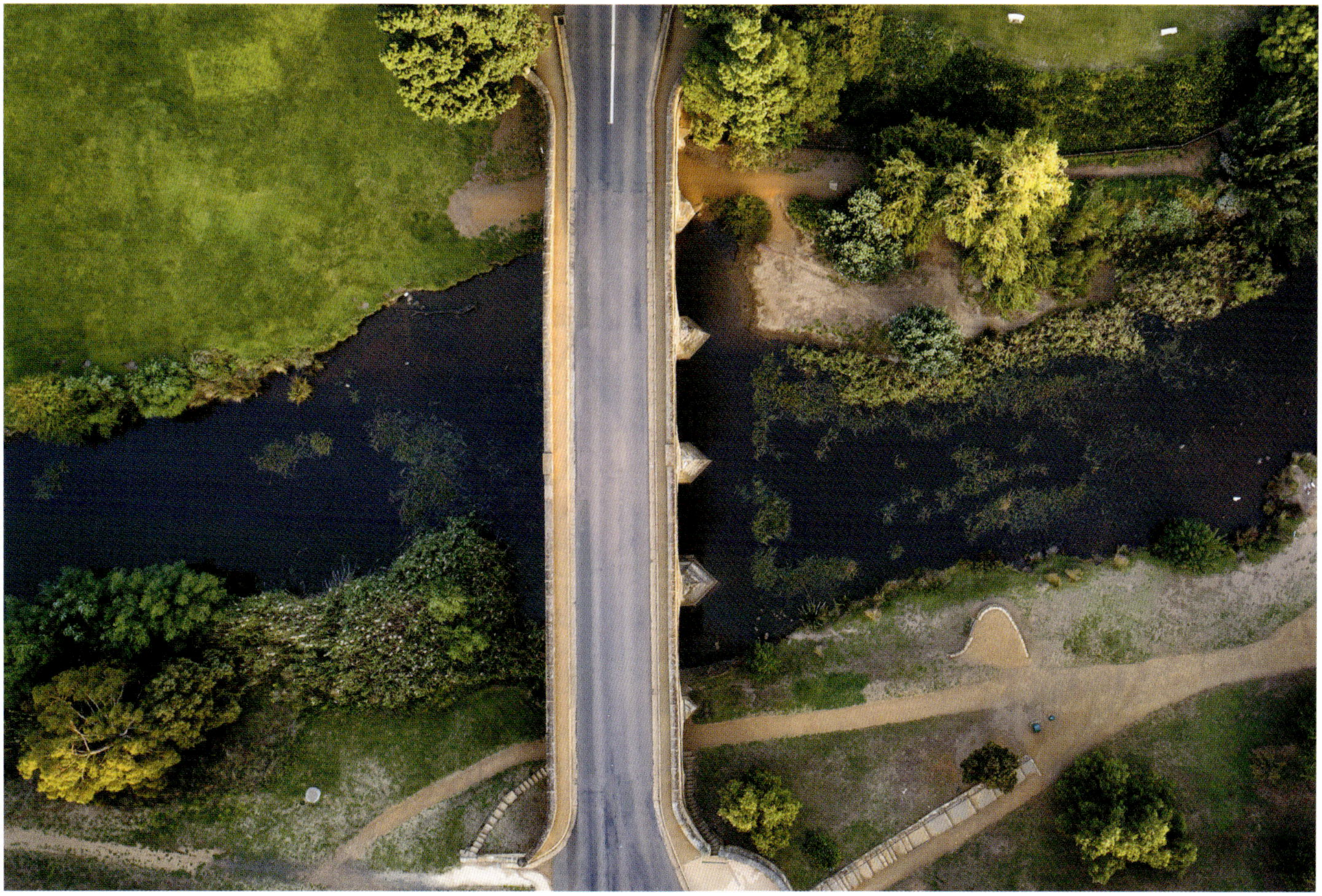

» **ABOVE** Australia's oldest bridge as seen from above, in Richmond

» **OPPOSITE** A stairway meanders through an ancient King Billy pines forest at Cradle Mountain–Lake St Clair National Park

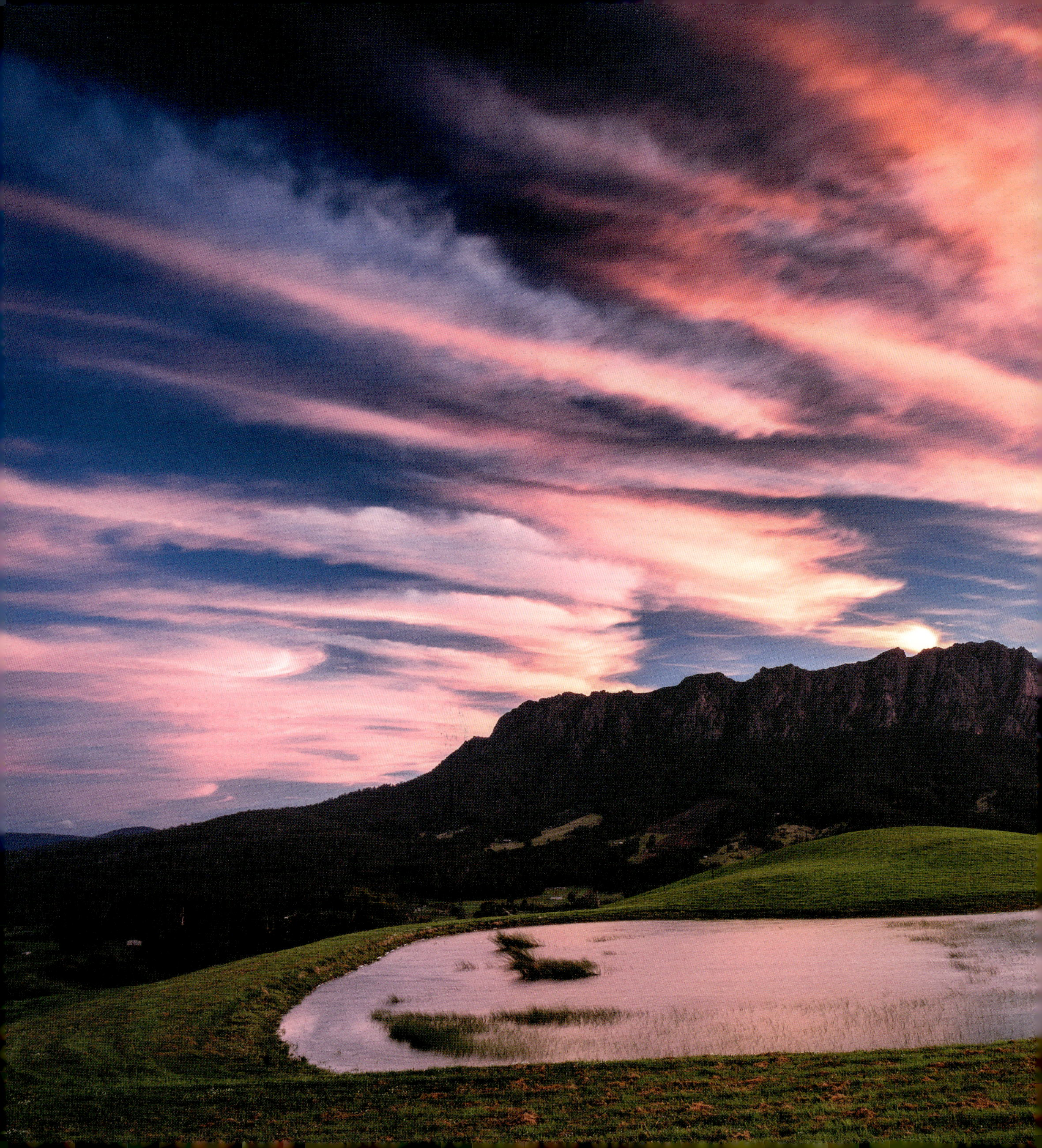

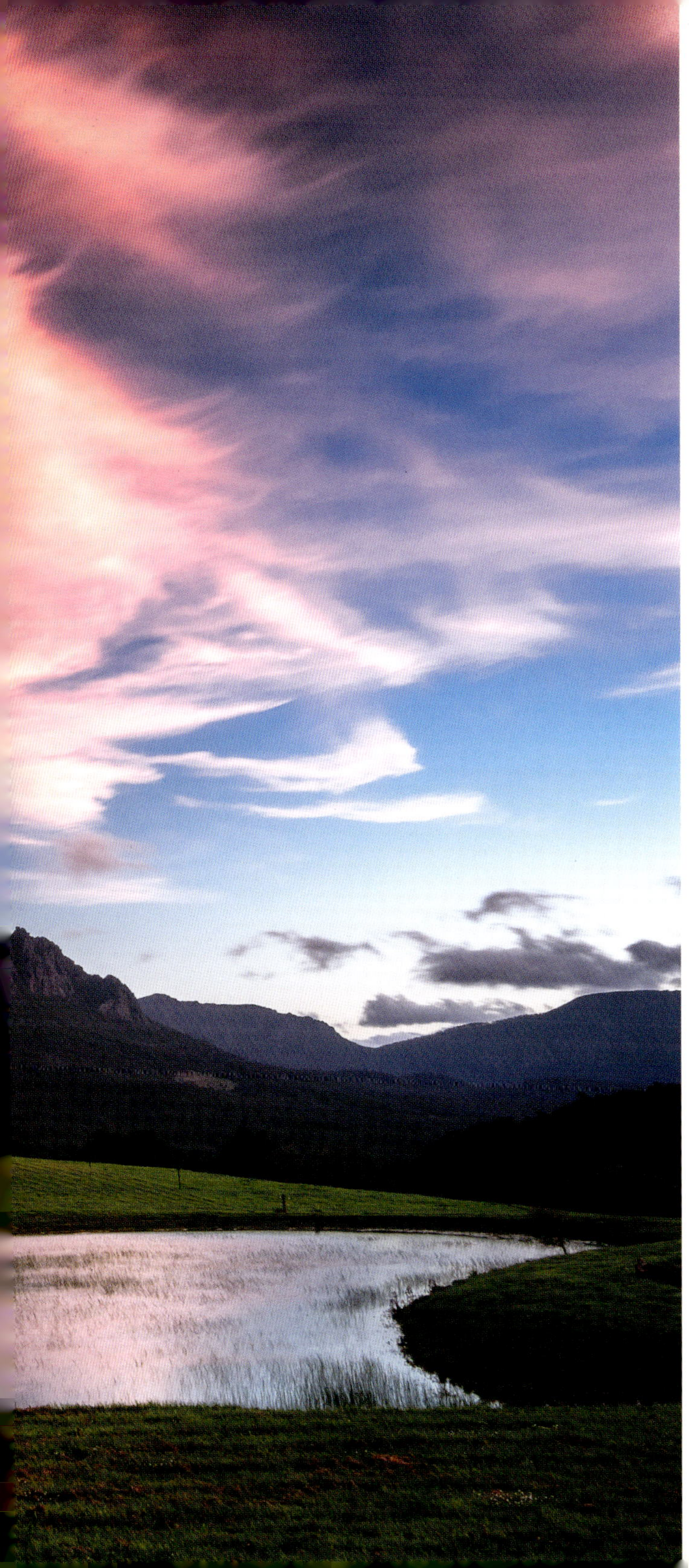

» **LEFT** A room with a view. Sunset from Eagles Nest Retreat in Sheffield

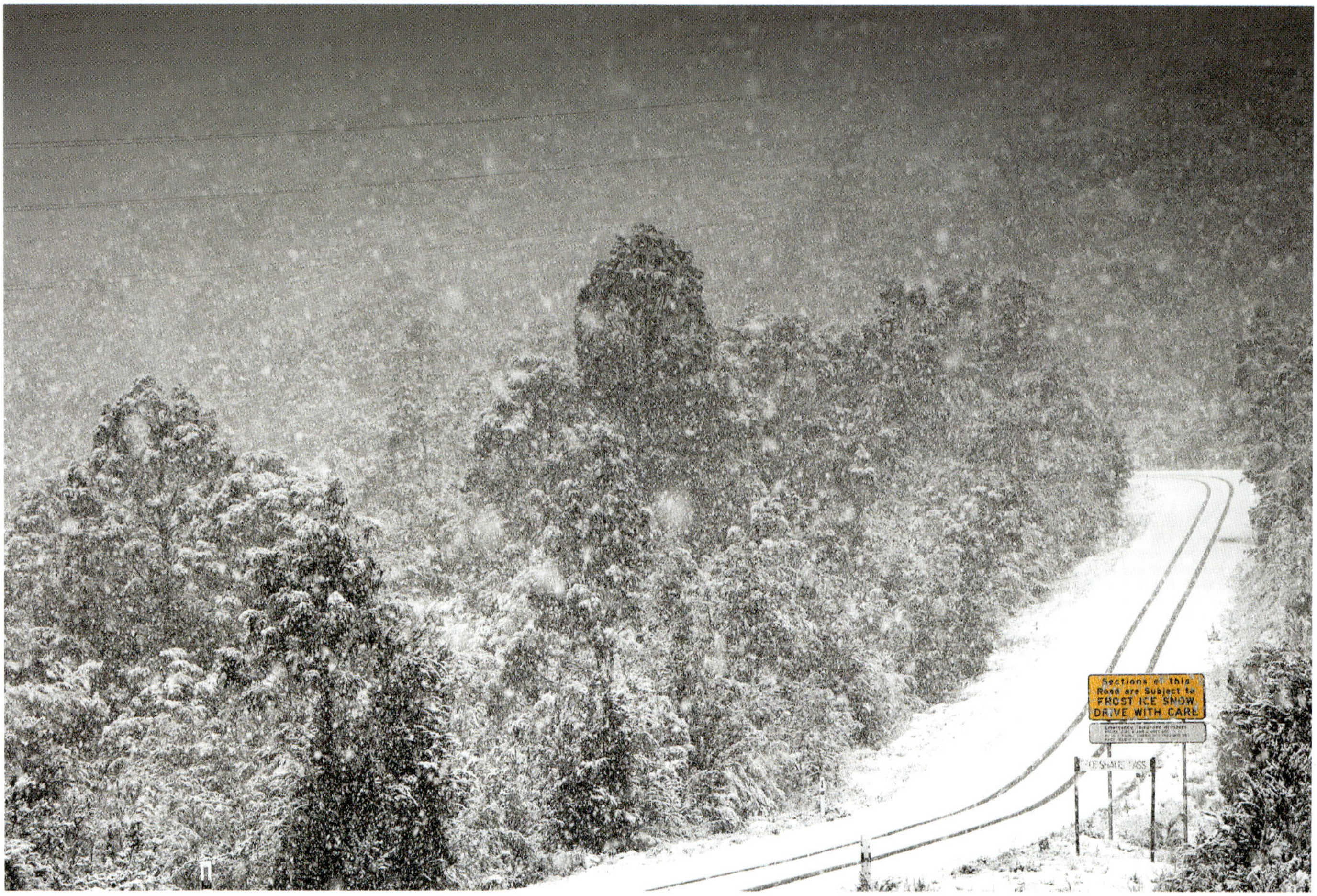

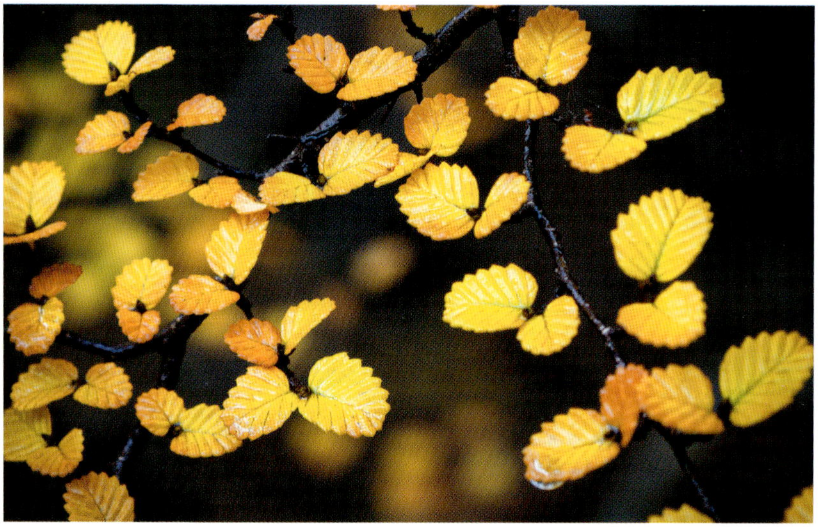

» **ABOVE** A winter blast covers Tasmania's south-west

» **RIGHT** The fagus – Tasmania's deciduous beech tree – during autumn

» **OPPOSITE** A bay to yourself at Bathurst Harbour in Southwest National Park

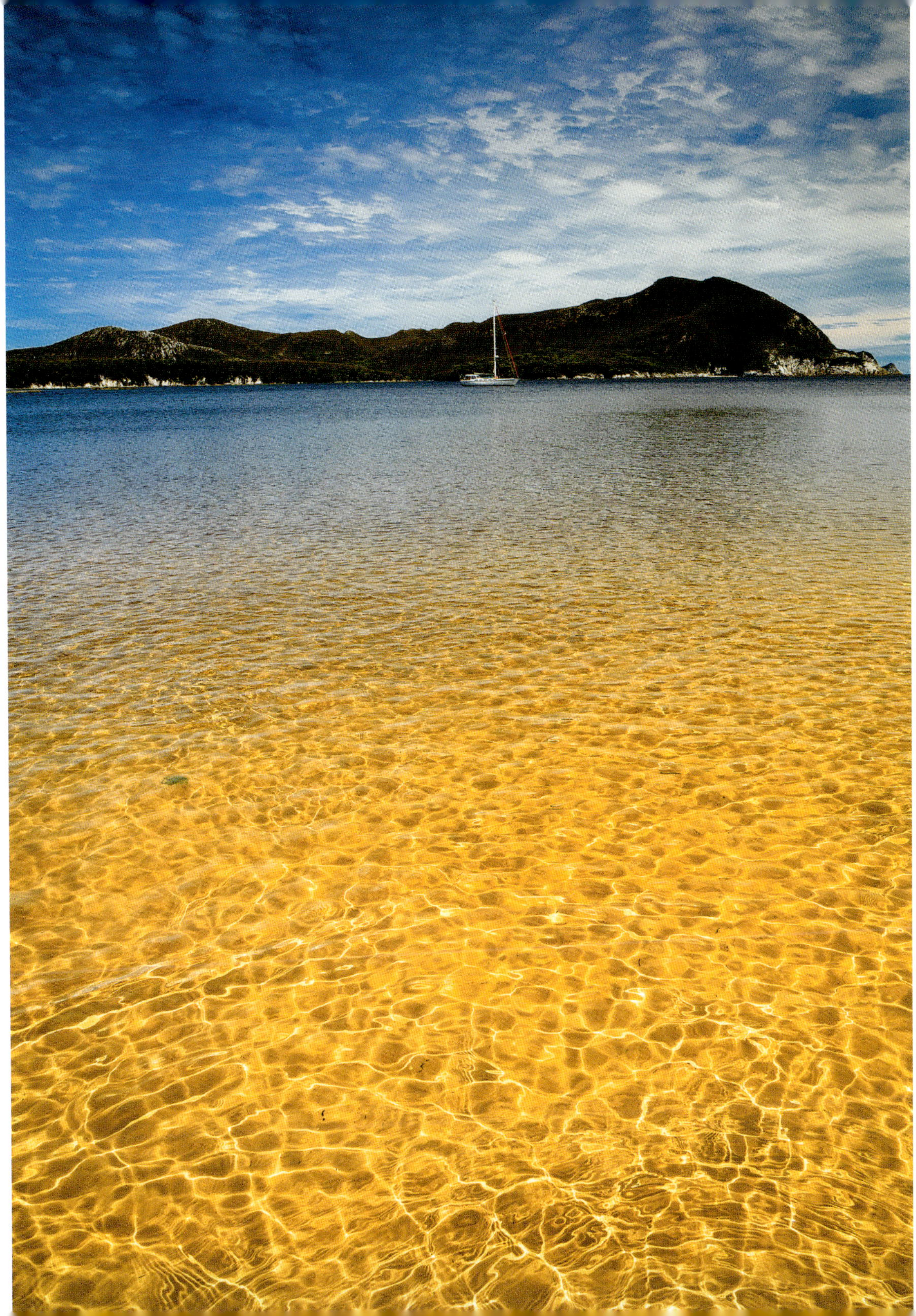

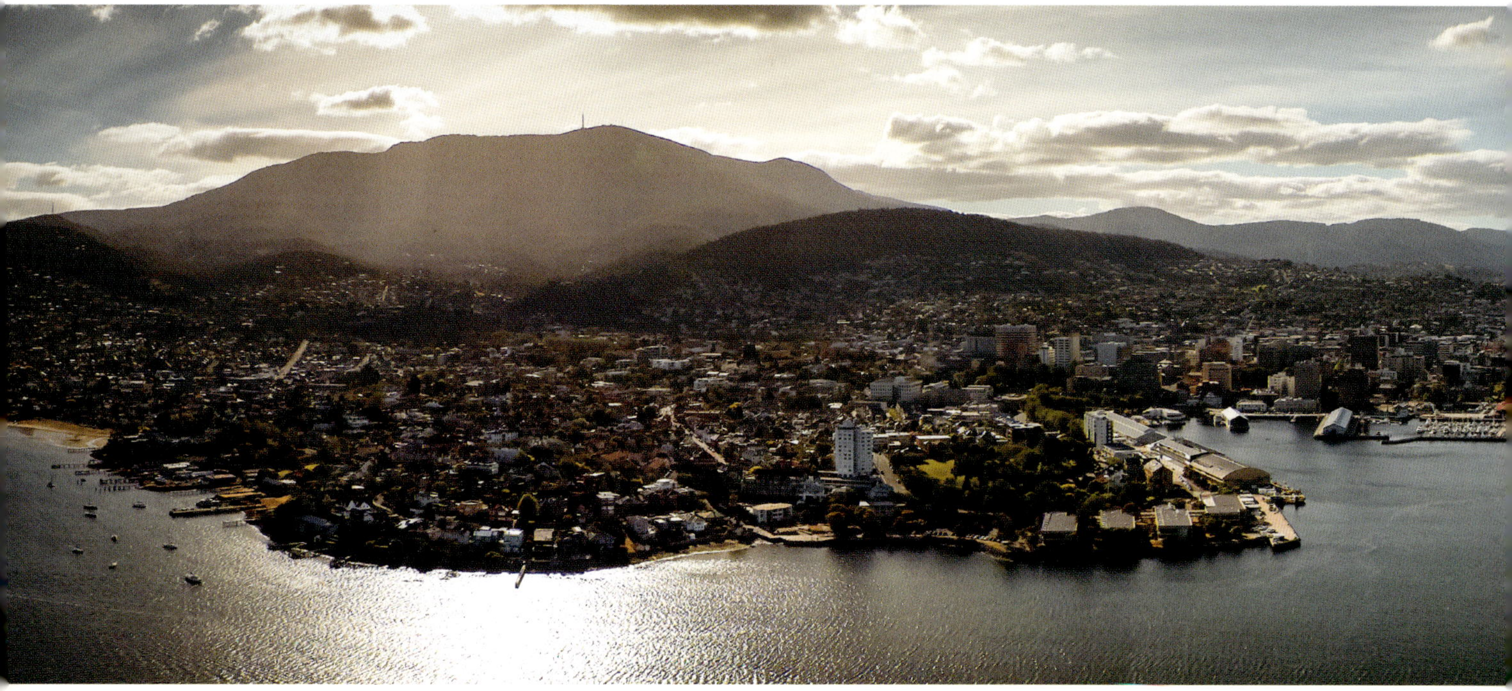

» **ABOVE** A bird's eye view of Hobart and its flurry of activity during the summer months

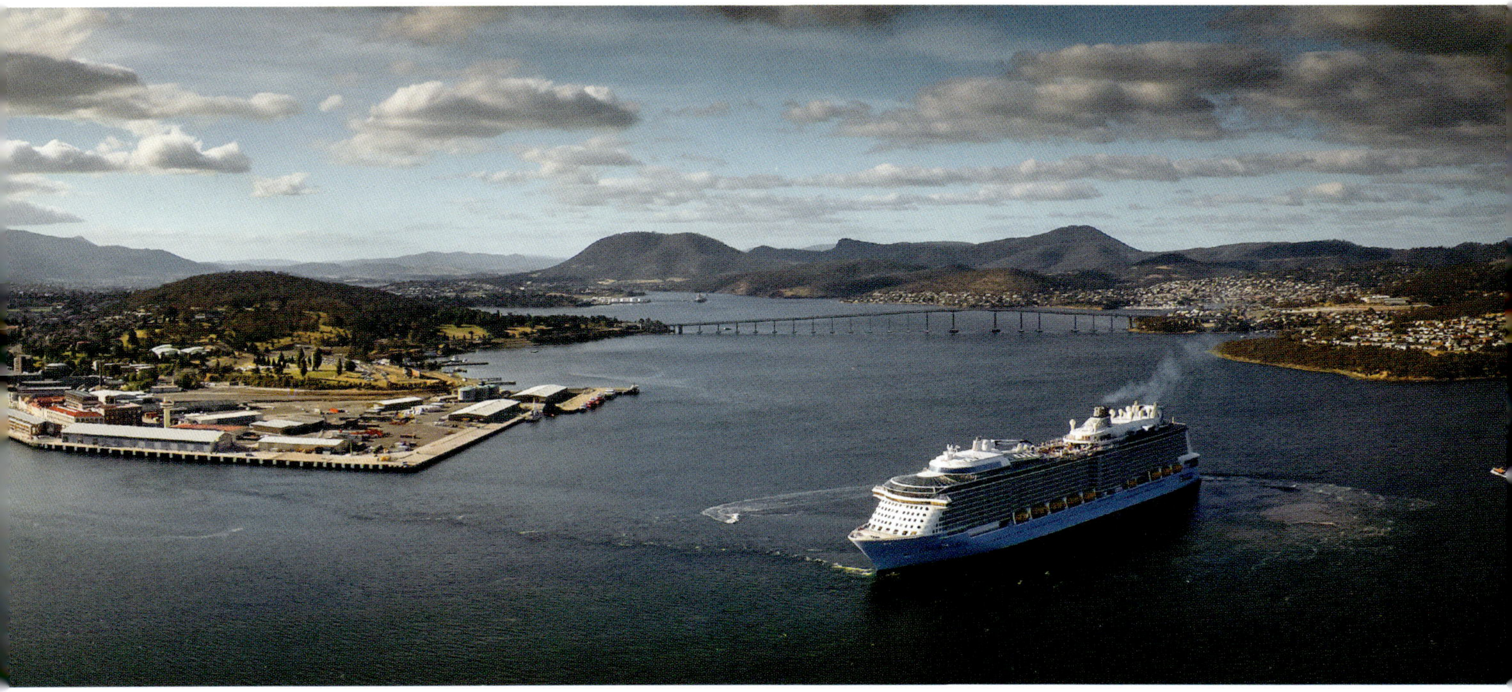

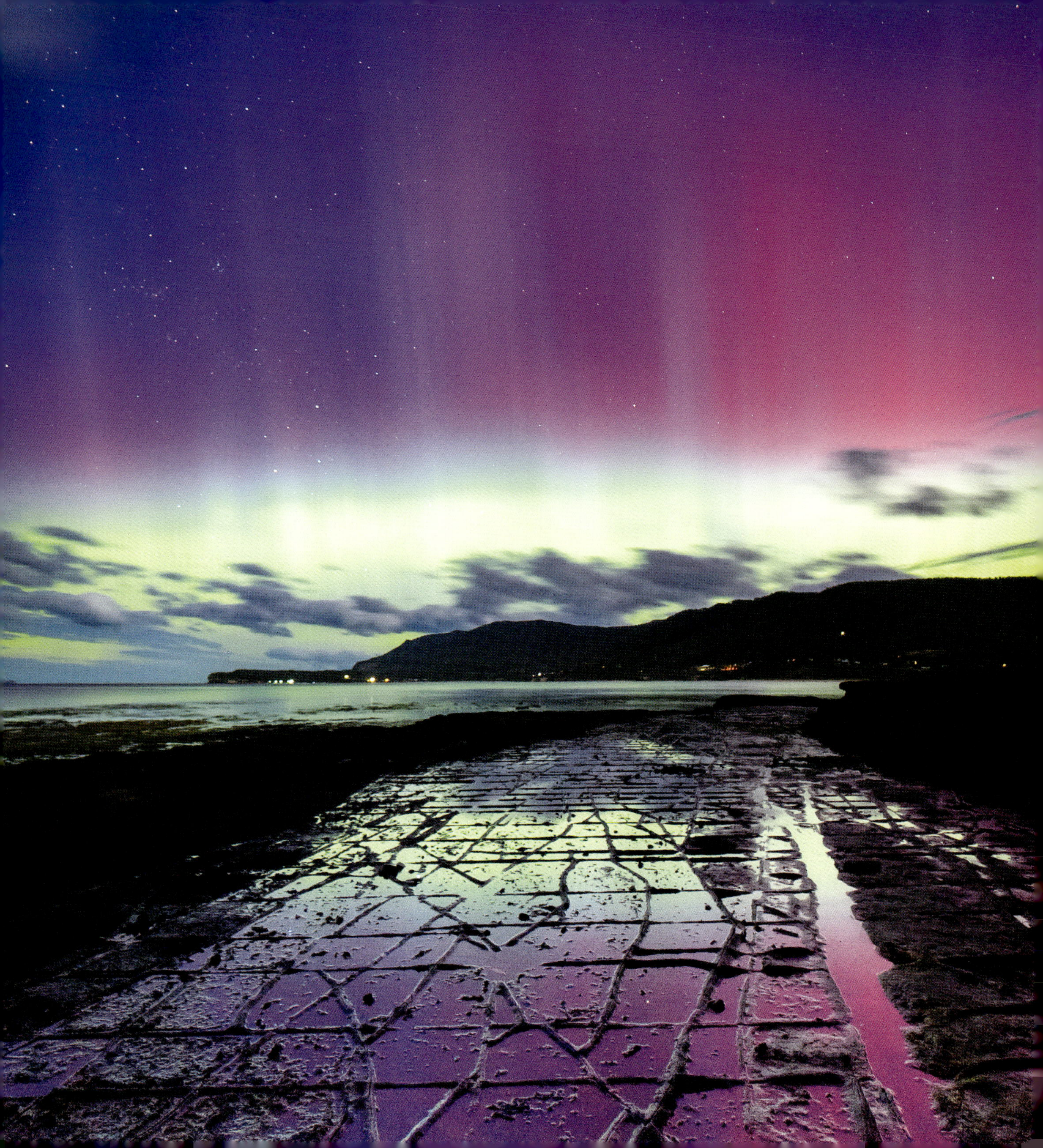

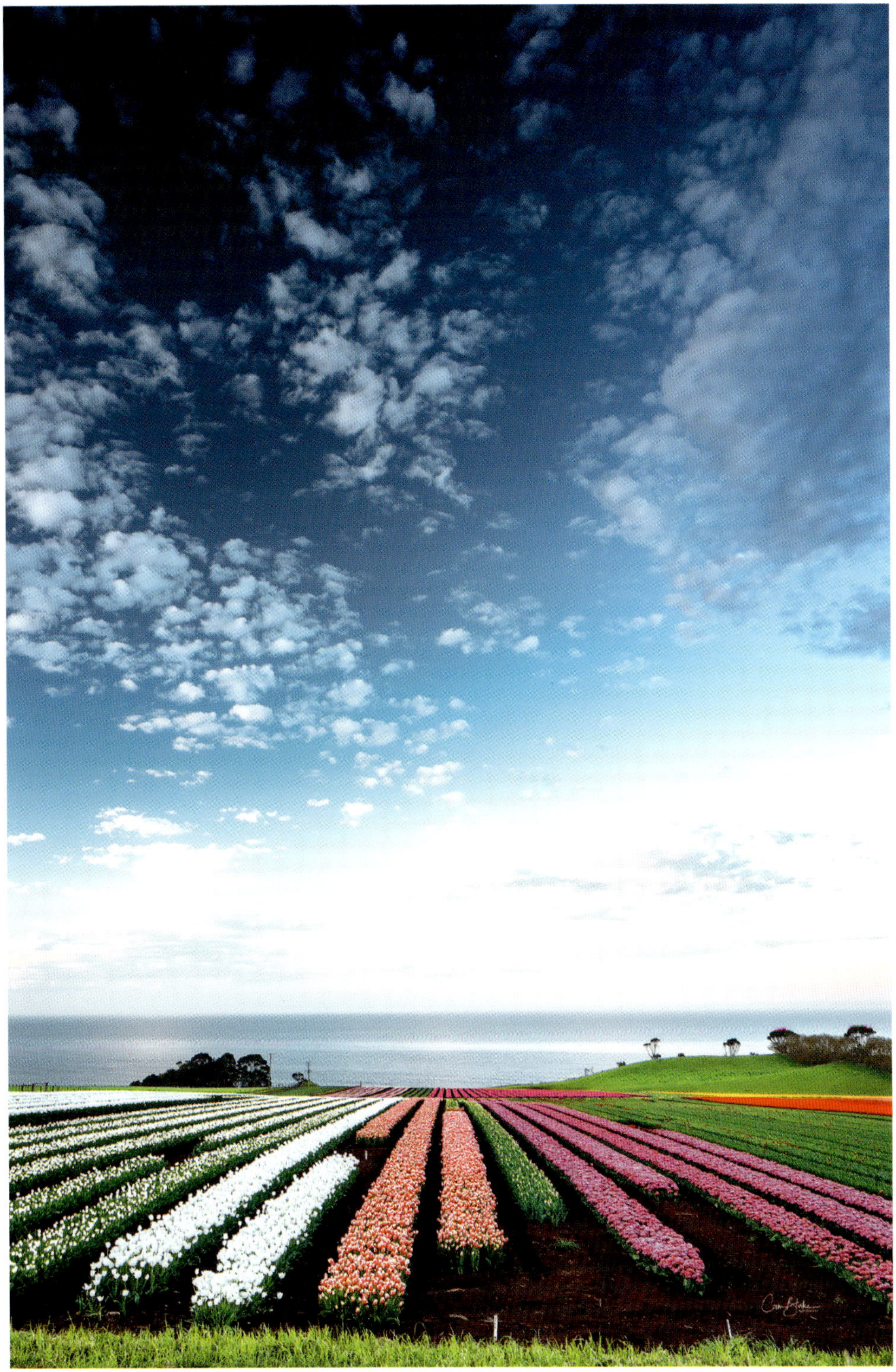

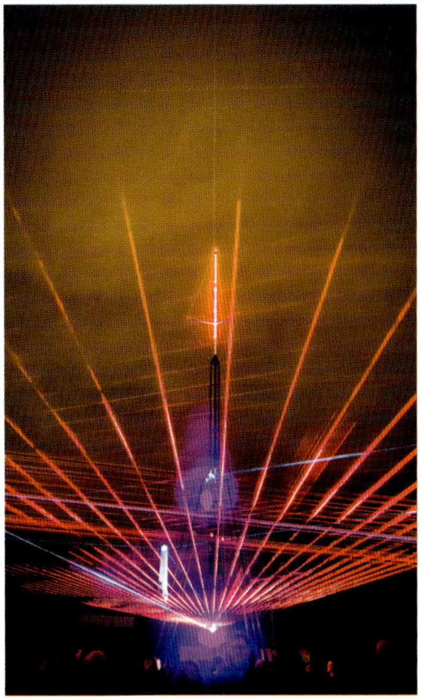

» **ABOVE** Light shows are aplenty during winter's Dark Mofo festival

» **LEFT** Table Cape tulips ready for picking and shipping to the Melbourne Cup

» **OPPOSITE** Also known as Lady Aurora, aurora australis lights up southern Tasmania

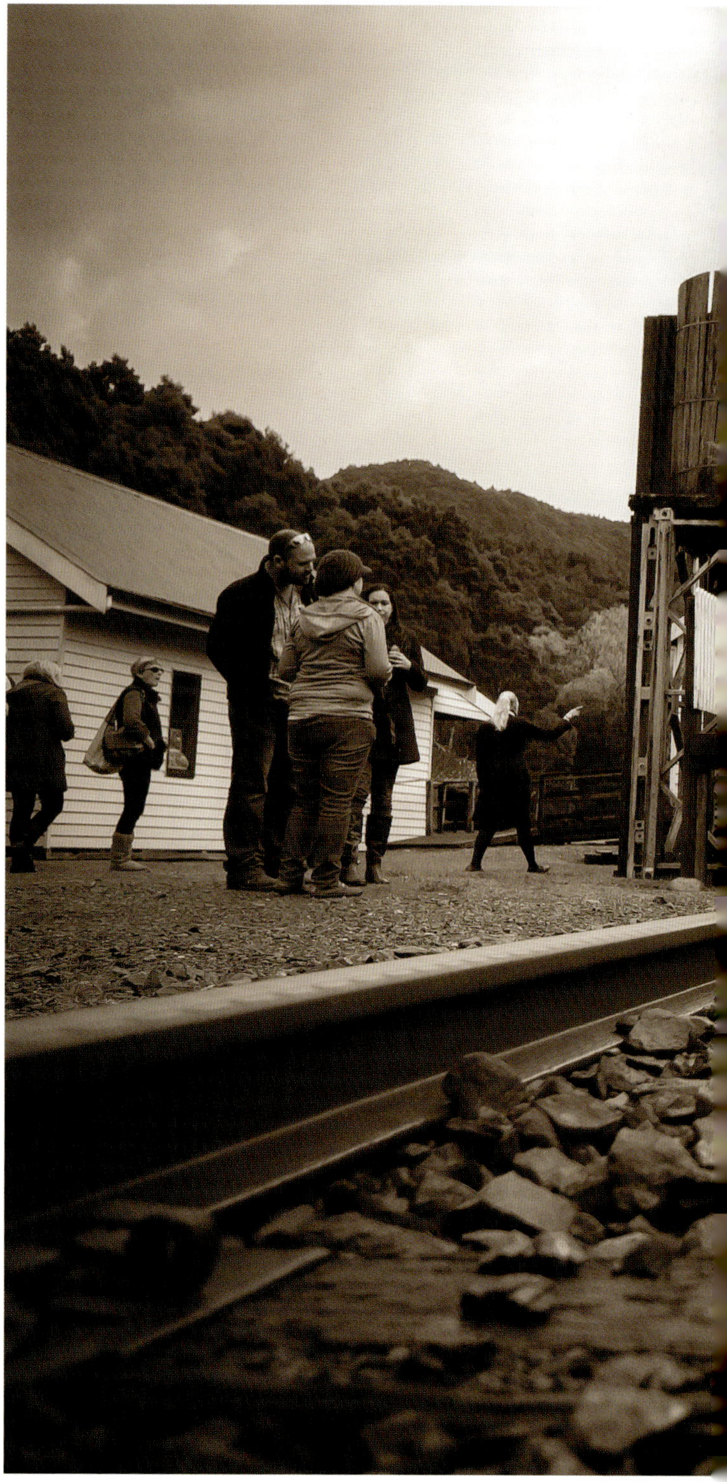

» **RIGHT** Tasmania's West Coast Wilderness Railway edges its way through olde time locations

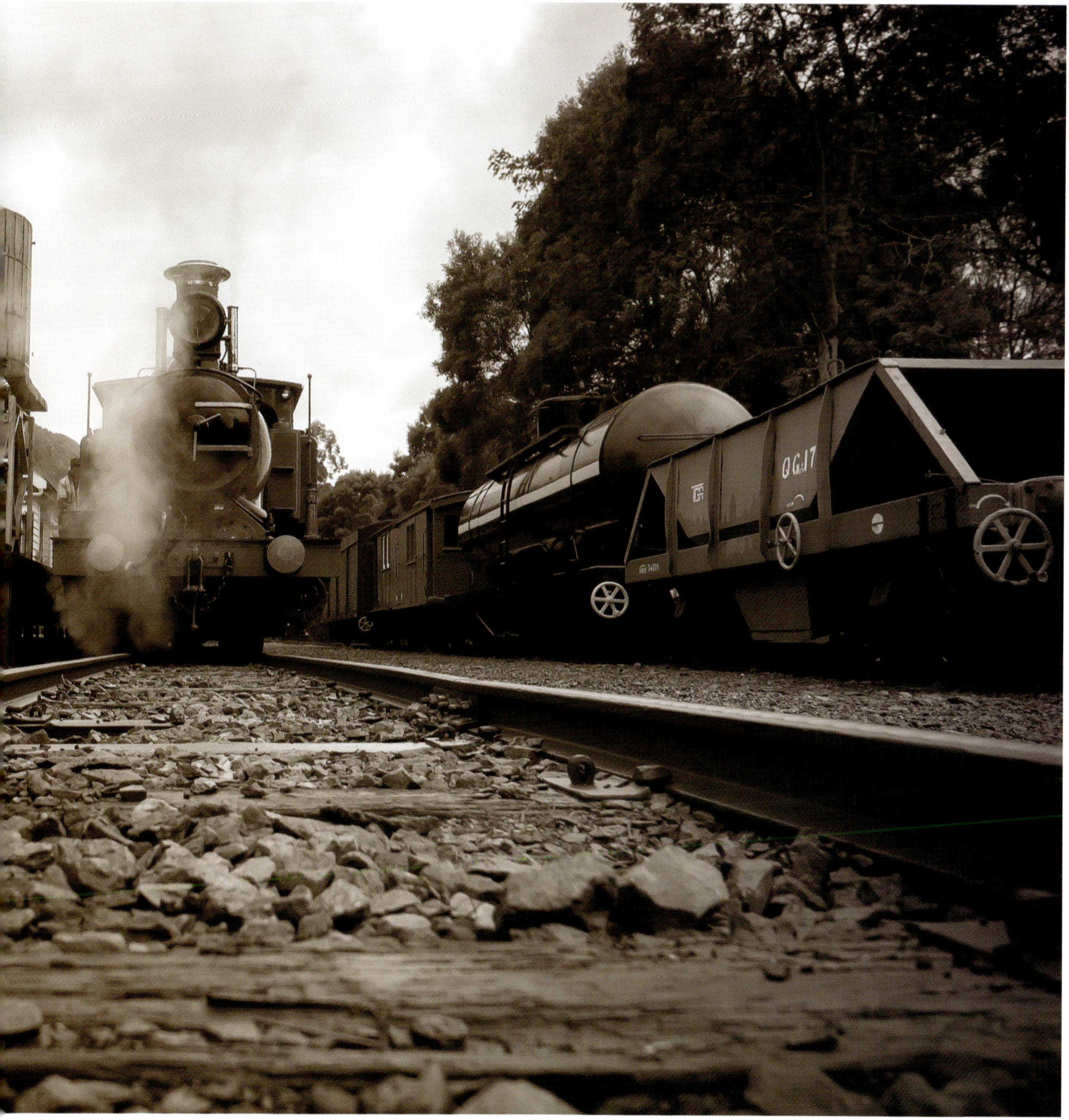
QG17

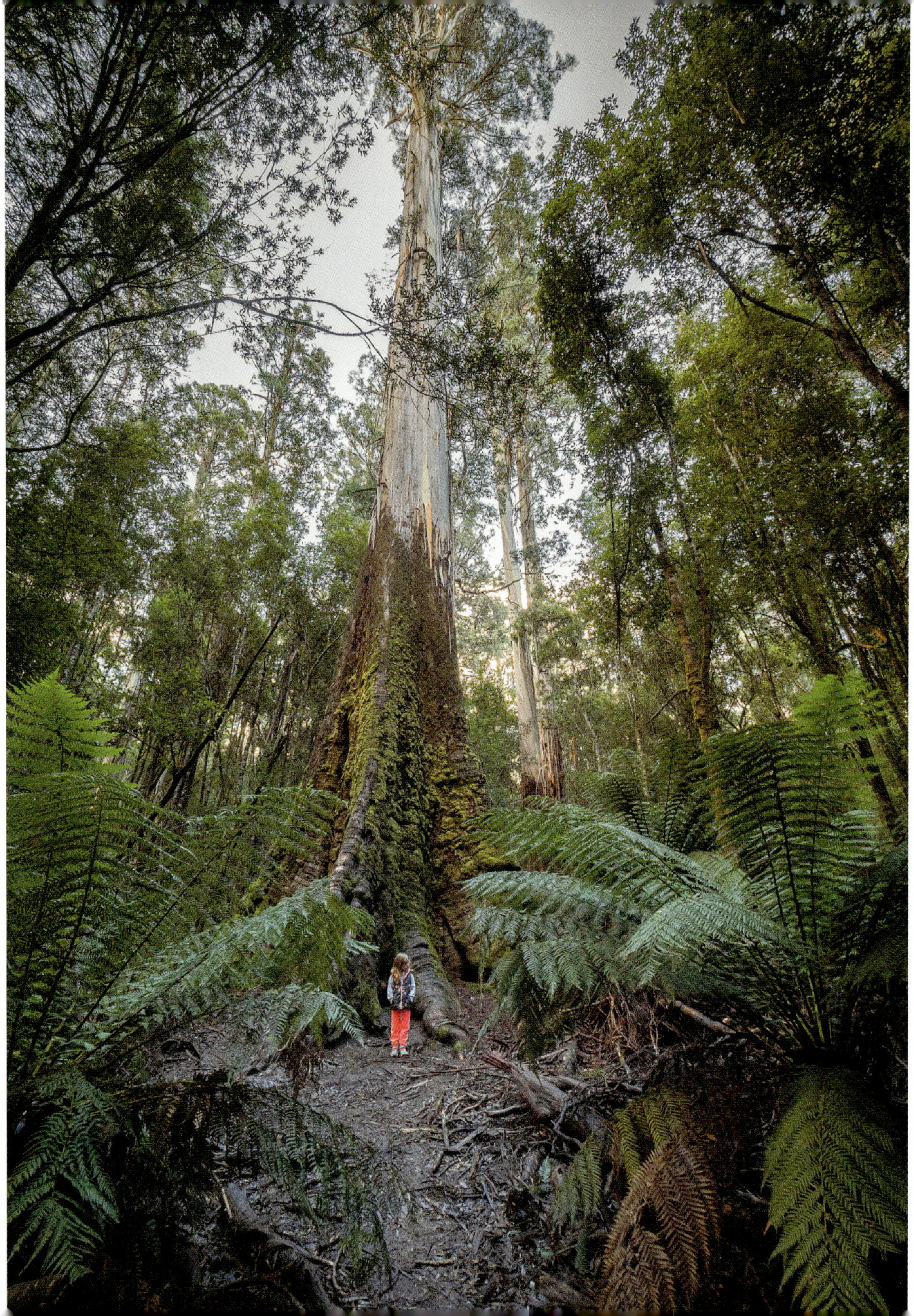

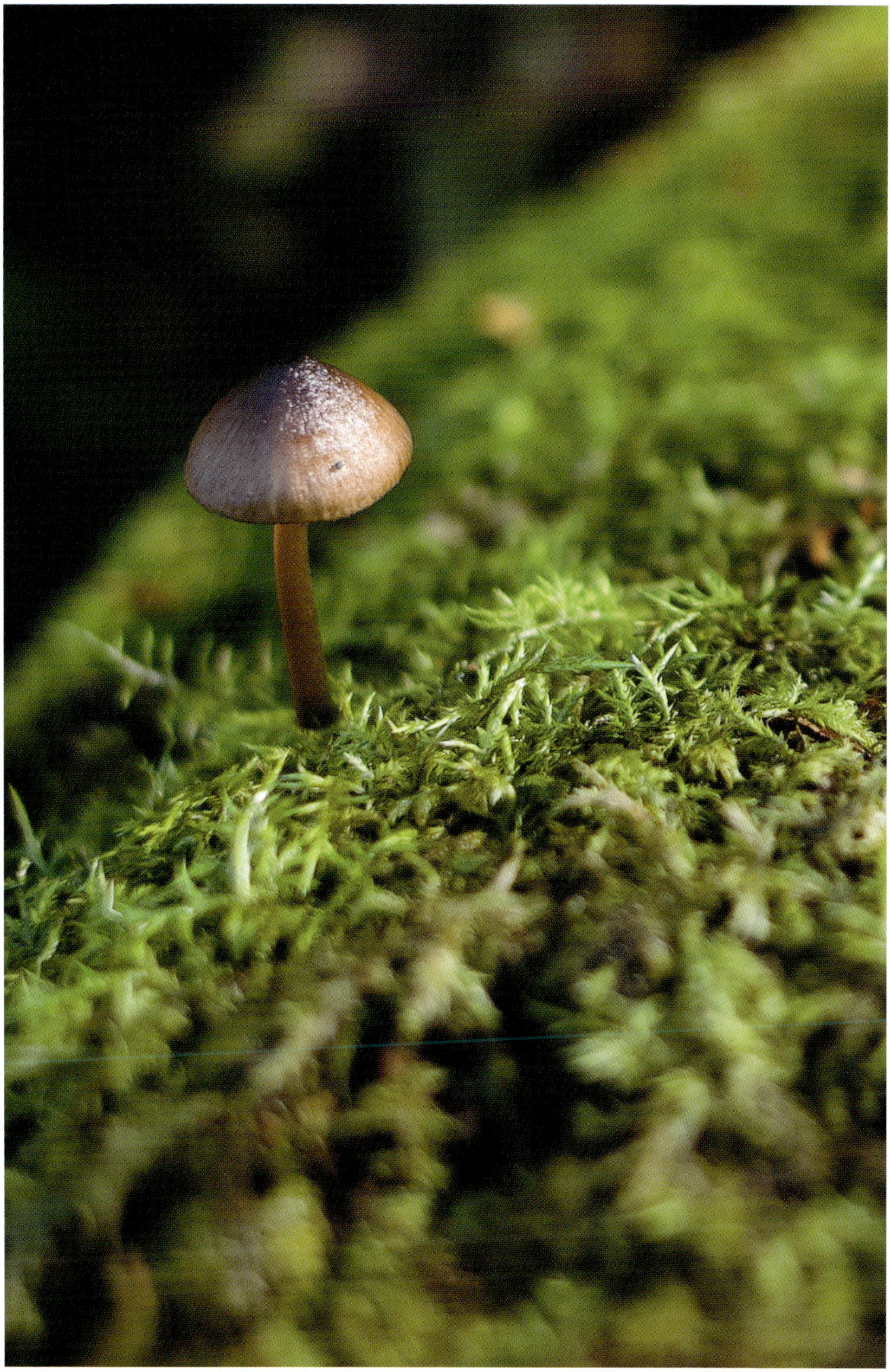

» **LEFT** Tiny marvels of the Tasmanian rainforests along the wild western coast

» **OPPOSITE** The giants among us in the Tall Trees Walk at Mount Field National Park

» **OVERLEAF** Binalong Bay and the Bay of Fires showcase the stunning east coast of Tasmania

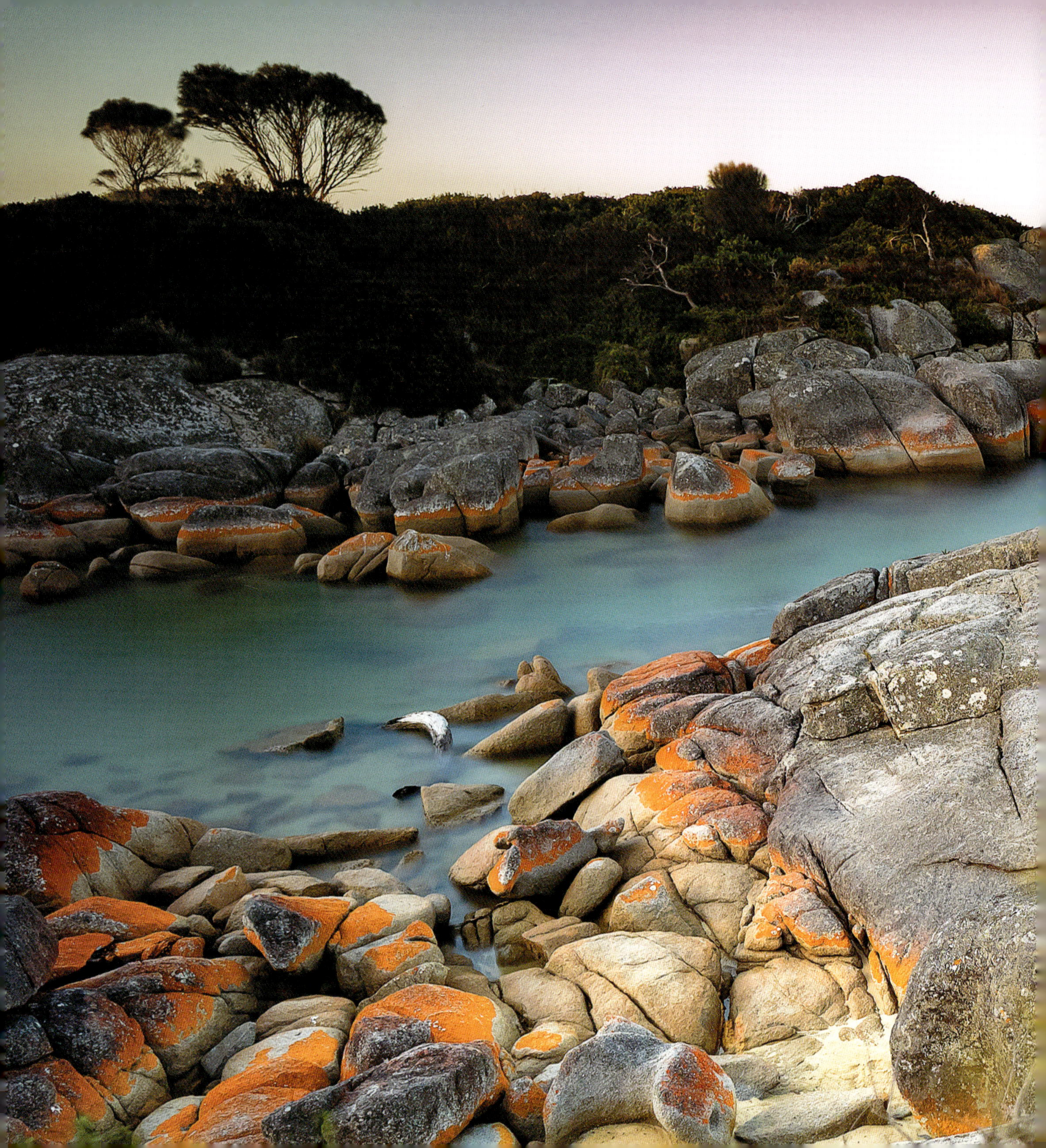

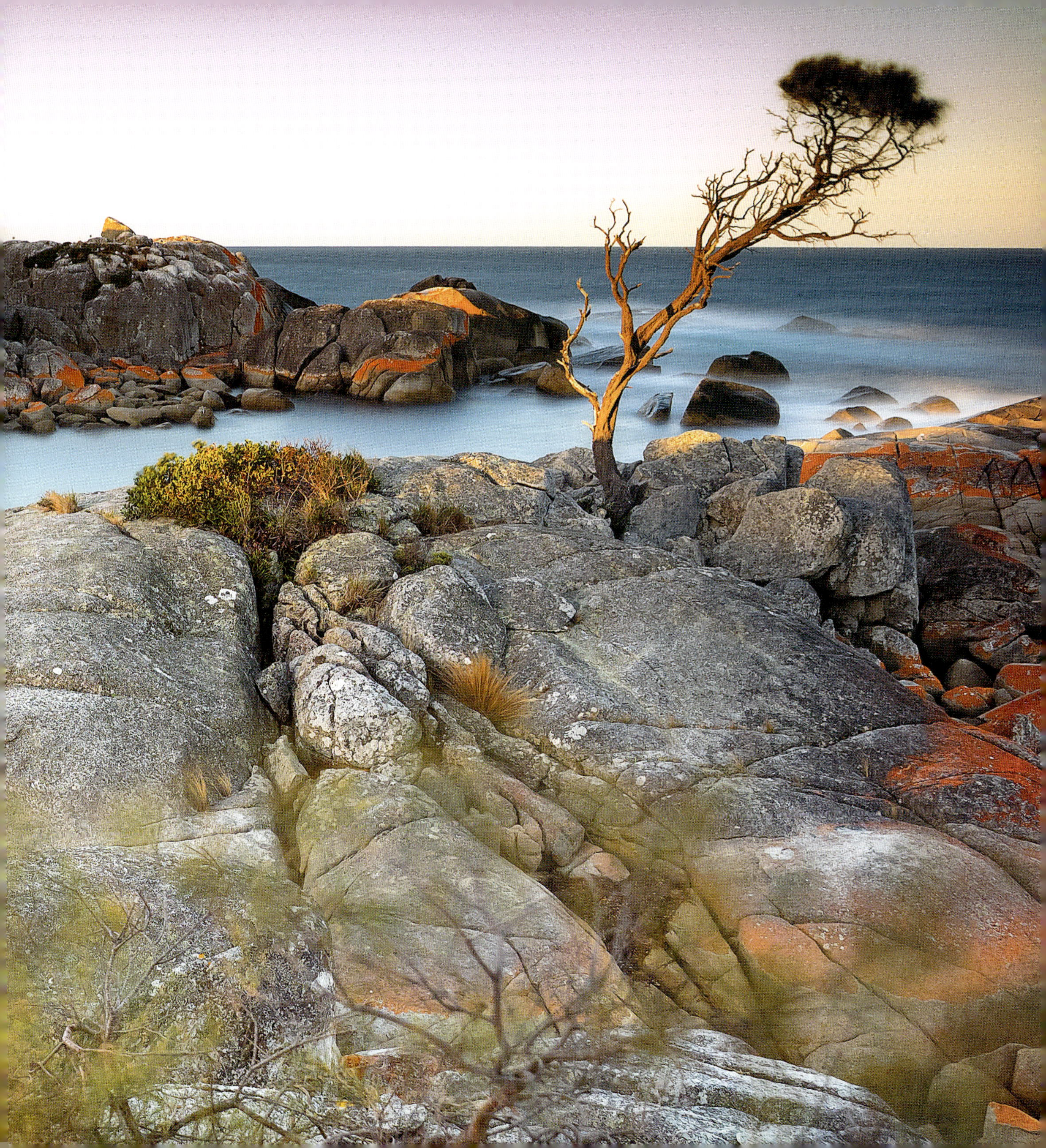

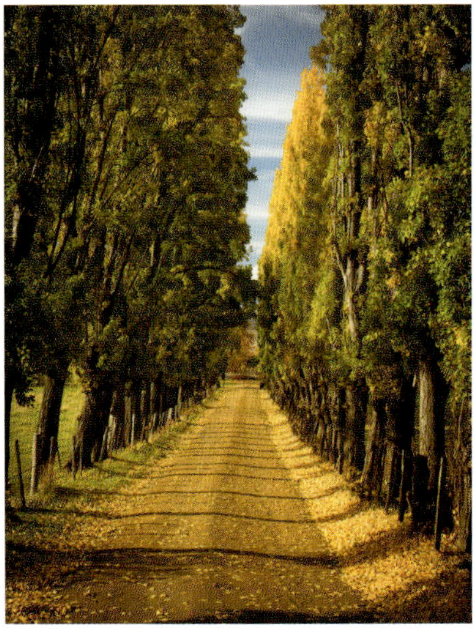

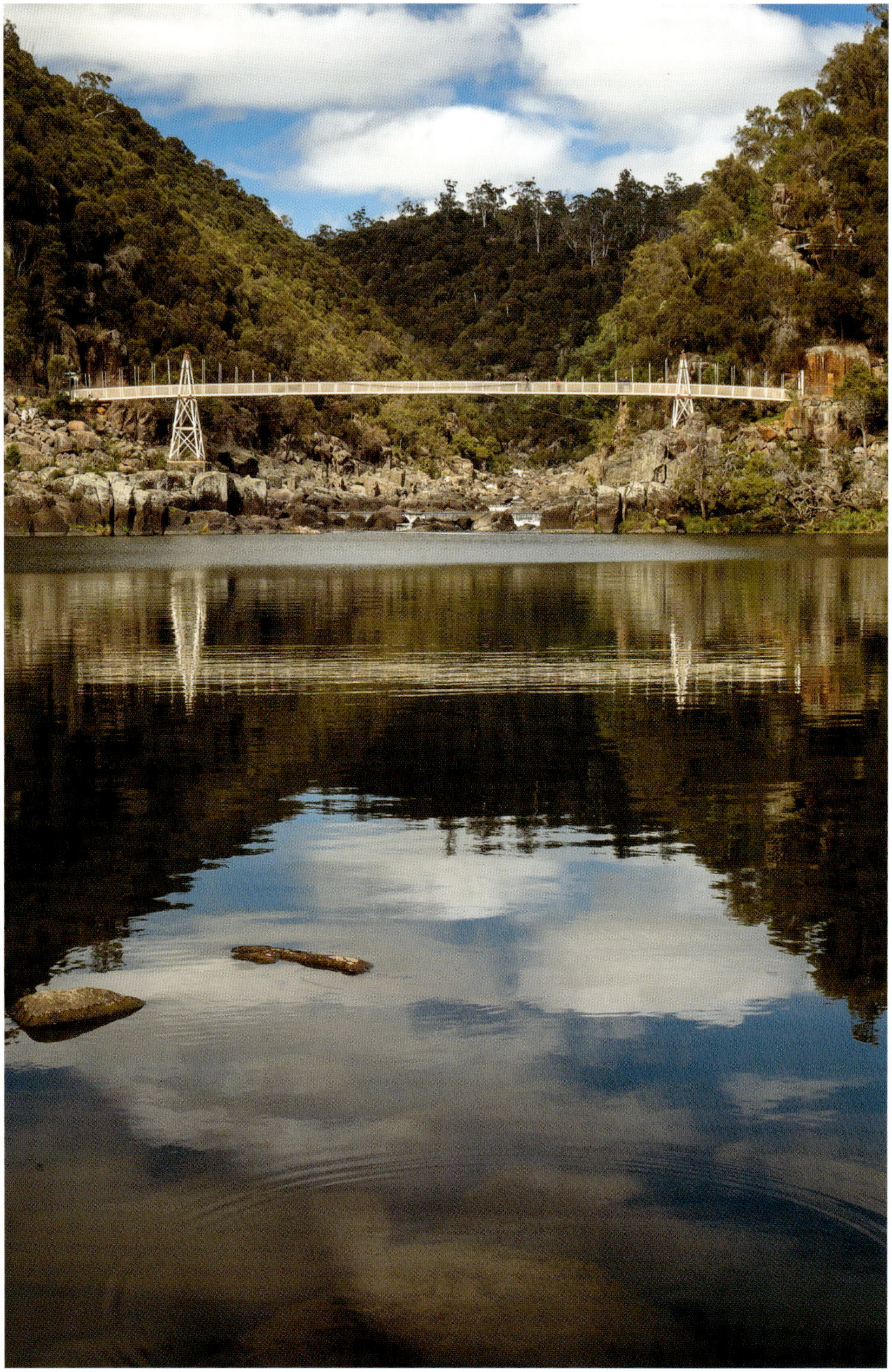

» **ABOVE** Autumn avenues line the Derwent Valley during this picturesque season

» **RIGHT** The walk around Launceston's Cataract Gorge is a must for any traveller

» **OPPOSITE** The Port Arthur Historic Site embodies the eerie history of convict life during Tasmania's early settlement

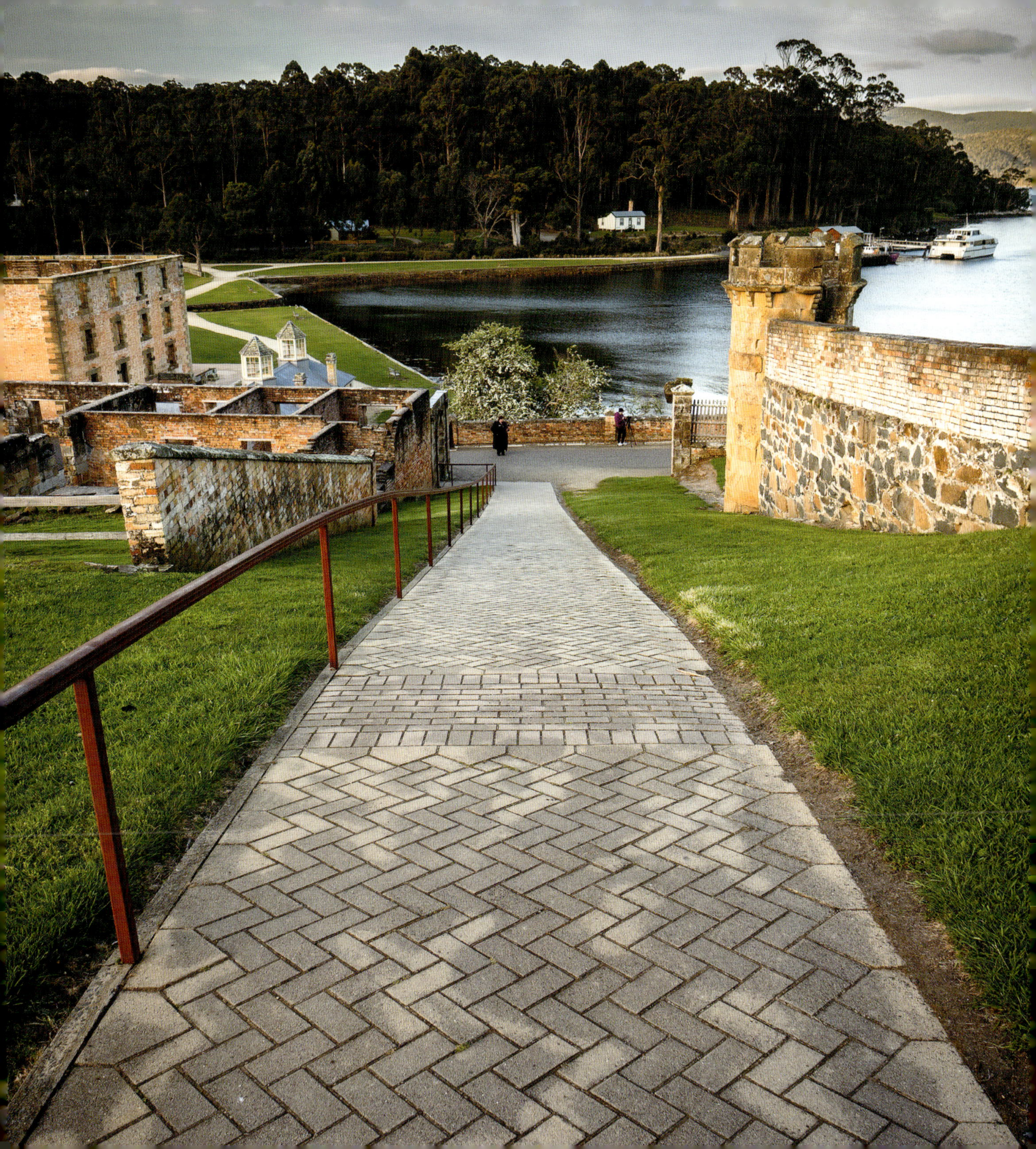

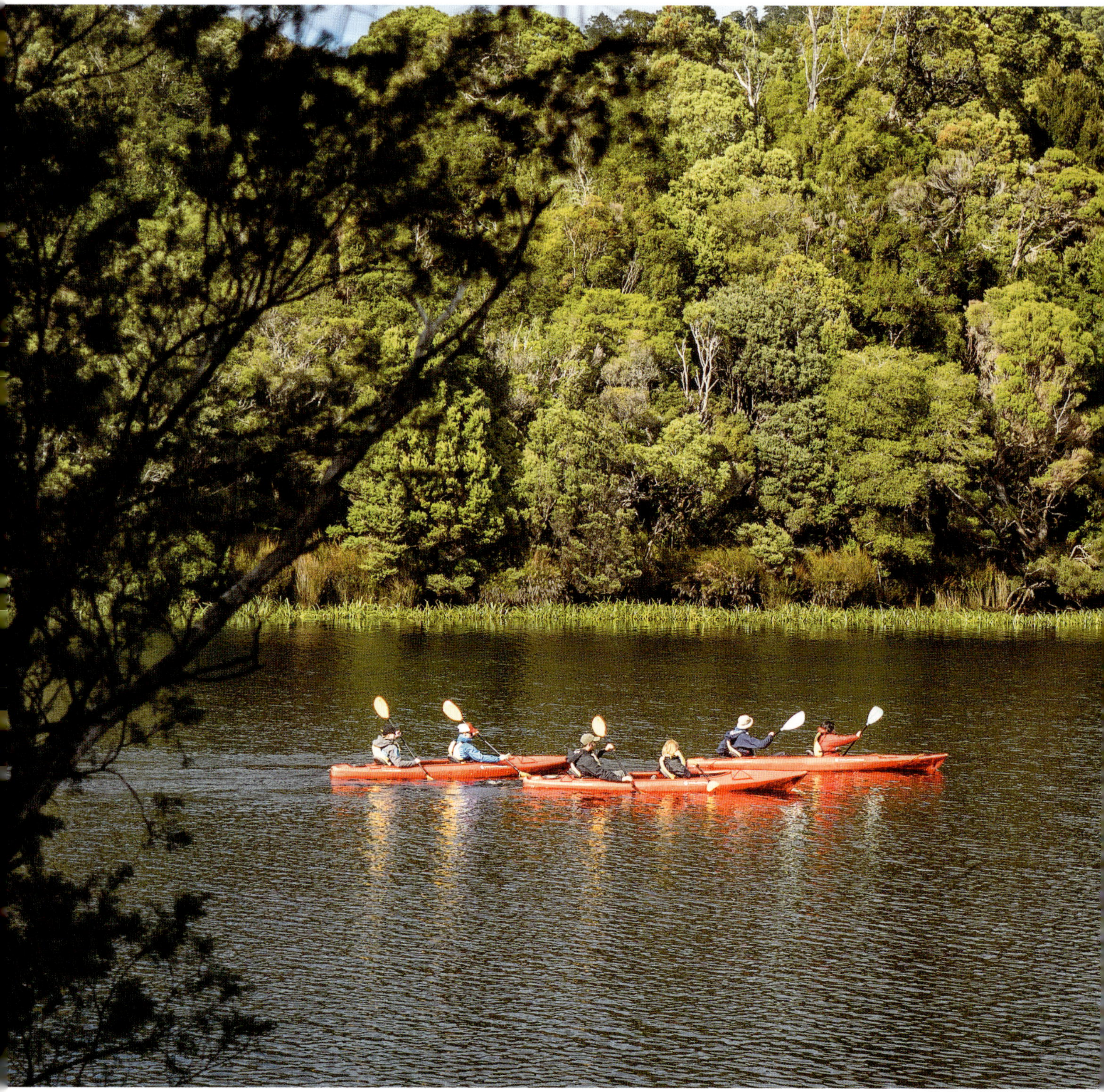

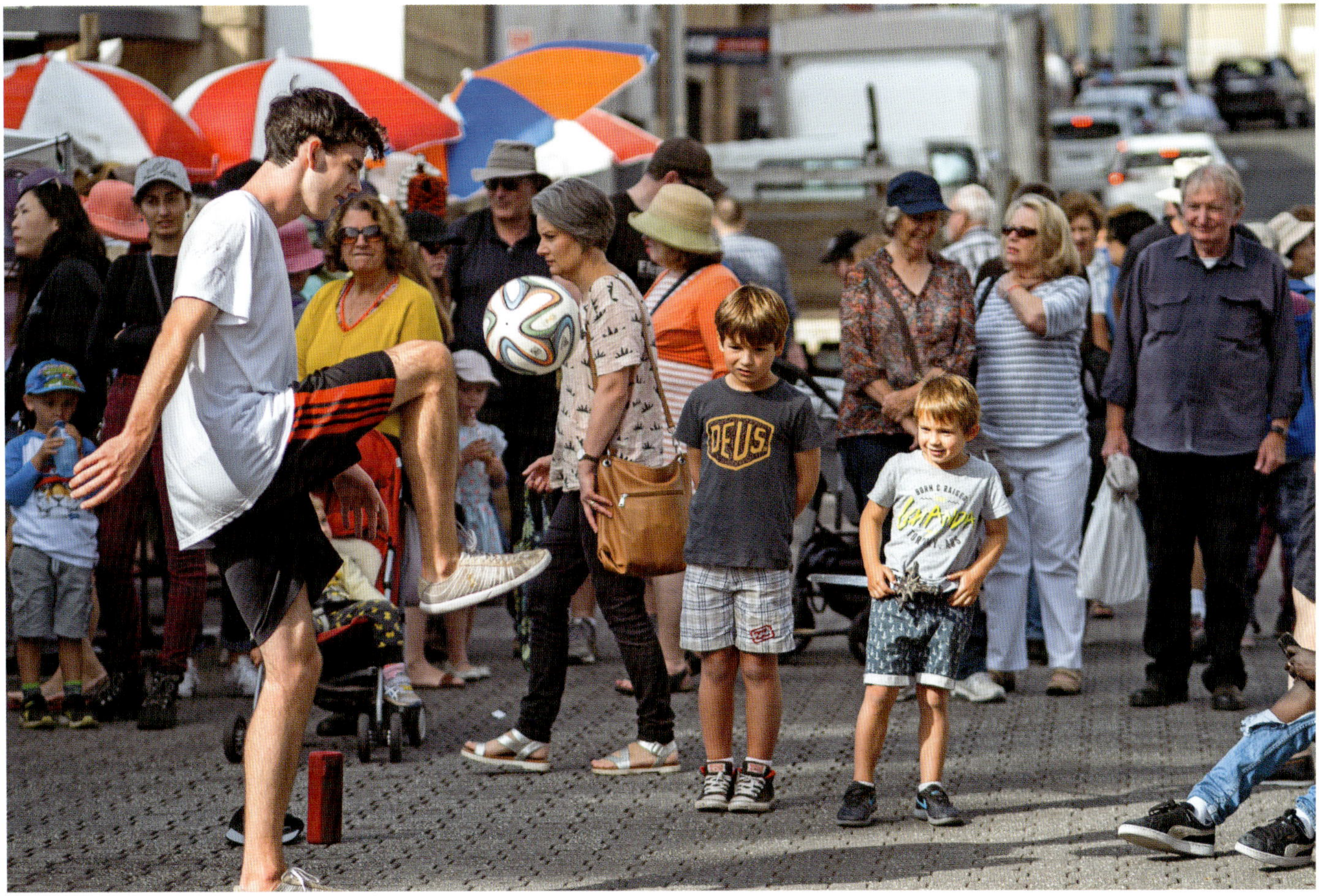

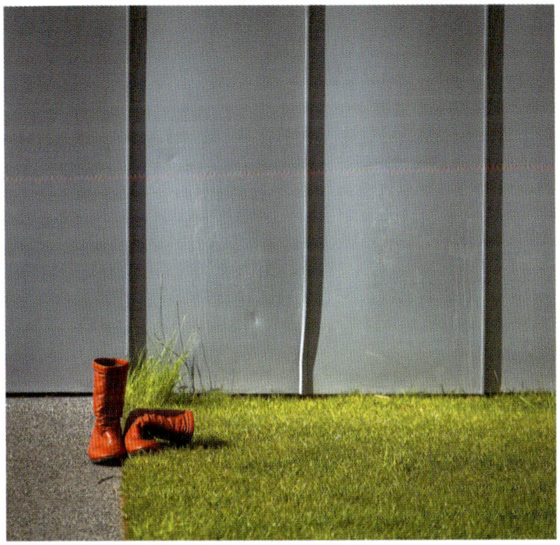

» **ABOVE** 'How many can you do?' a little fan asks this skilful street performer at Salamanca Market

» **LEFT** Simplicity at its finest at the MONA art museum, where anything goes in the name of art

» **OPPOSITE** Corinna and the Pieman River offer these keen explorers kilometres of rivers and rainforests to enjoy within the takayna/Tarkine region

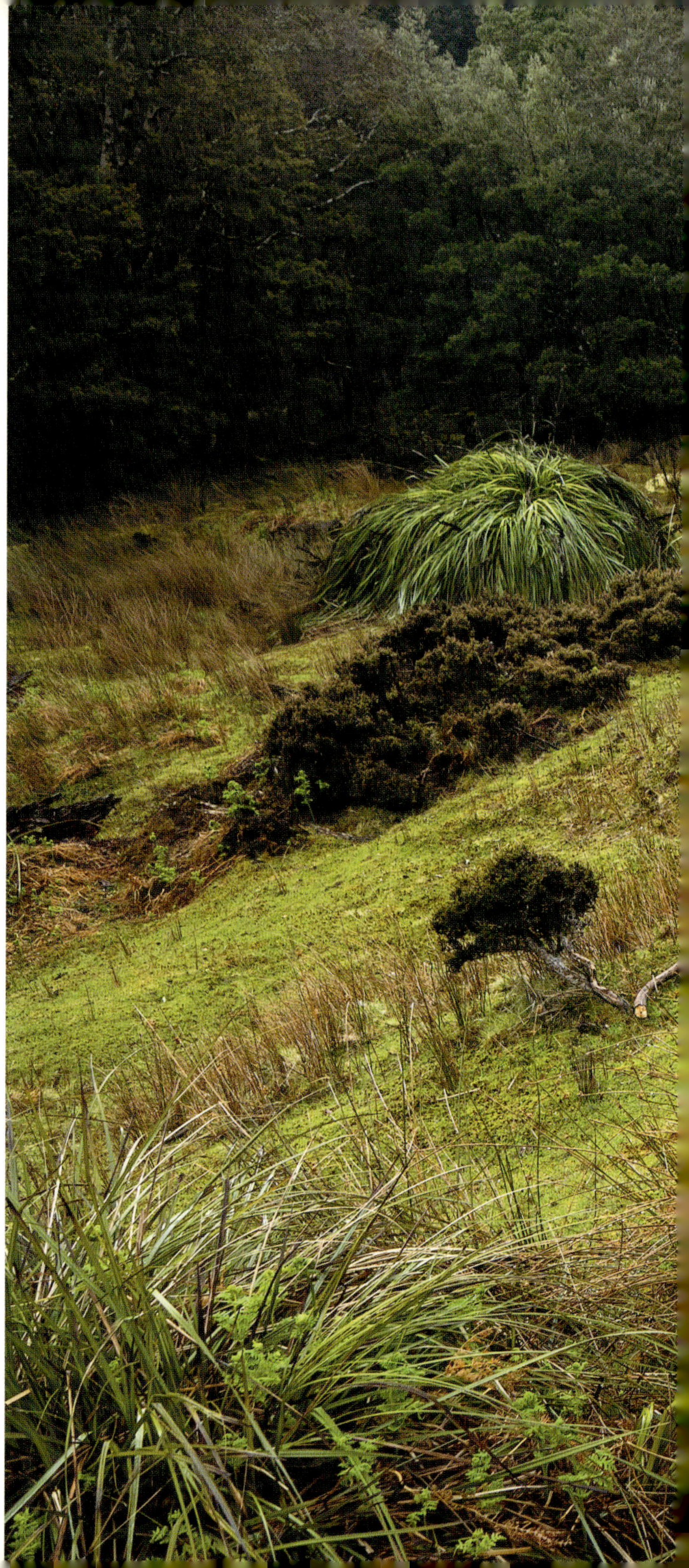

» **RIGHT** The famous Du Cane Hut was once a home for animal trappers along the Overland Track region

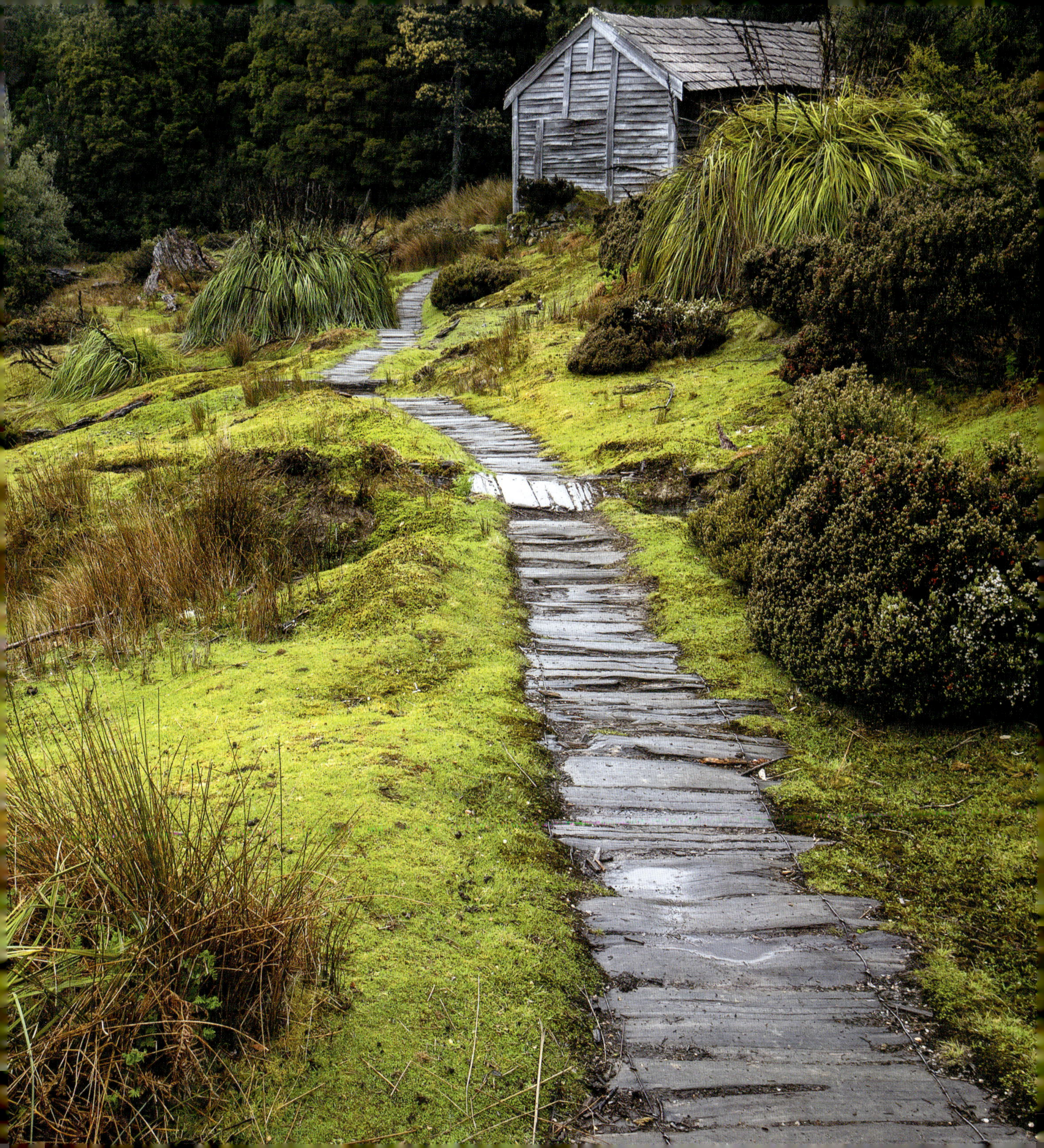

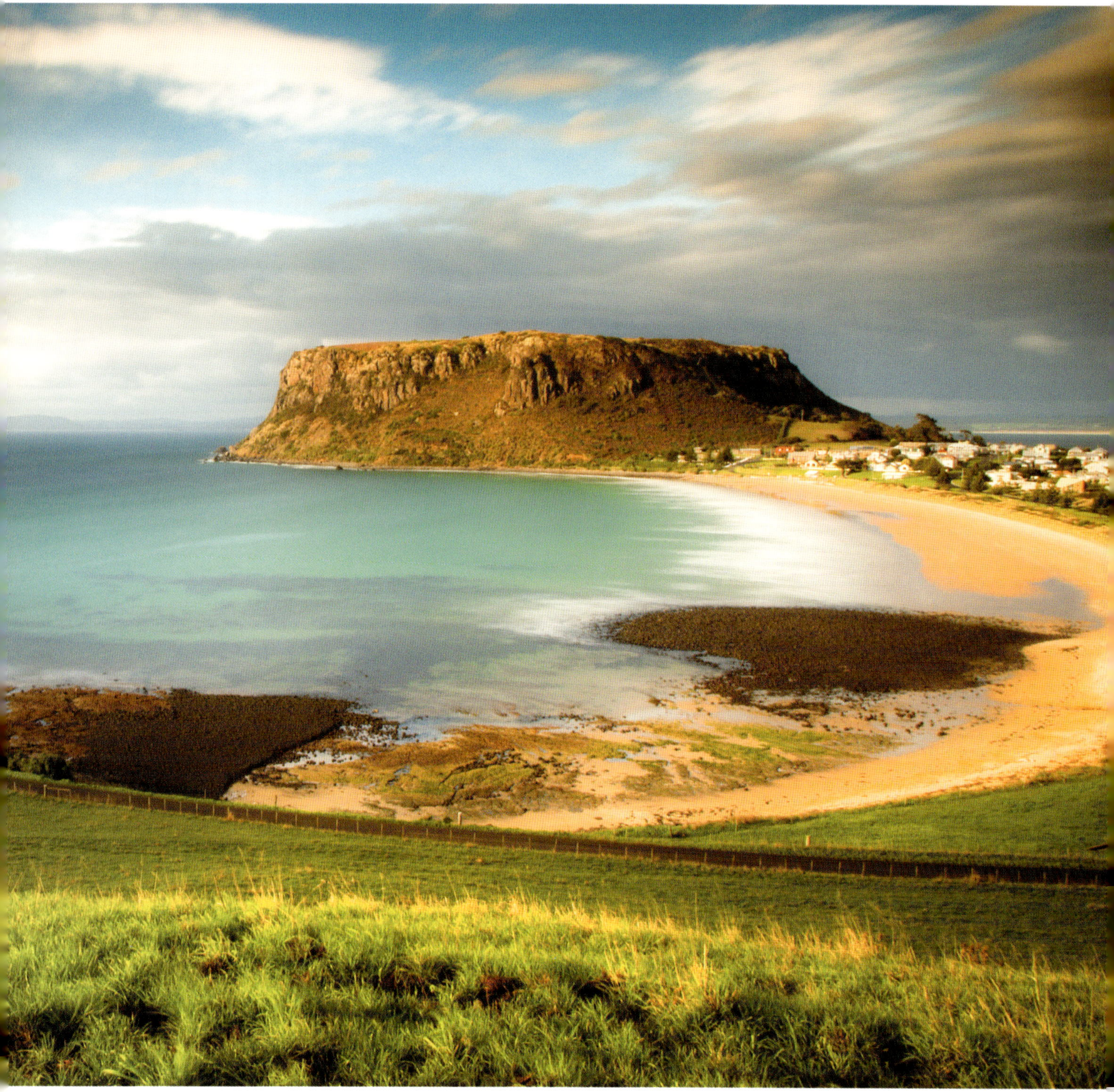

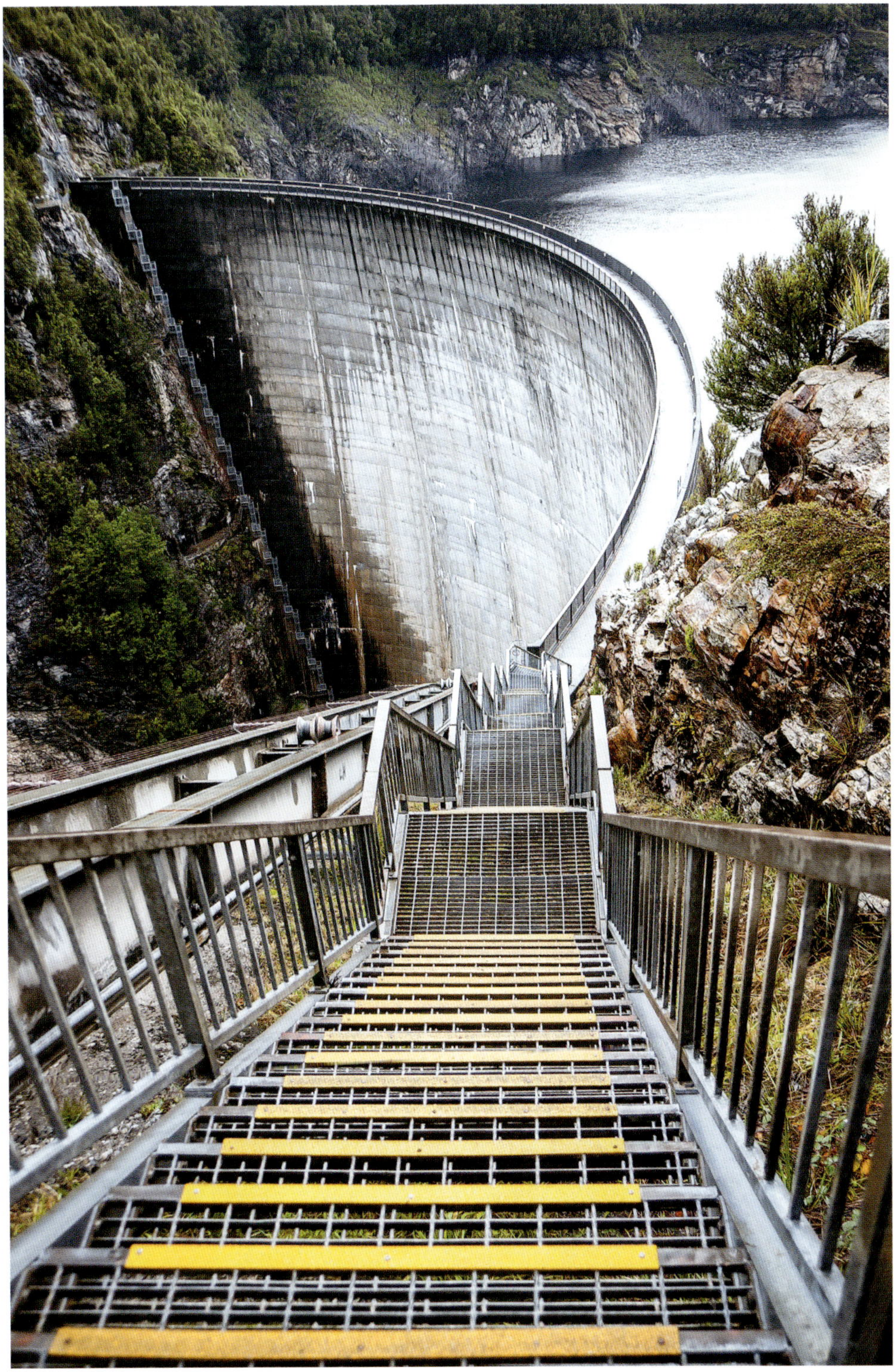

» **LEFT** Australia's highest dam wall holds back the pressure from the Gordon River

» **OPPOSITE** The Nut towers over the quaint seaside town of Stanley in Tasmania's north-west

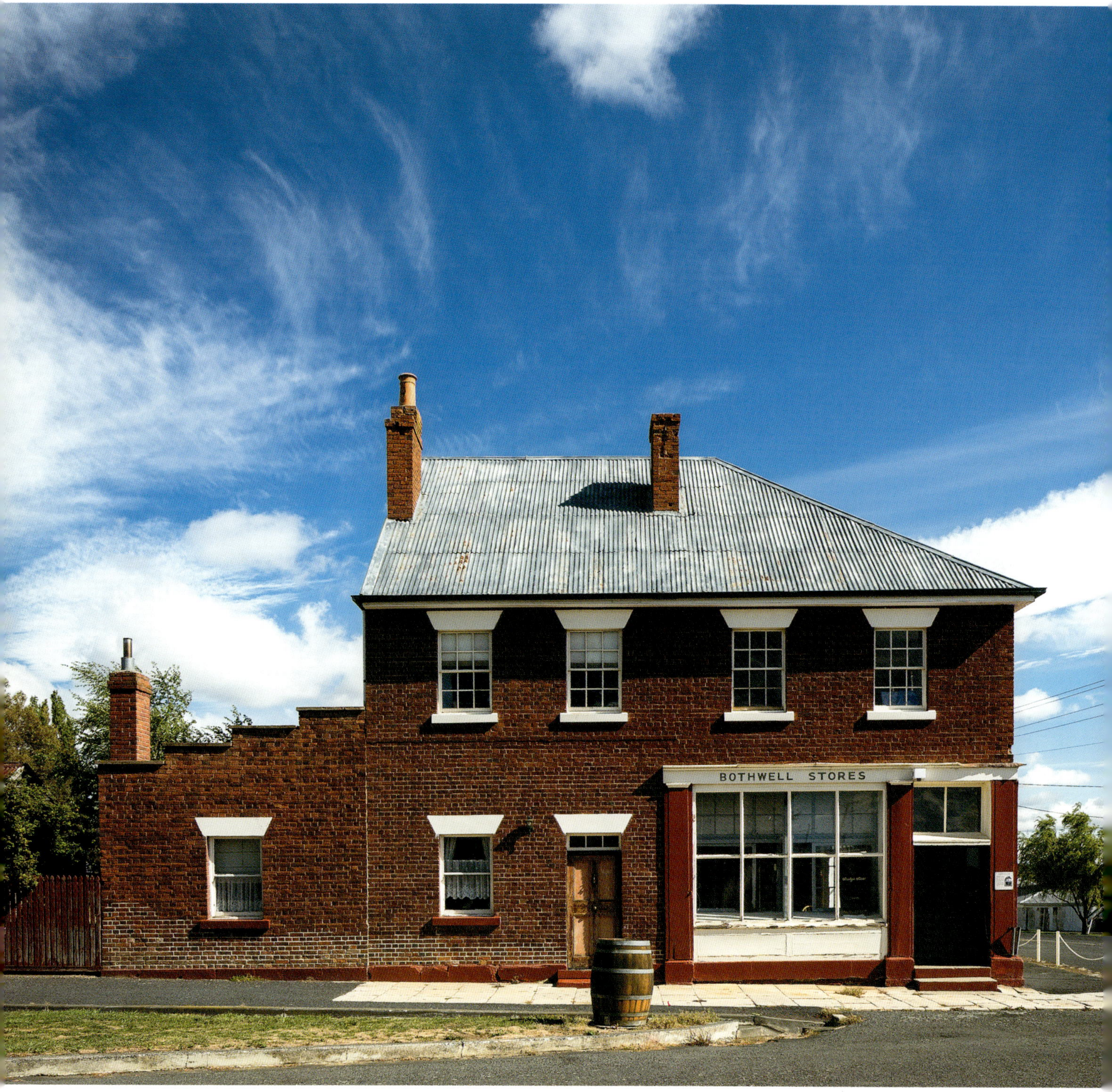
BOTHWELL STORES

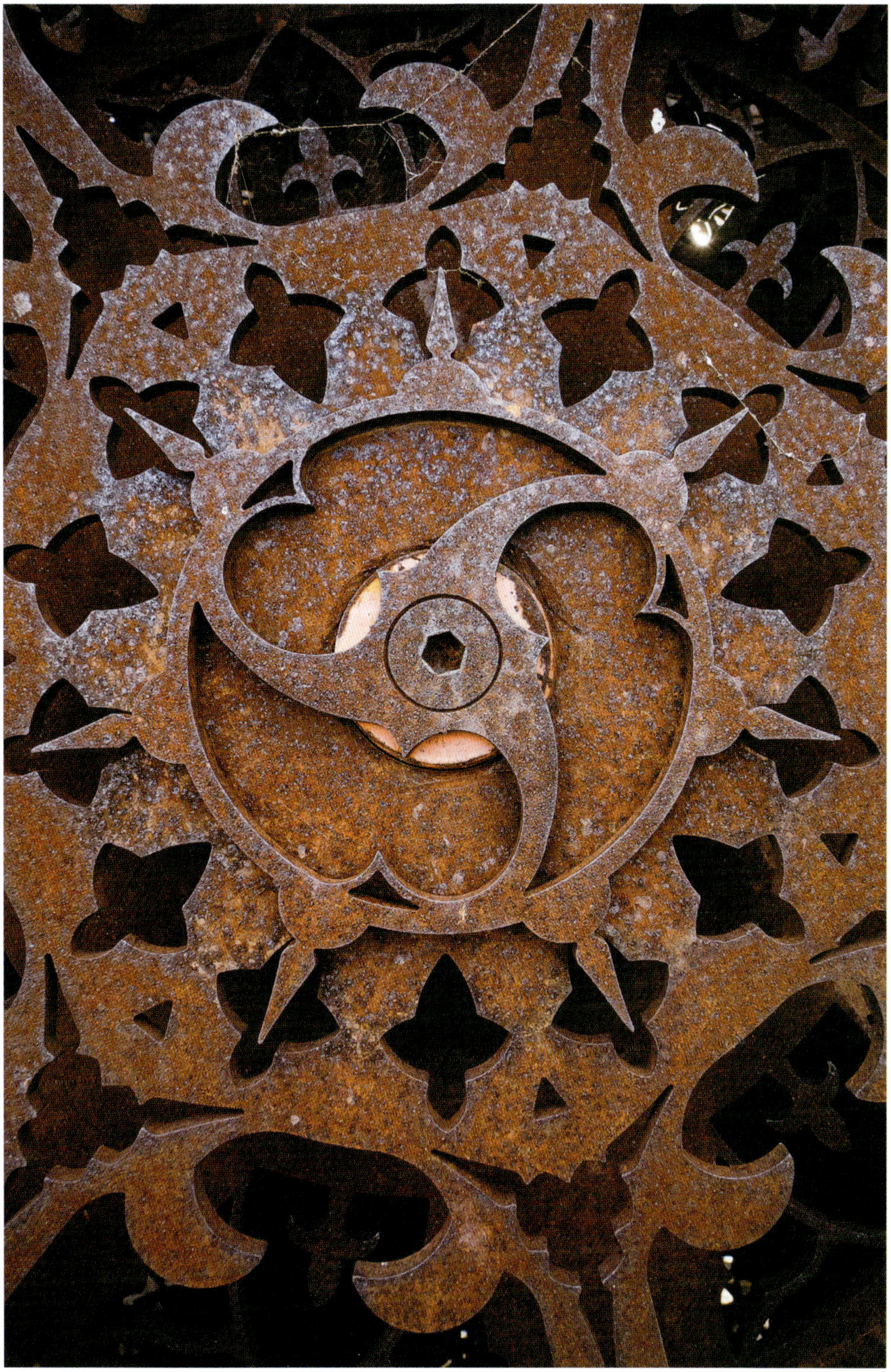

» **LEFT** The rustic features of a MONA outdoor sculpture

» **OPPOSITE** Hobart has plenty of beautiful old buildings still standing

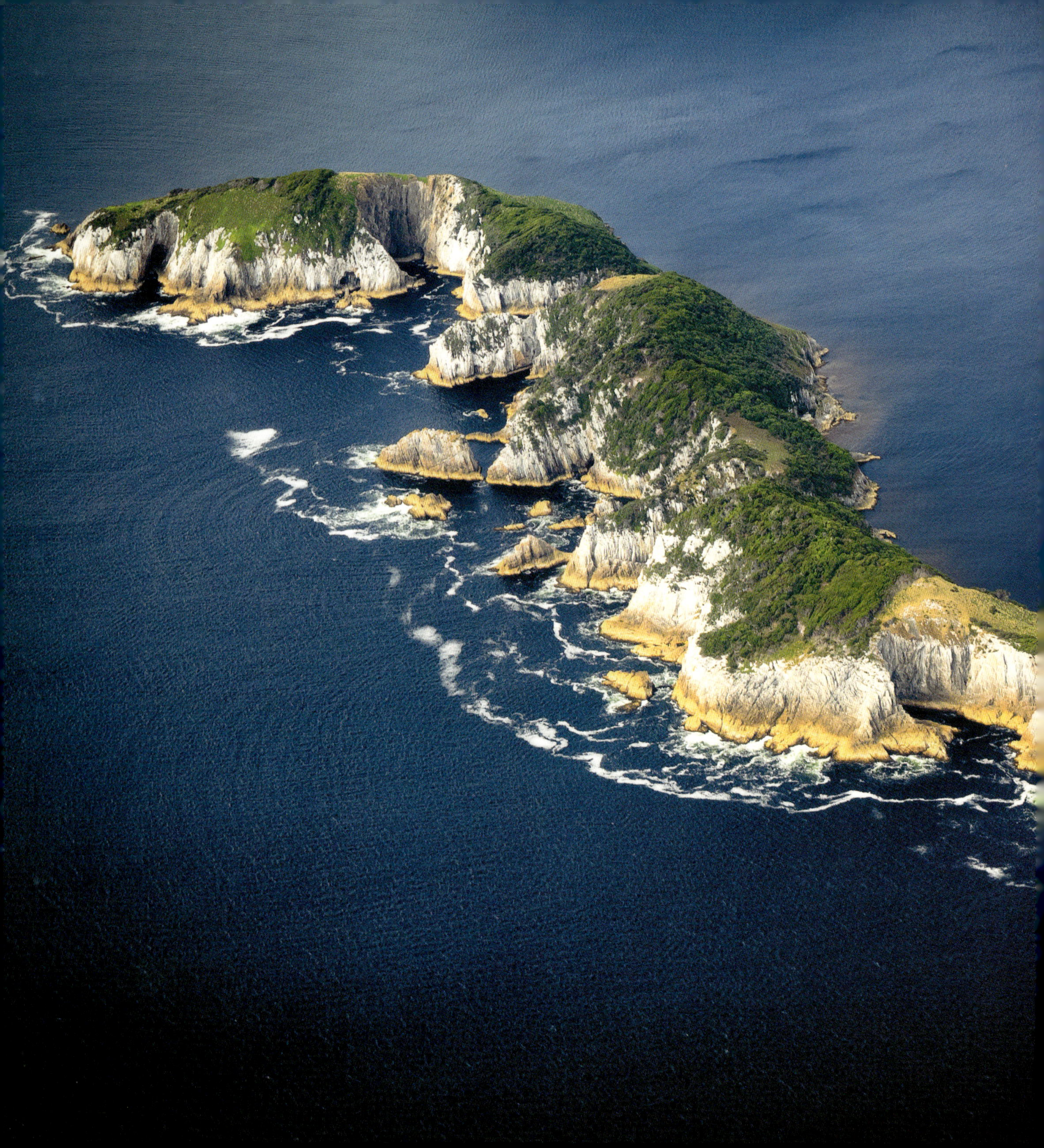

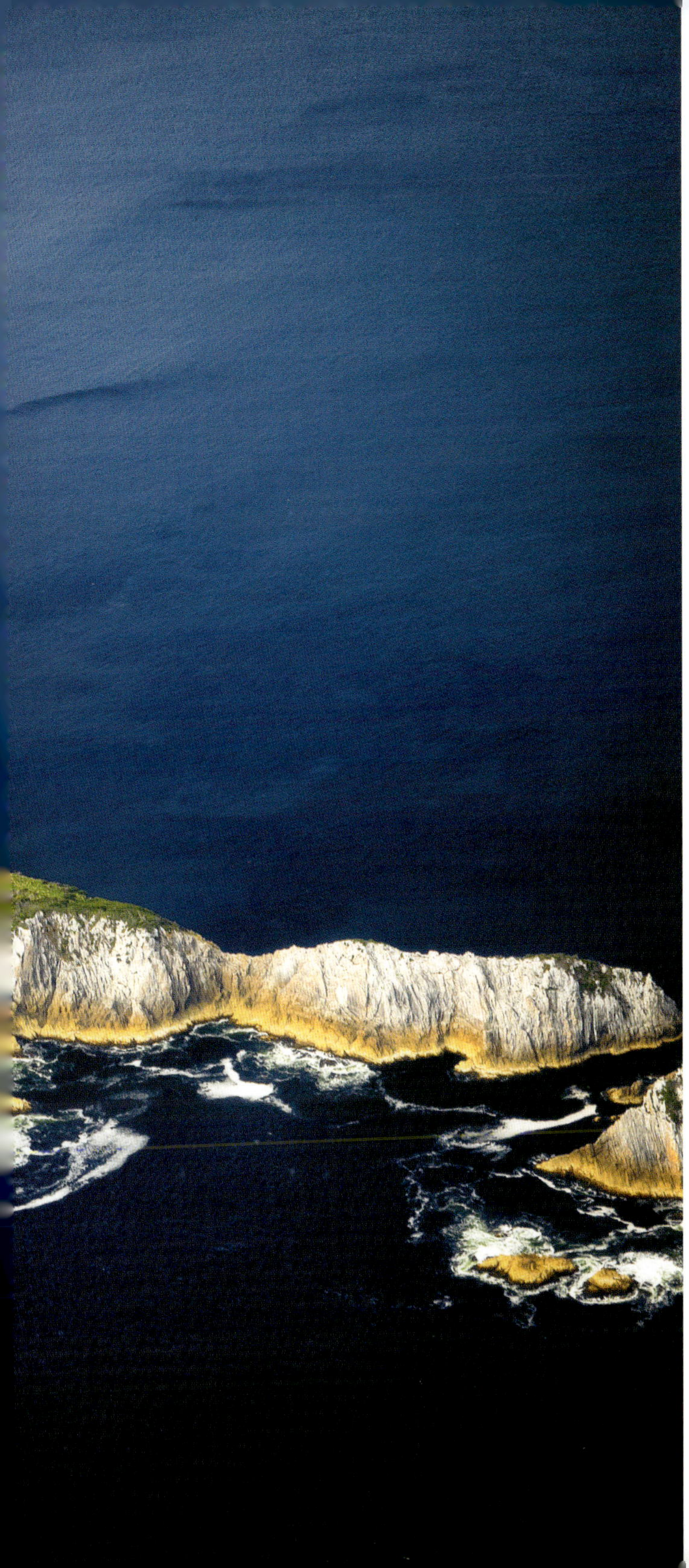

» **LEFT** One can only imagine what types of wild weather the Breaksea Islands have witnessed

» **OVERLEAF** A majestic pair of endangered wedge-tailed eagles grace the Tasmanian Midlands' sky

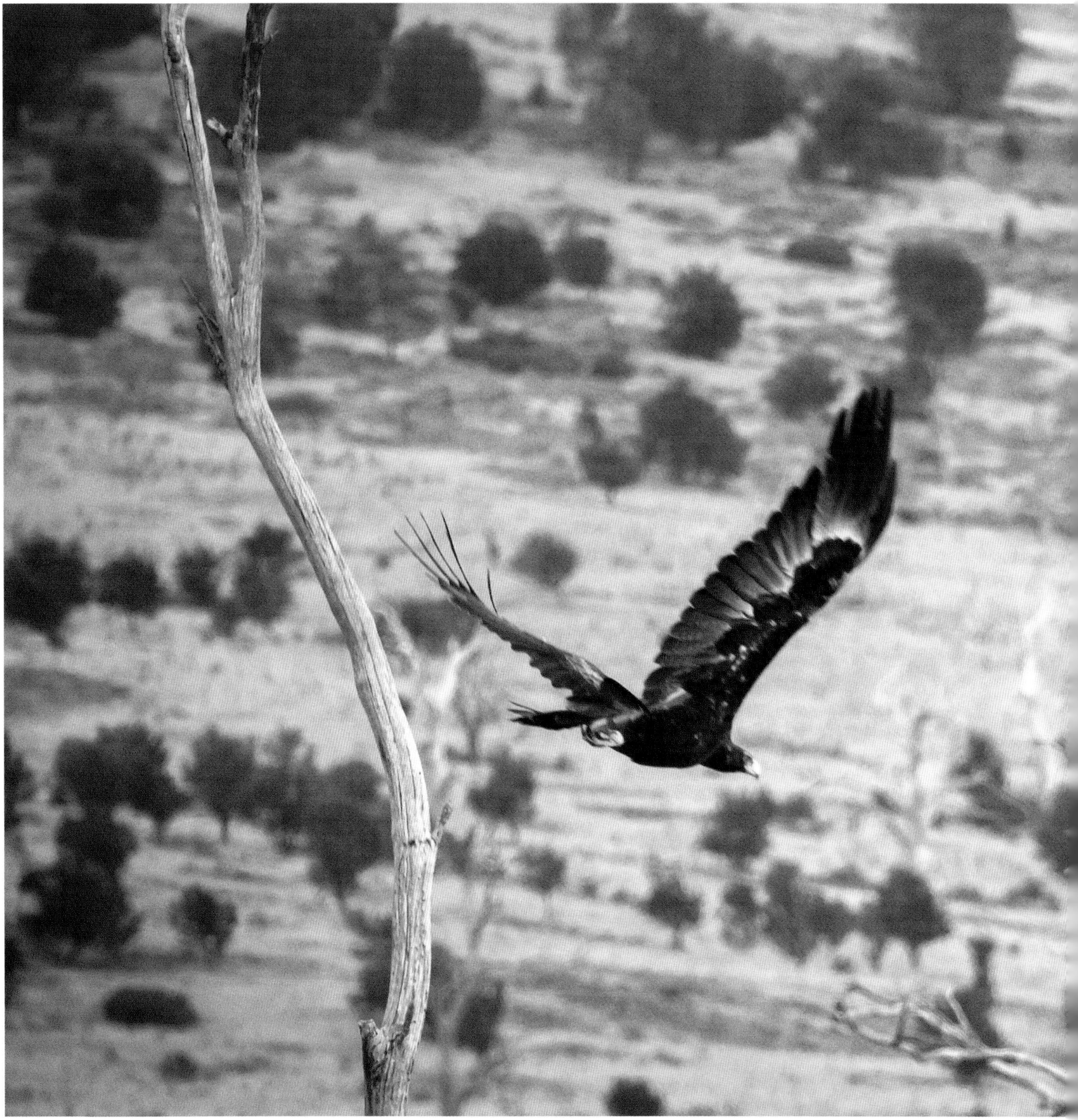

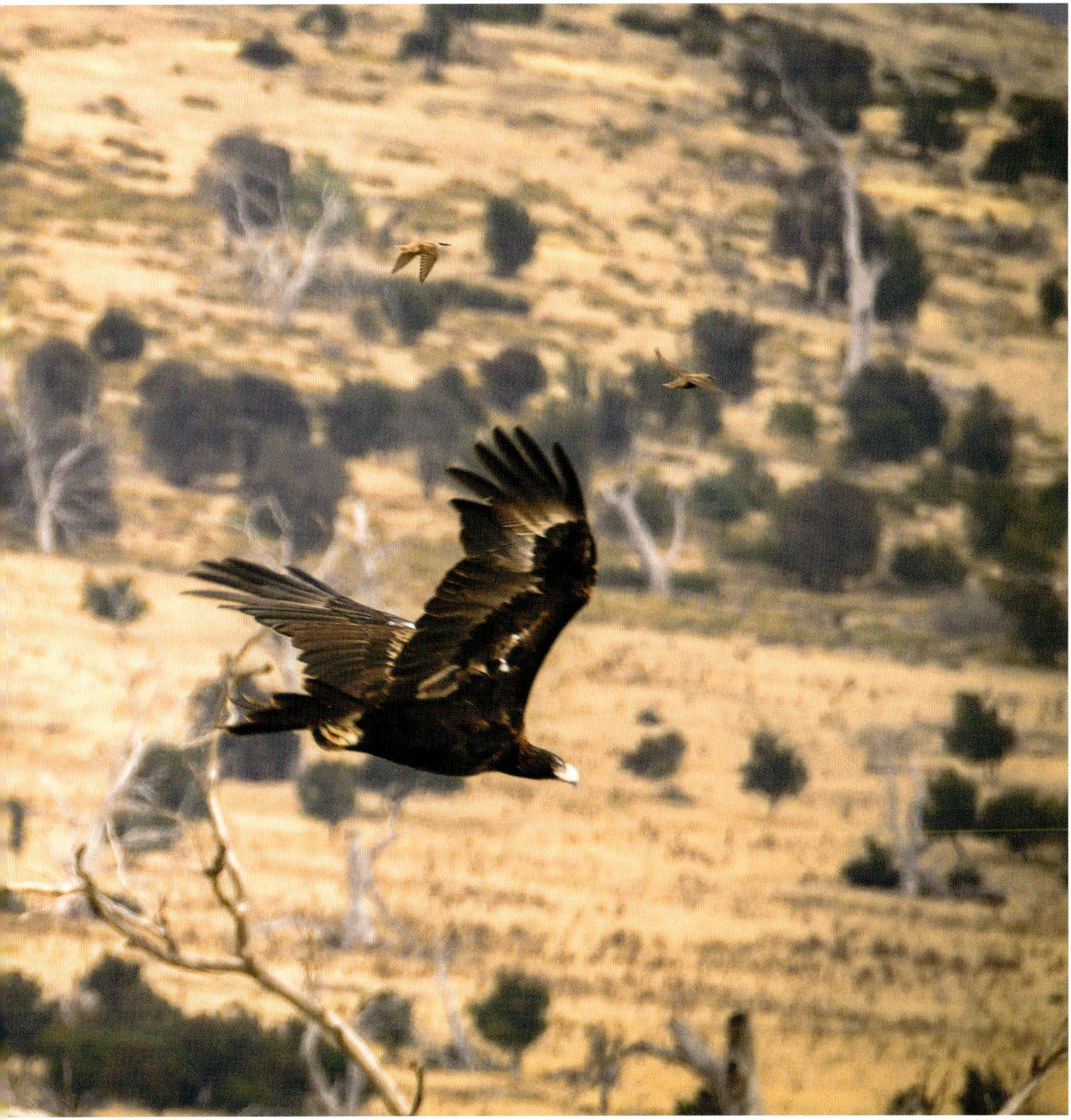

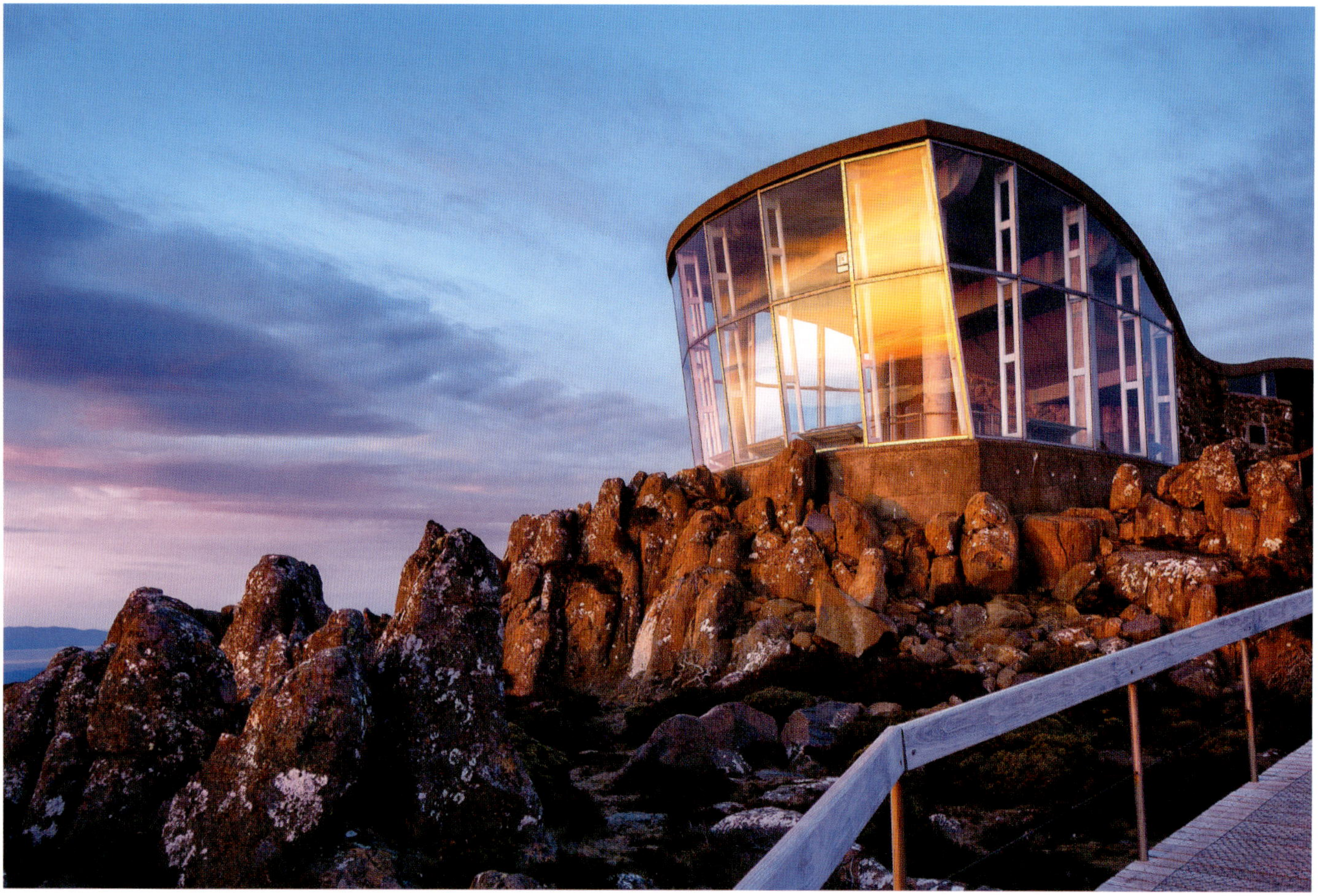

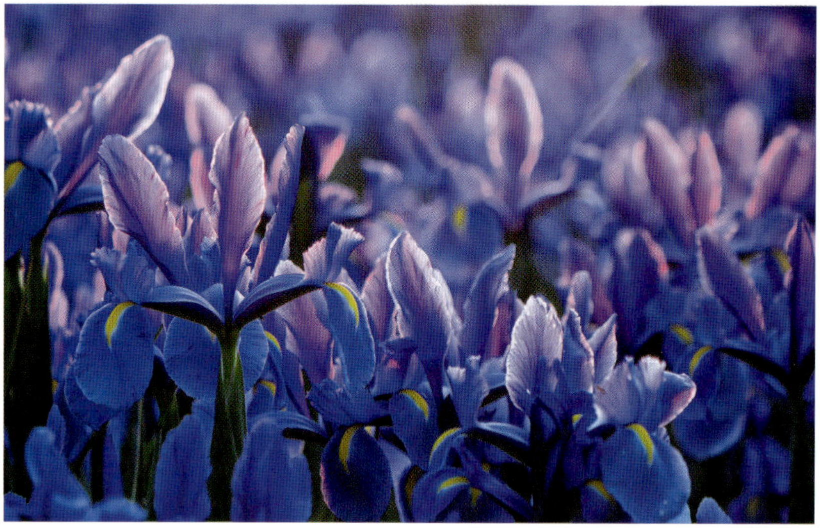

» **ABOVE** The sun breaks on another beautiful day, as seen from the top of Hobart's kunanyi/Mt Wellington

» **RIGHT** Colourful violets catch the day's last rays on Table Cape

» **OPPOSITE** Tasmania's Midlands come to life during spring with bright canola fields and magical sunsets

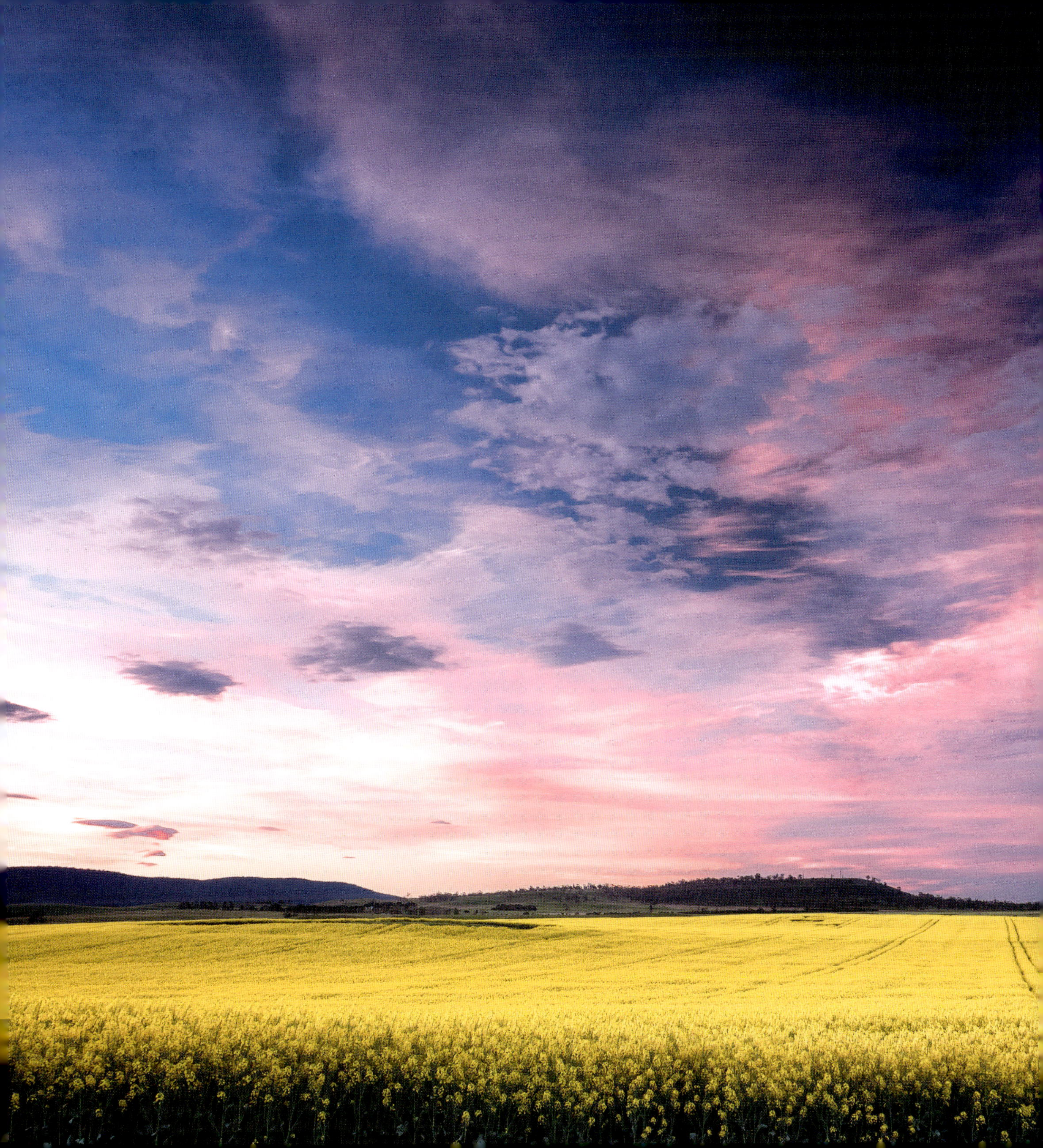

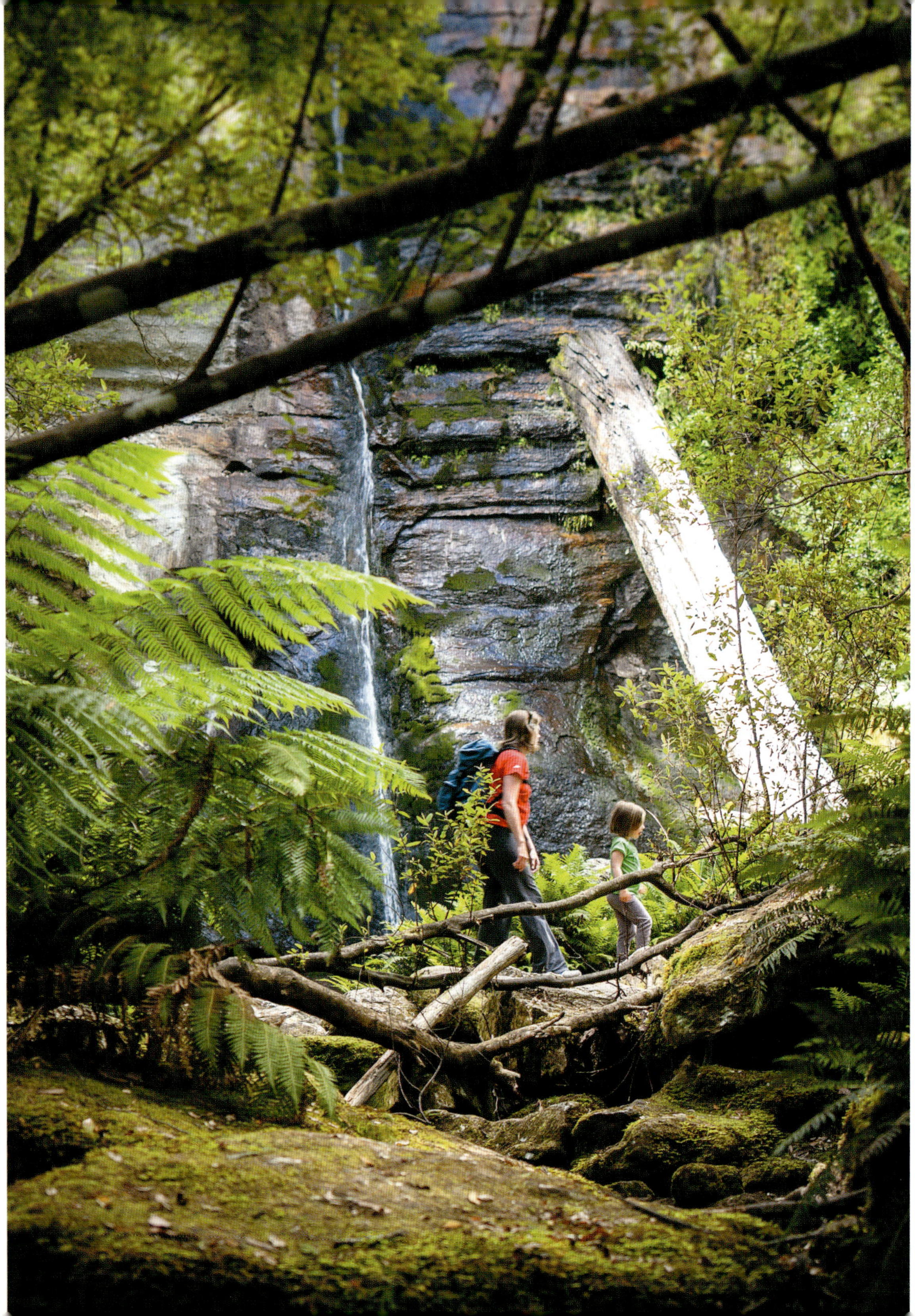

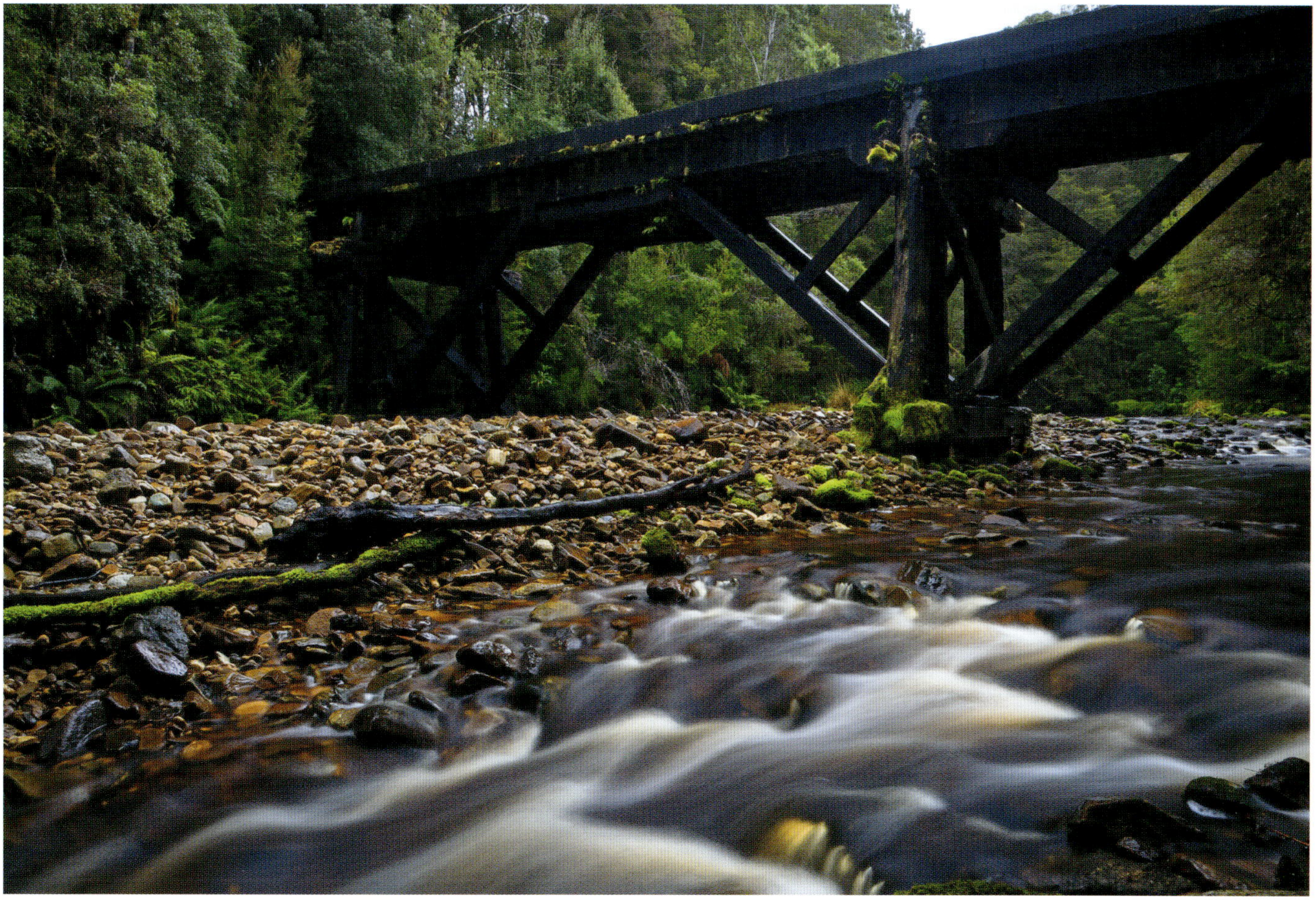

» **ABOVE** The Bird River caresses its way through the breathtaking Kelly Basin region

» **OPPOSITE** Explorers of all ages can enjoy Tasmania's waterfalls, including Snug Falls

» **OVERLEAF** The wild west of Tasmania, where beauty greets you from every angle

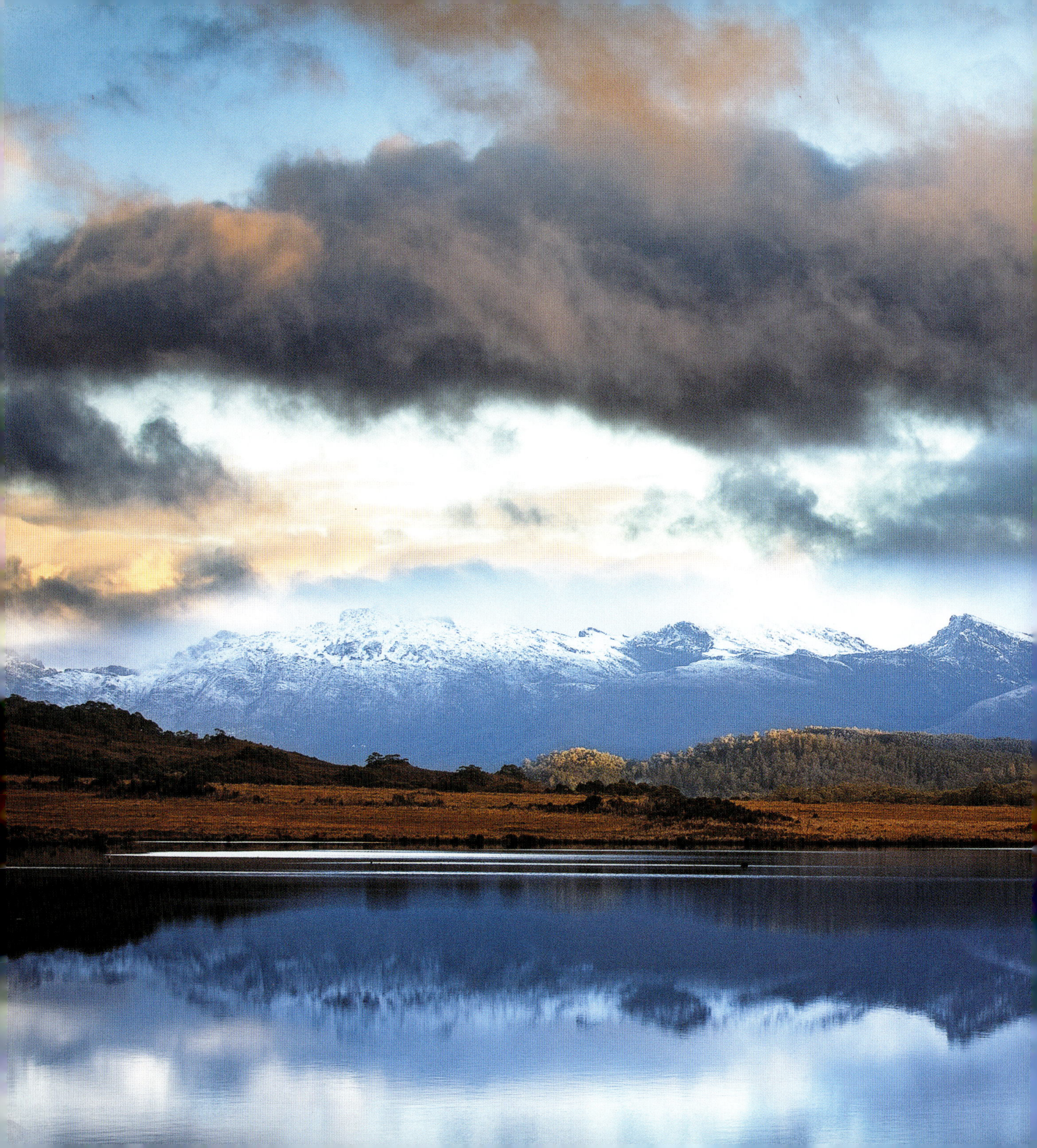

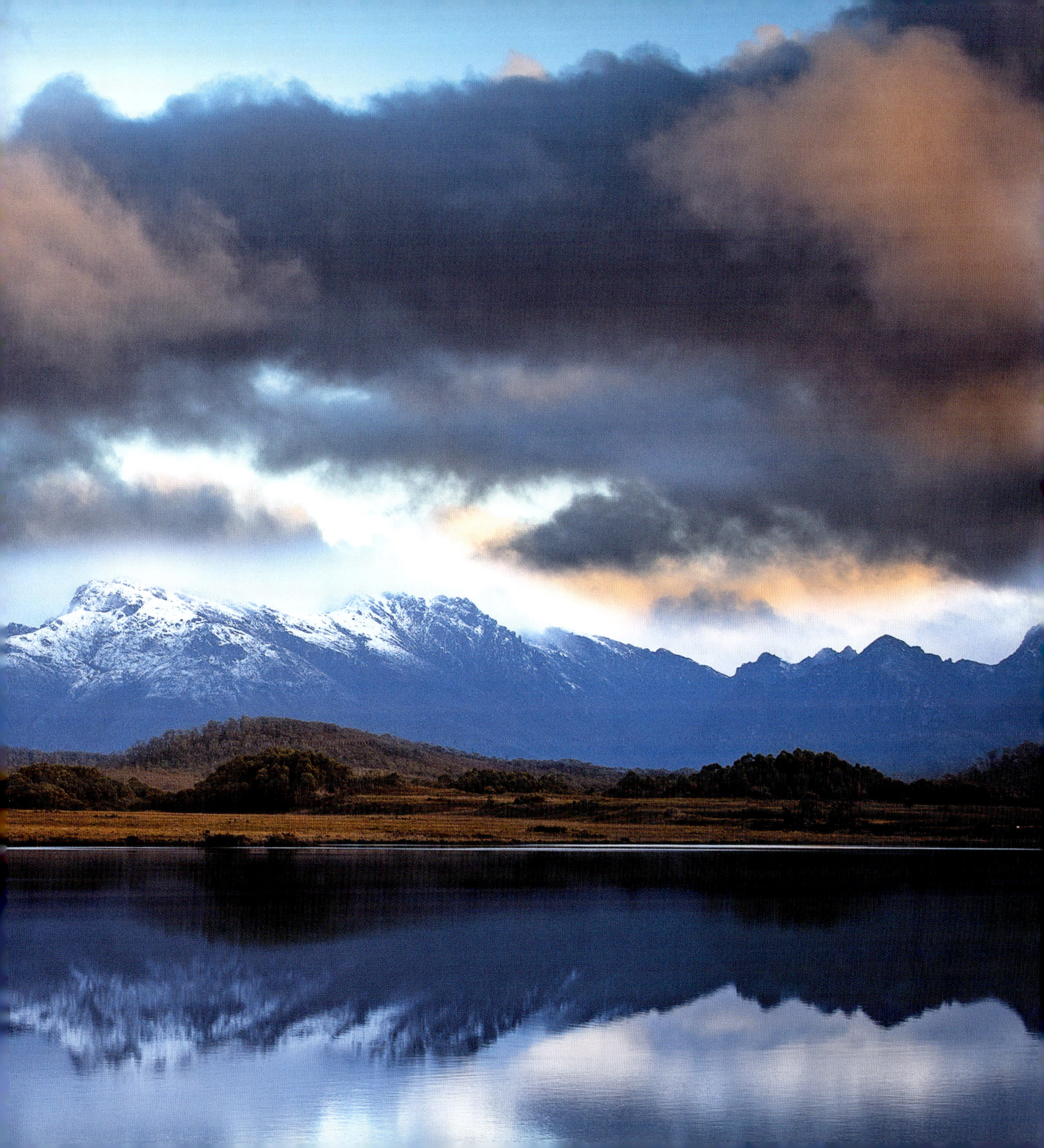

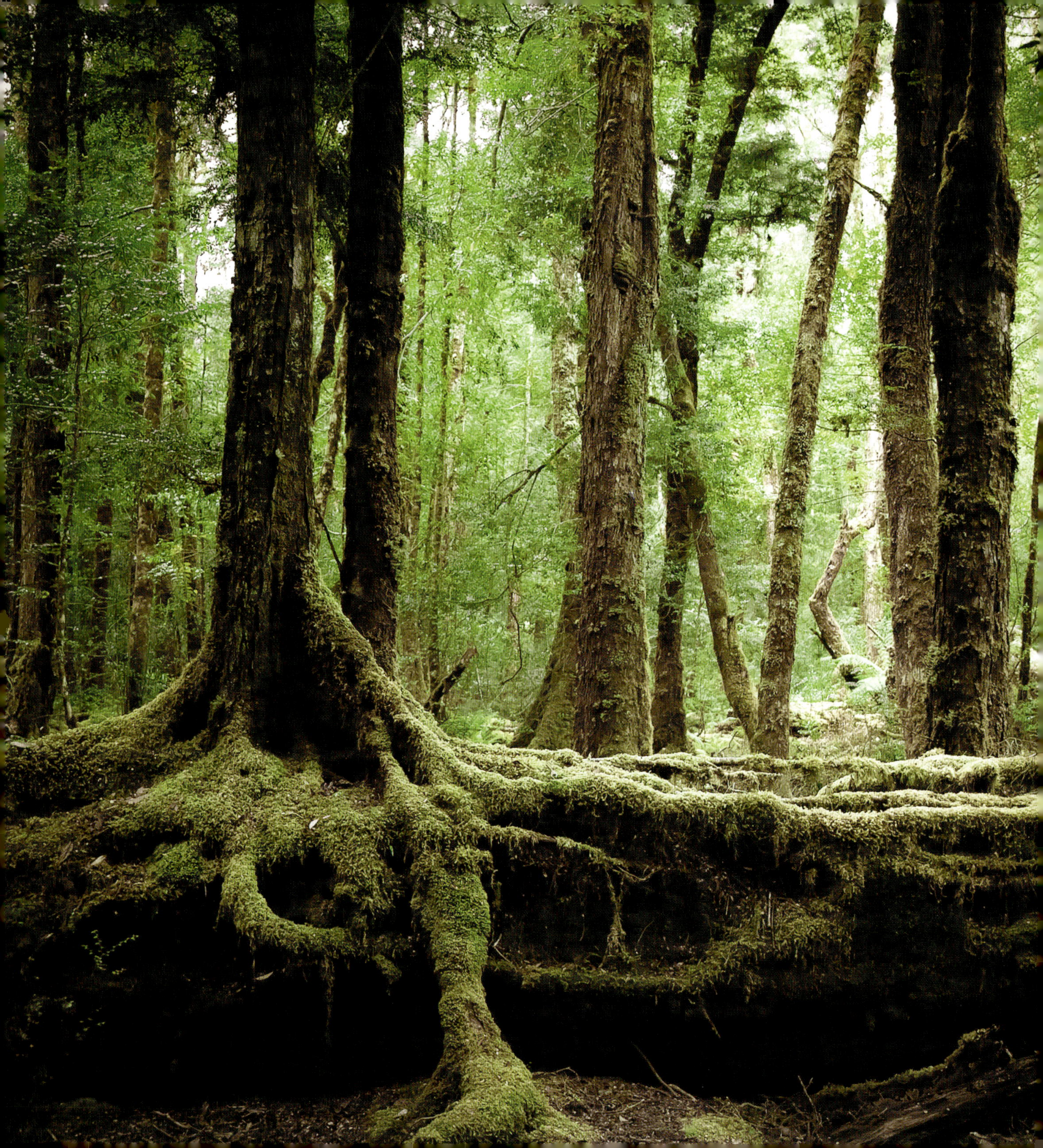

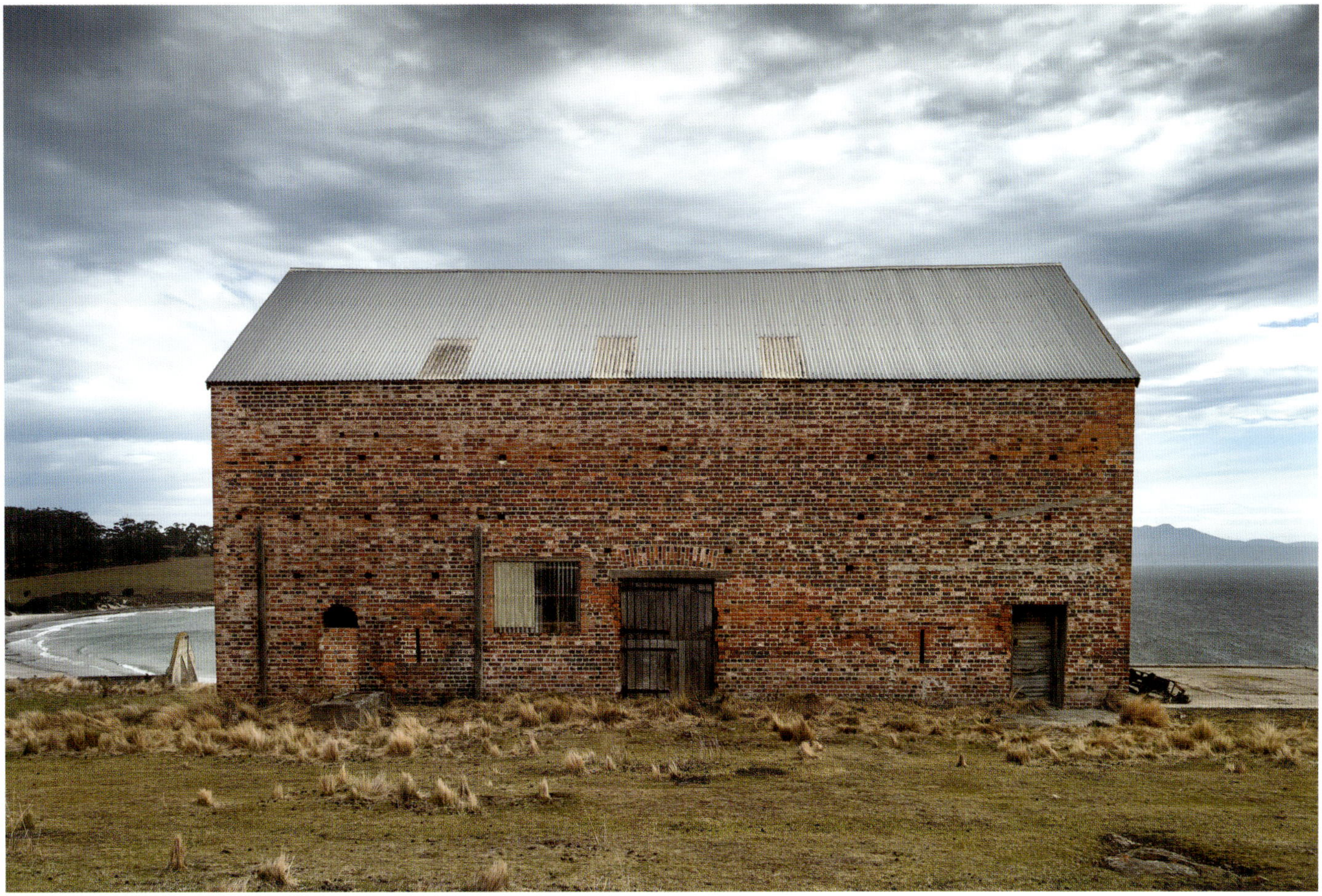

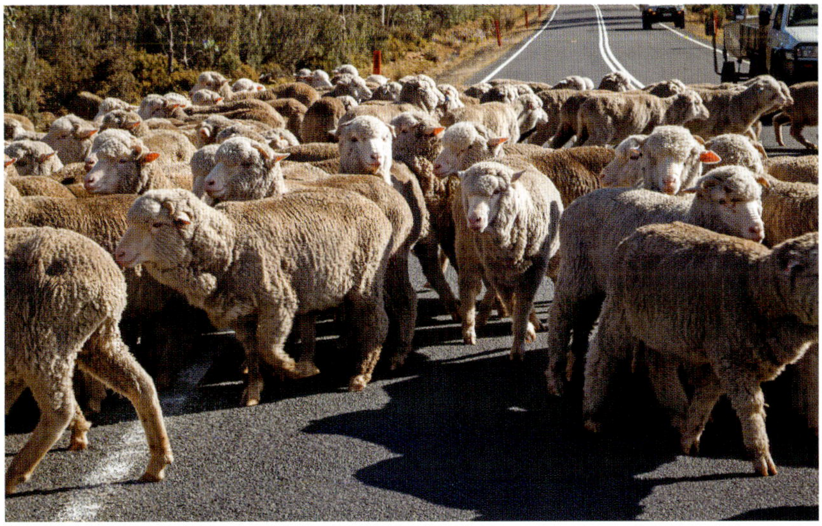

» **ABOVE** An old barn on Maria Island – still exuding character after all this time

» **LEFT** A quick stop as the locals make their way back home

» **OPPOSITE** Its easy to find yourself lost in a world long gone in these jurassic forests in the Cradle Mountain region

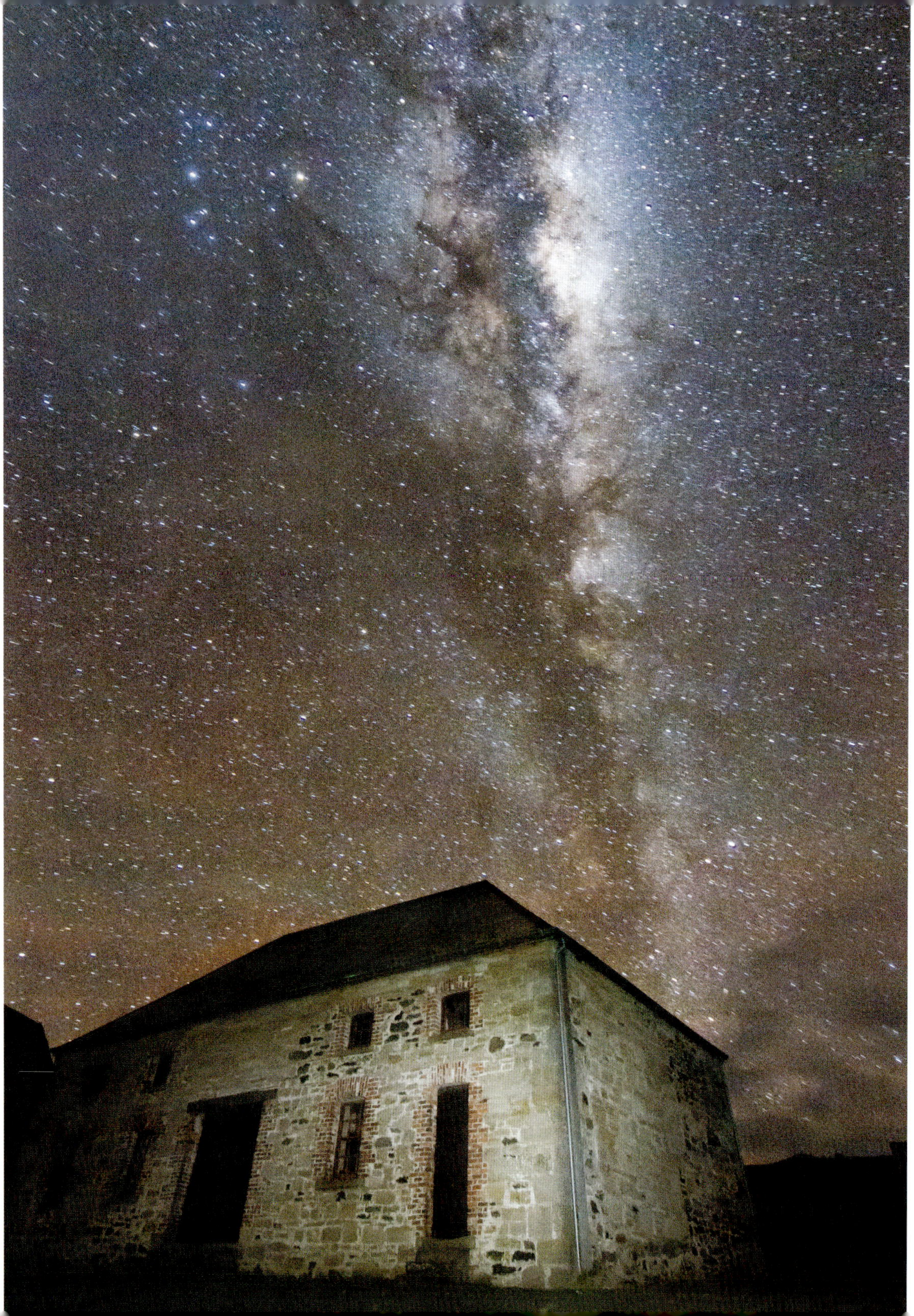

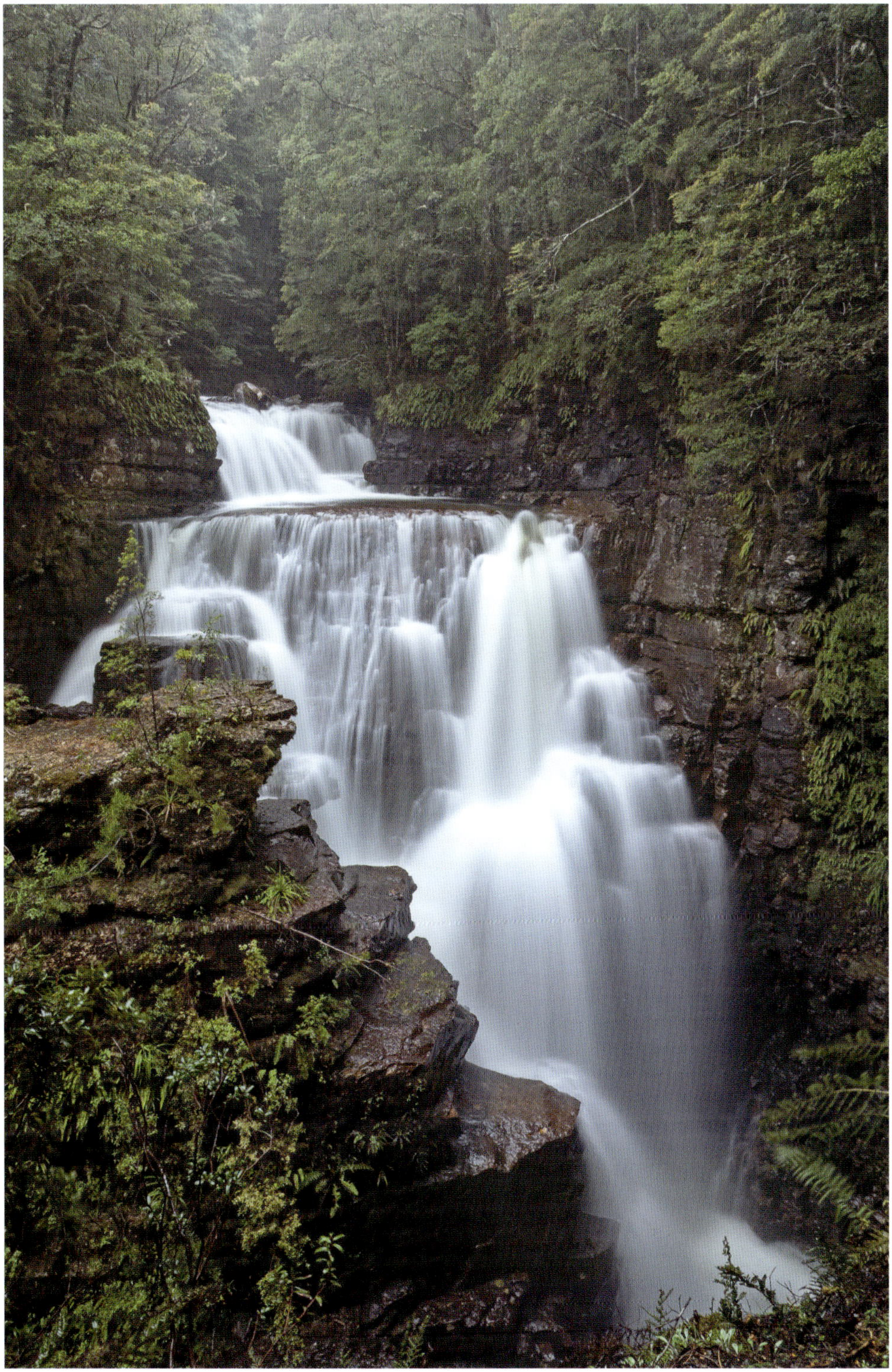

» **LEFT** Deep in the Tasmanian wilderness, D'Alton Falls is a breathtaking sight

» **OPPOSITE** If you're lucky, you may have the whole of remote Maria Island to yourself

» **OVERLEAF** Bringing in the New Year with a bang at Wrest Point Casino, Hobart

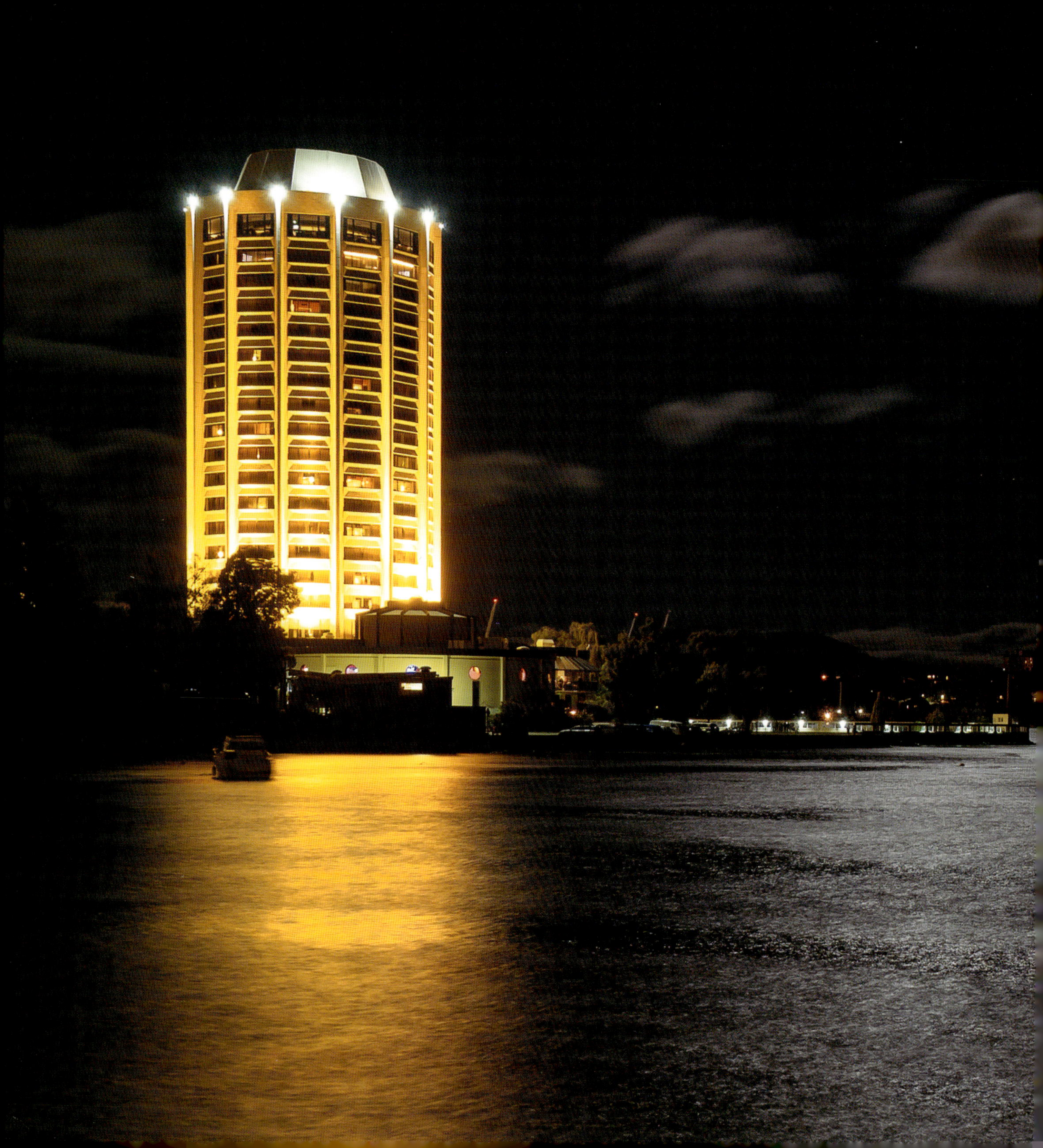

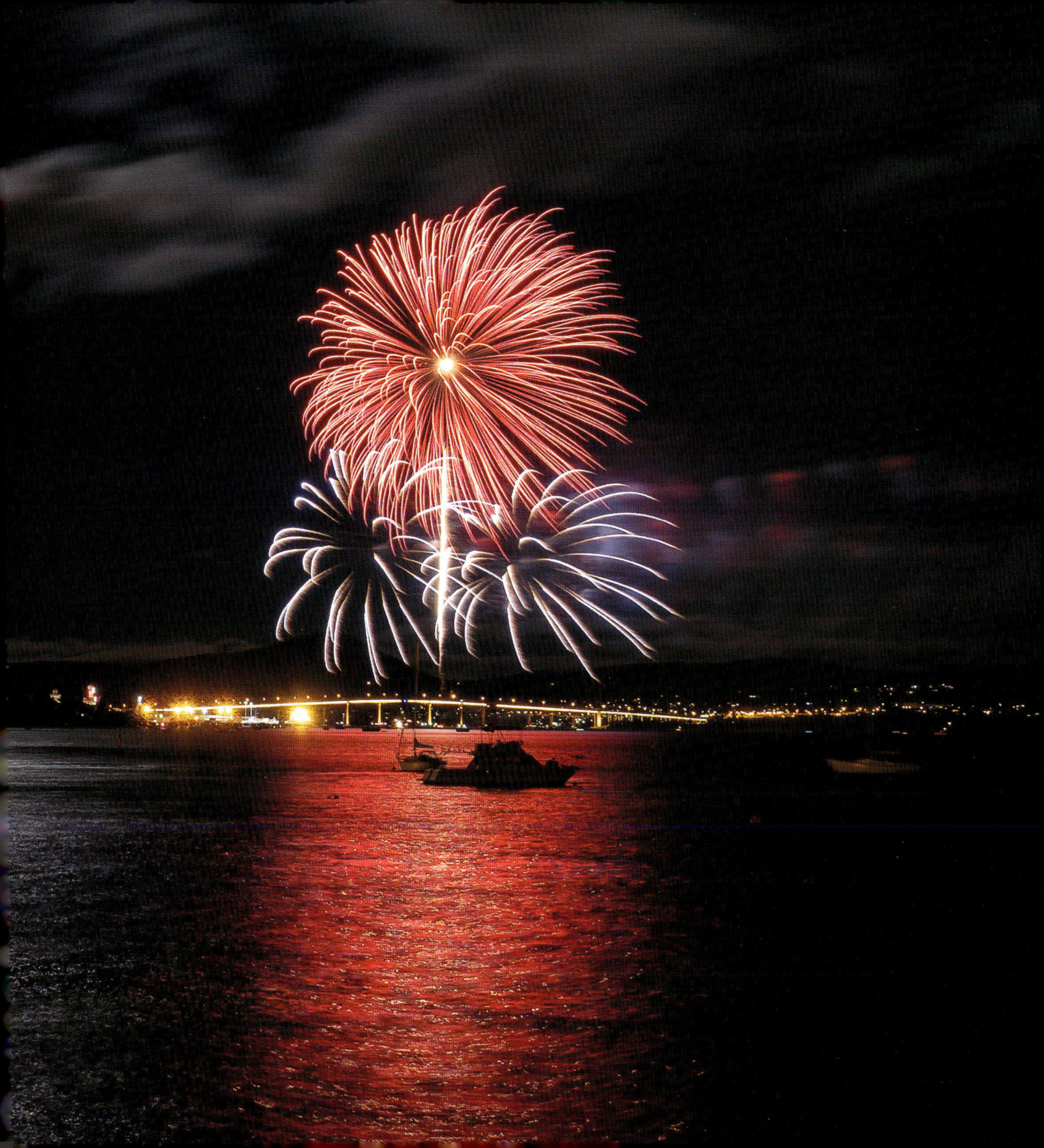

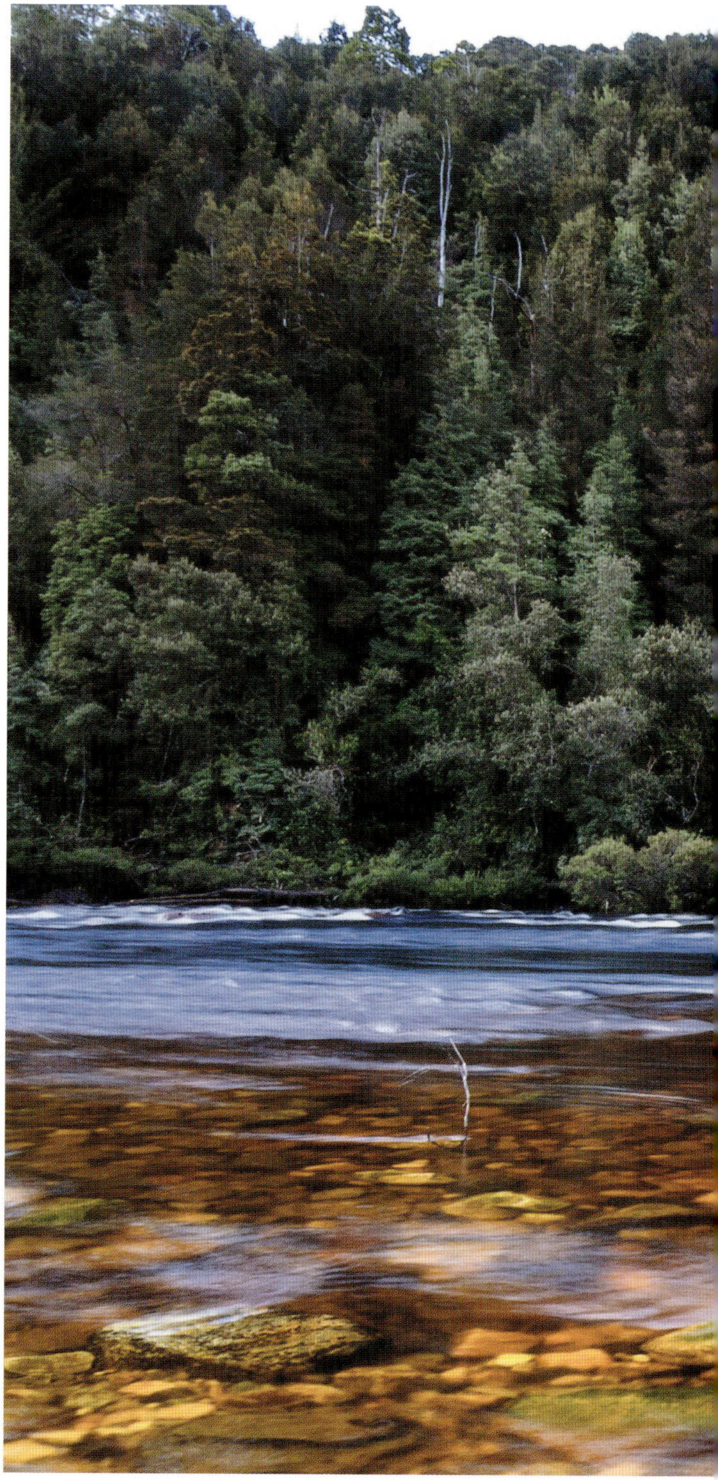

» **RIGHT** Time stands still along the Franklin River

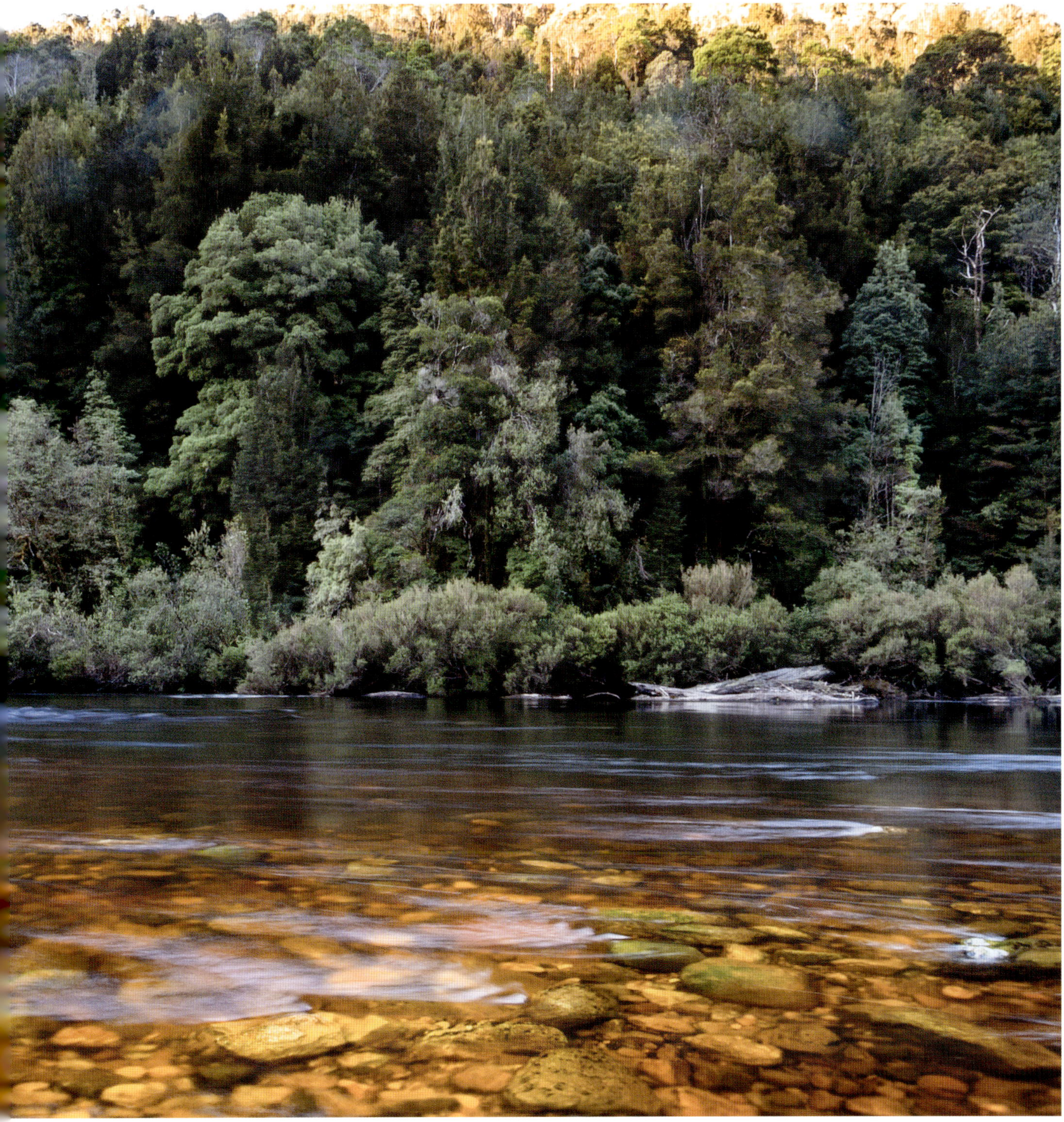

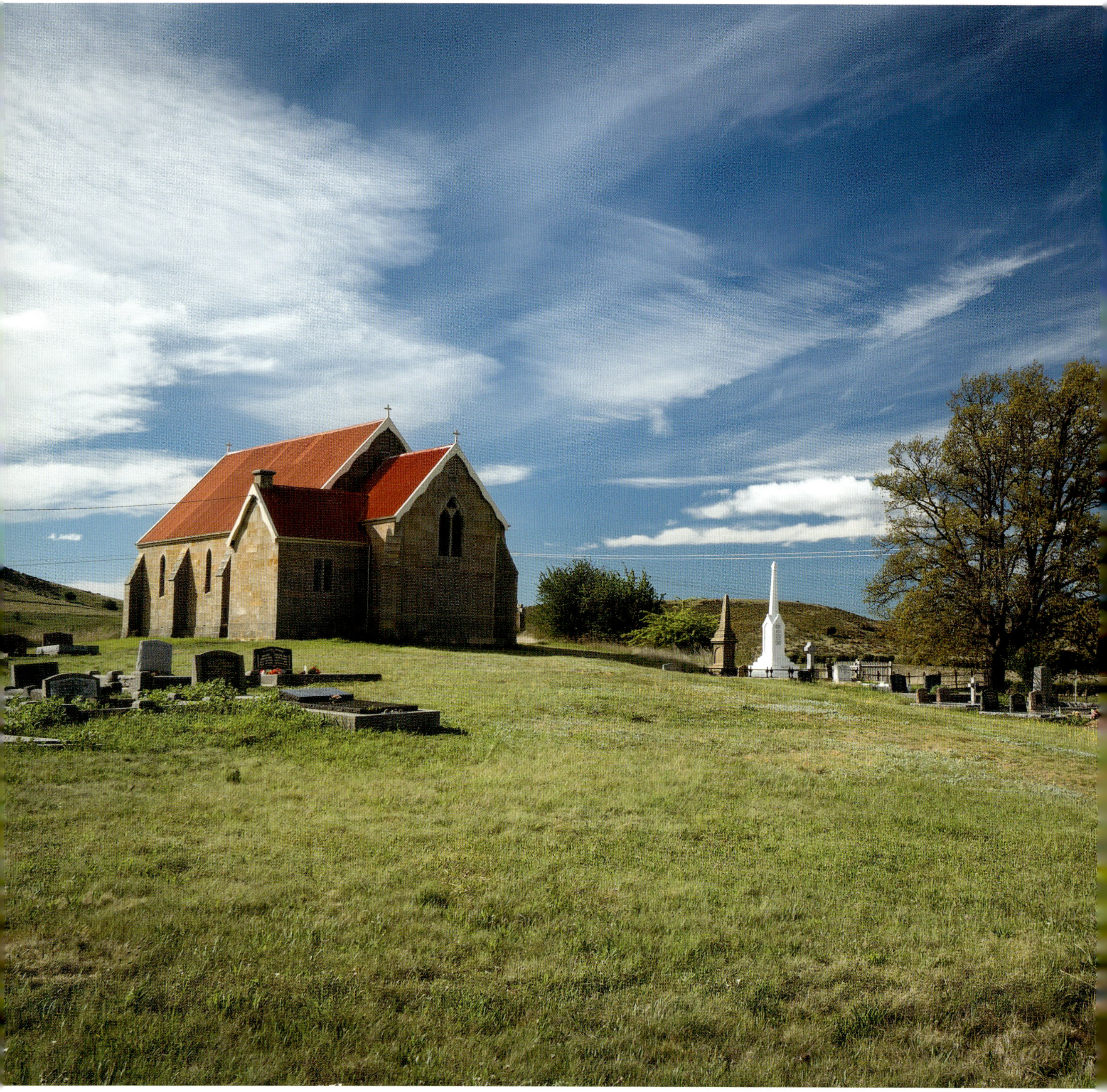

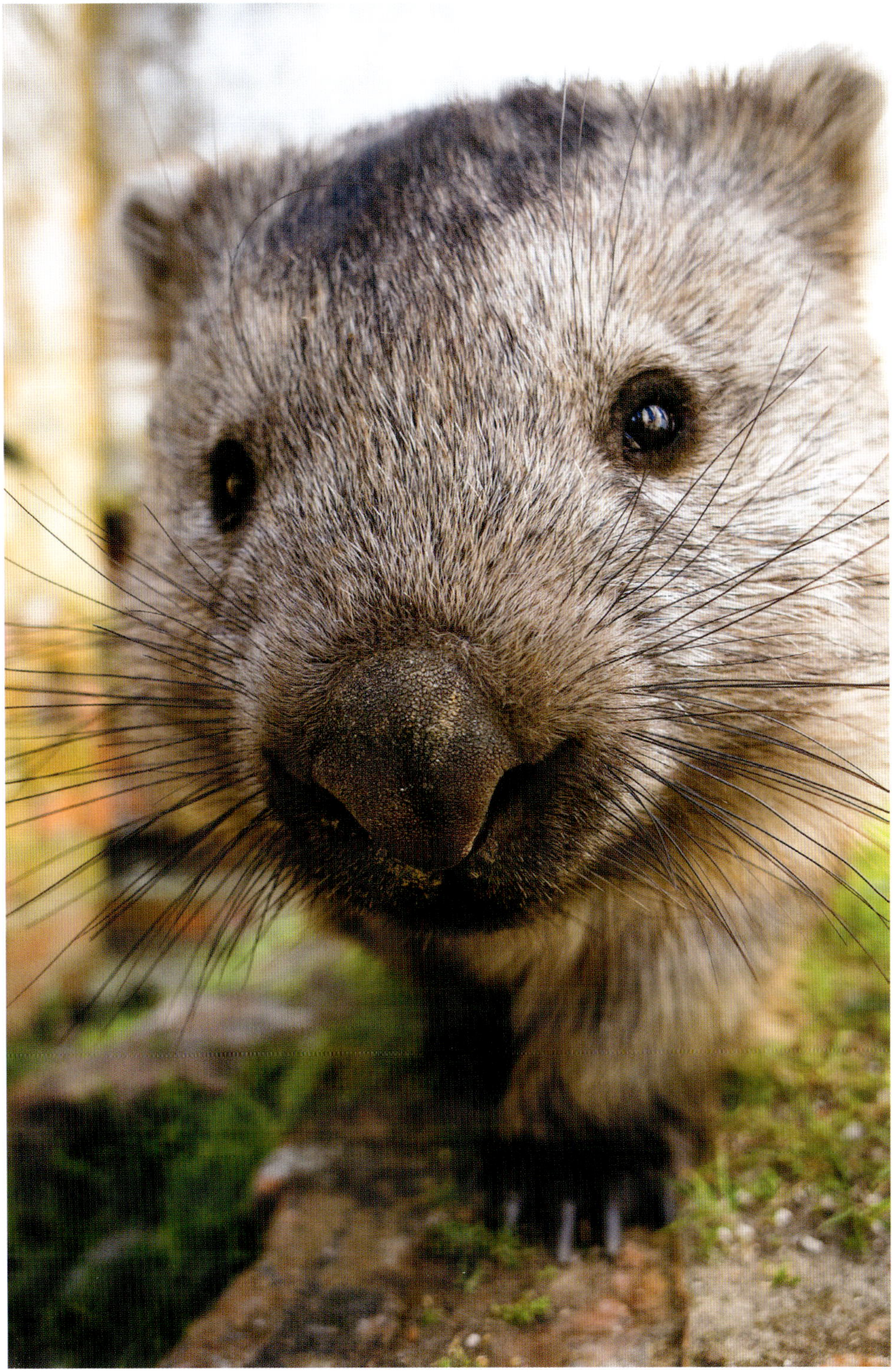

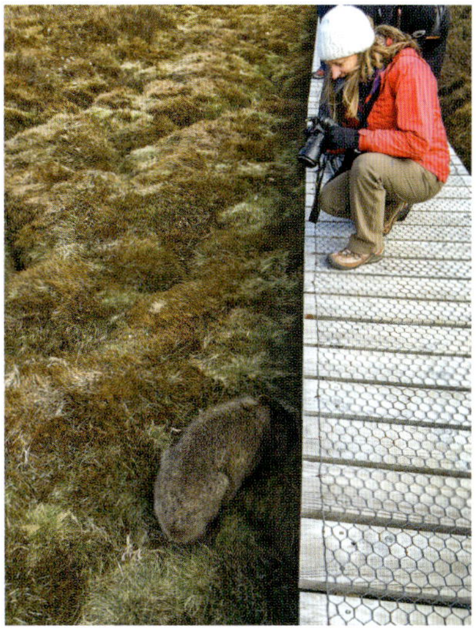

» **ABOVE** Wombats stock up on food in the lead up to wild weather, and on this day there were wombats aplenty

» **LEFT** The Maria Island wombats are extremely friendly and inquisitive

» **OPPOSITE** Located at Jericho, in the Midlands of Tasmania, is one of Australia's oldest churches

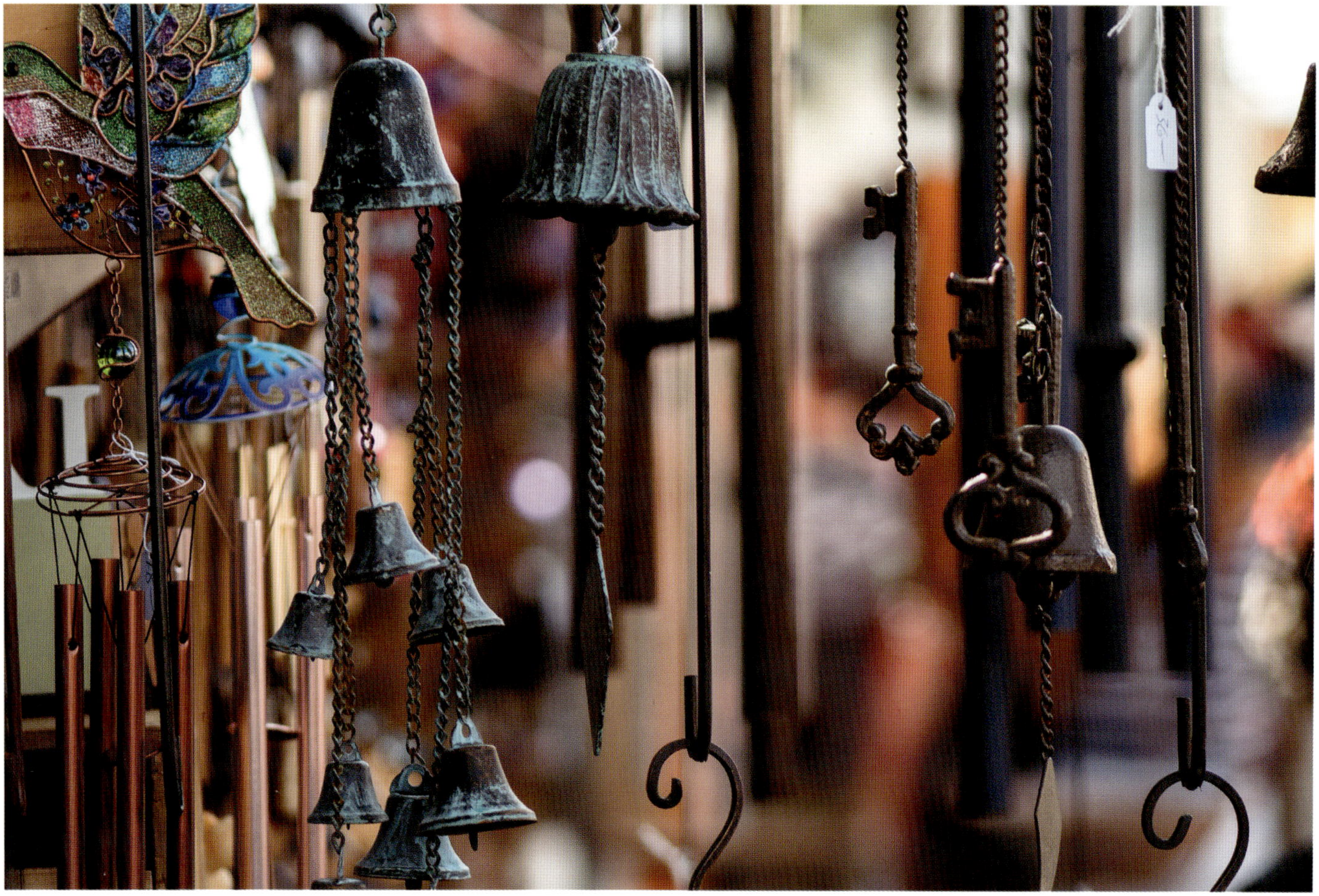

» **ABOVE** Arts and crafts line the historic streets of Salamanca every Saturday

» **OPPOSITE** A family of pandani nestled under a giant deciduous beech tree, commonly known as the fagus

» **OVERLEAF** Does anything beat the smell of a fresh rainforest after rainfall, especially in Mount Field National Park?

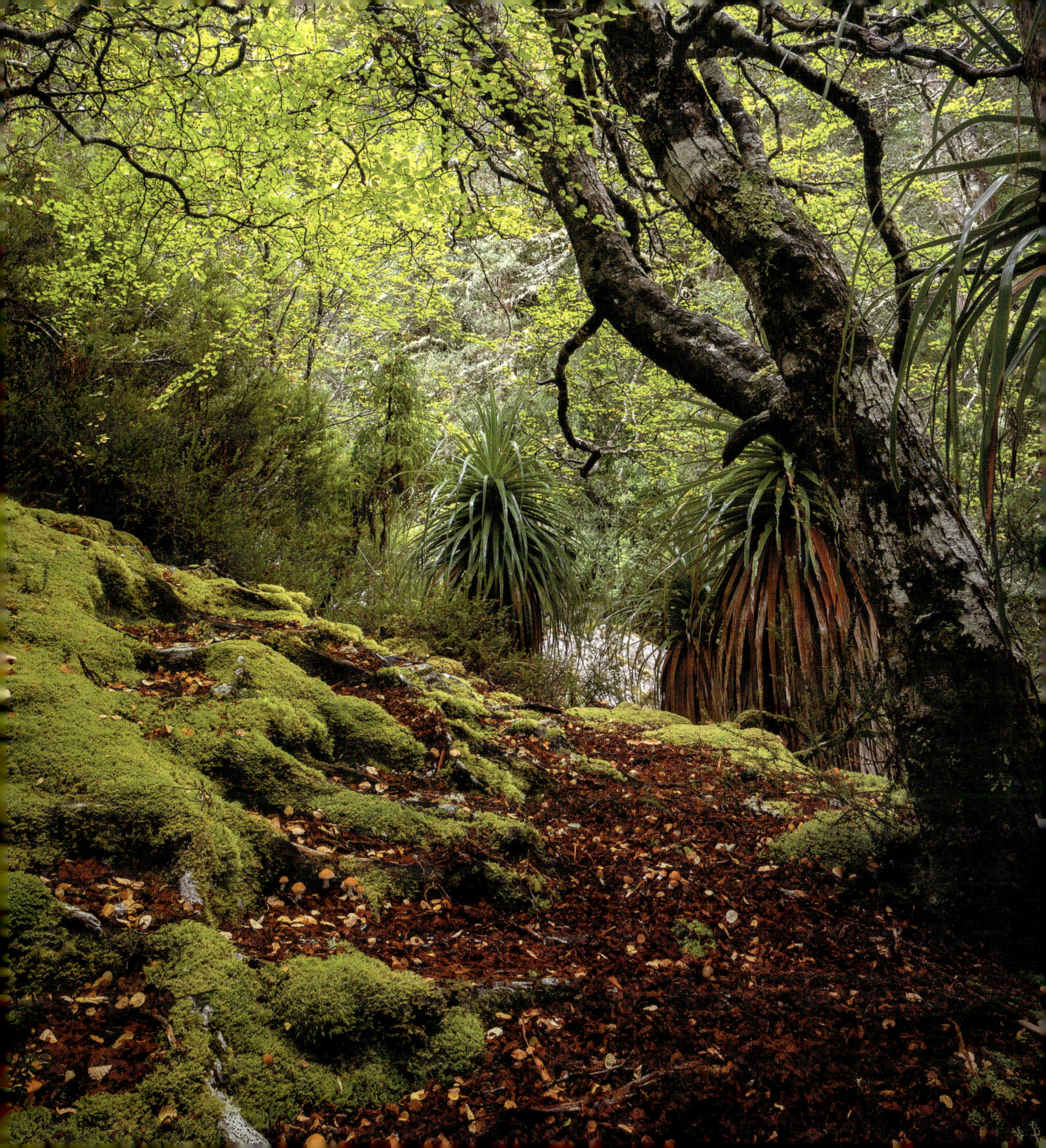

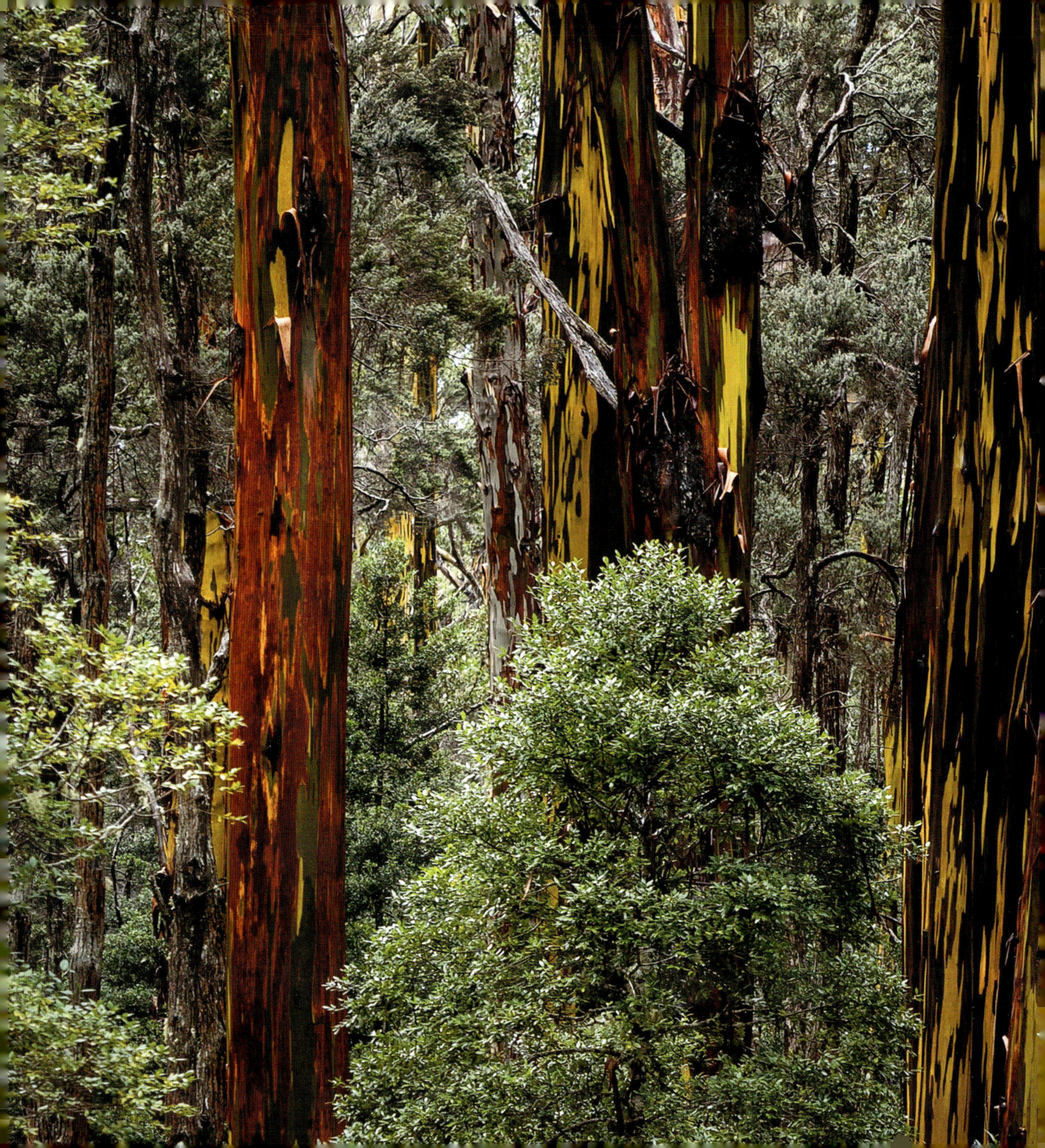

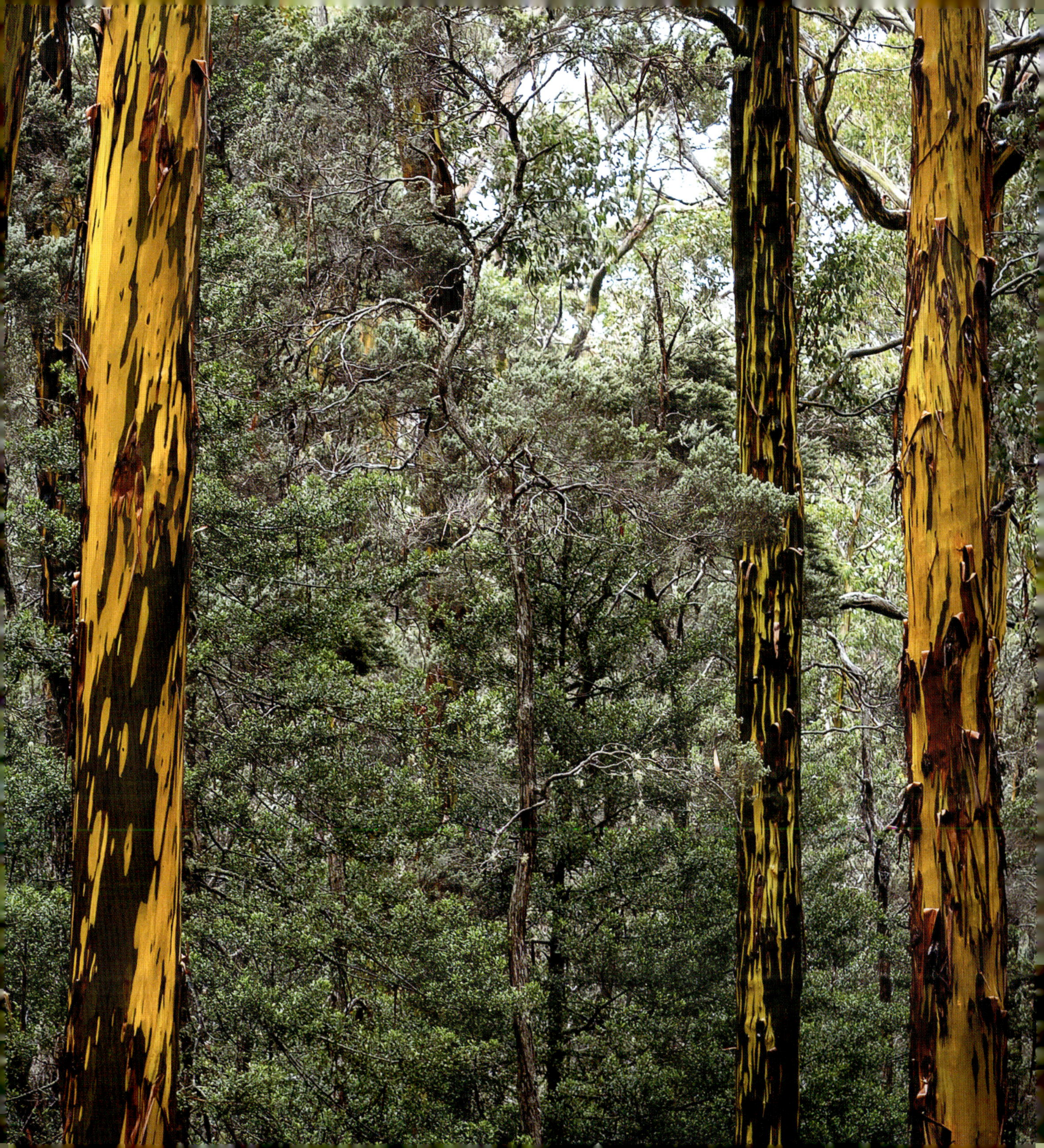

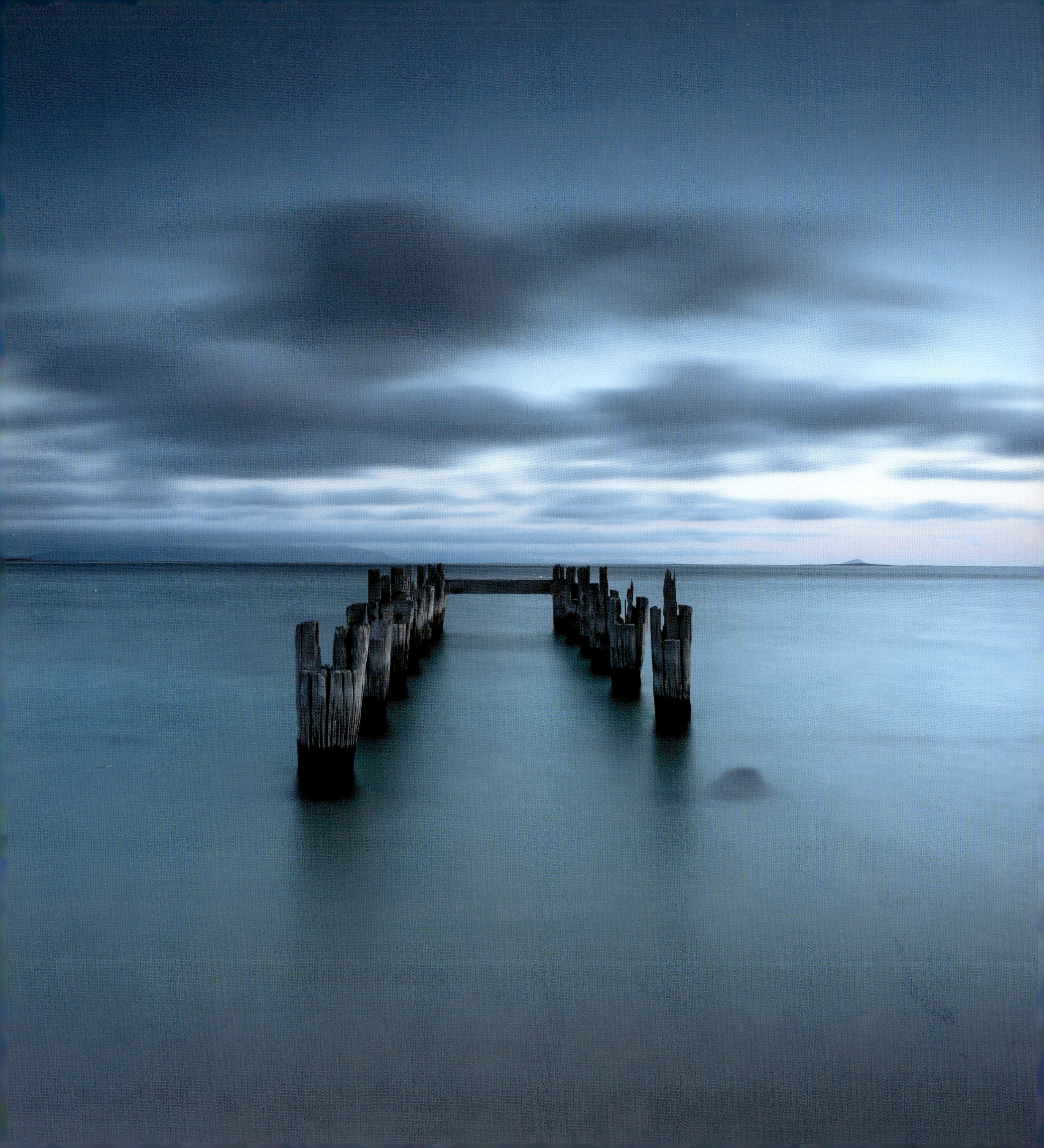

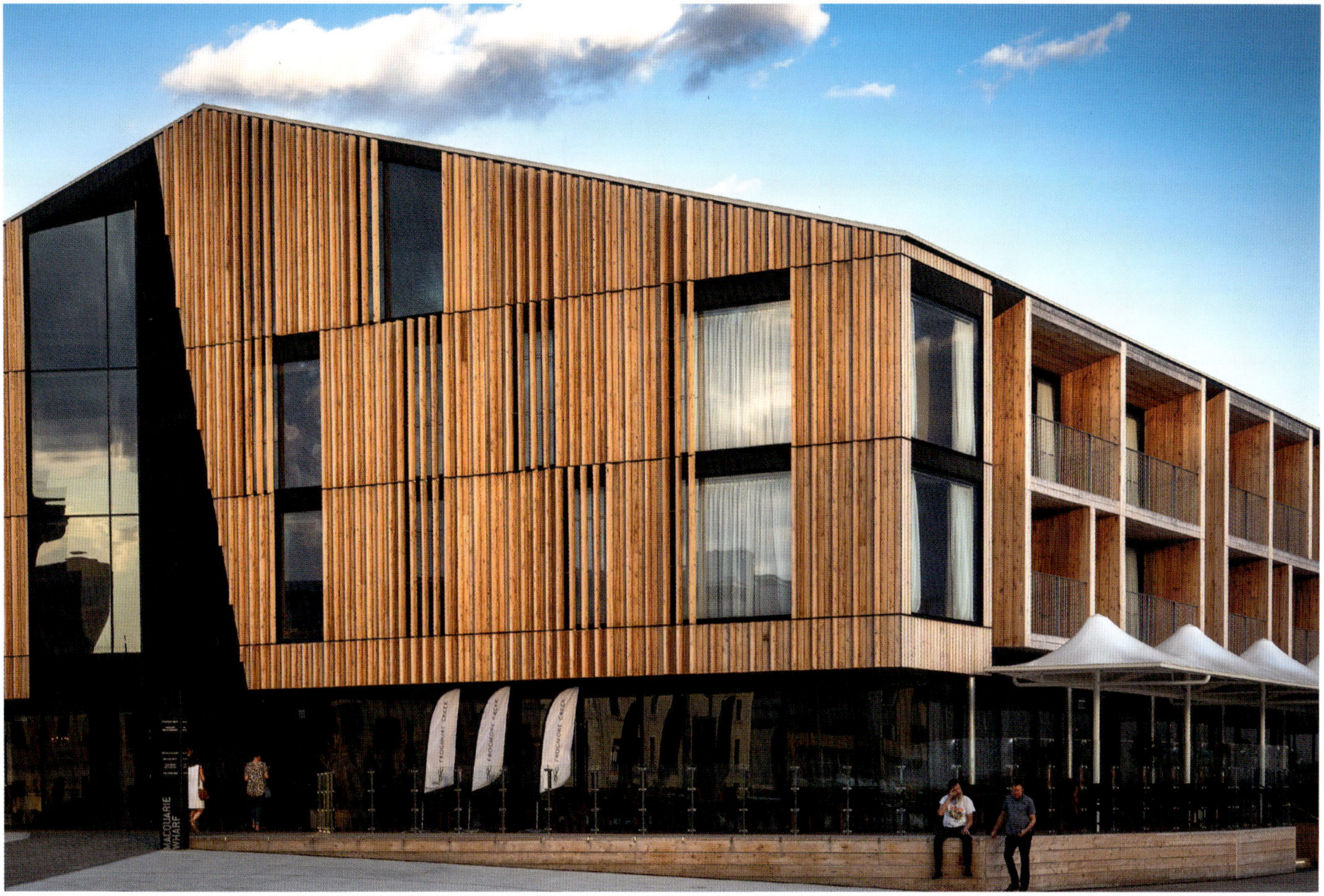

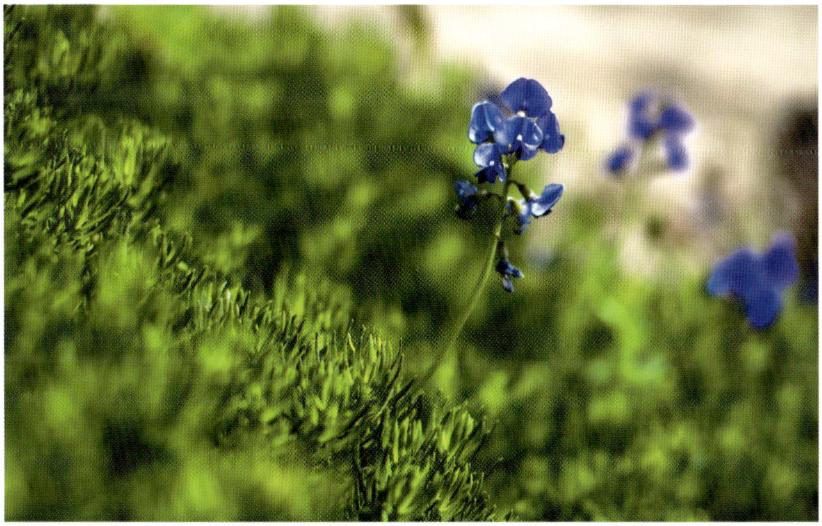

» **ABOVE** One of Hobart's newest and most impressive hotels, the MACq 01, is a beauty to photograph in the late afternoon

» **LEFT** Wildflowers grow in abundance along the coastline of King Island

» **OPPOSITE** A peaceful repose at Sawyer Bay on Flinders Island

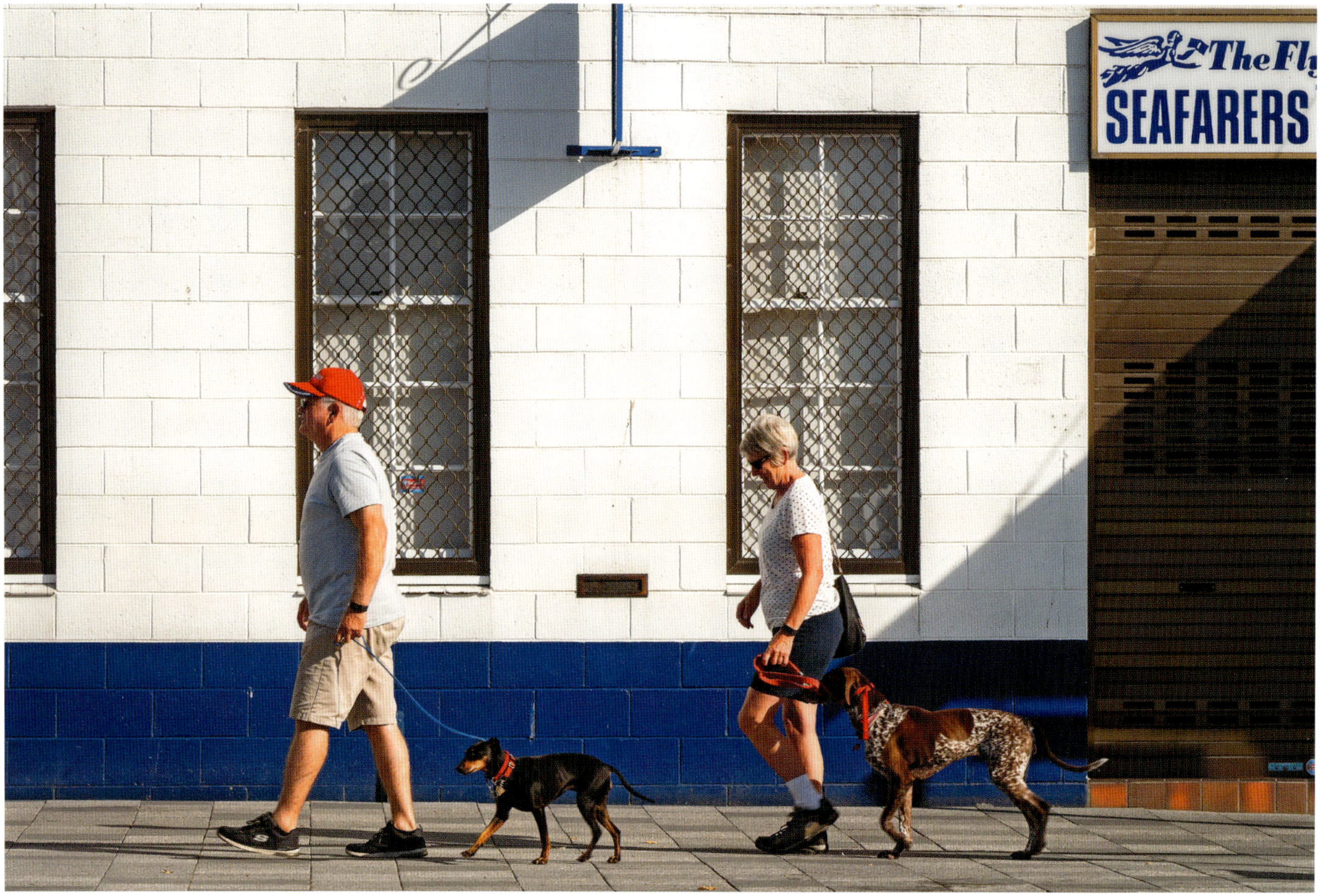

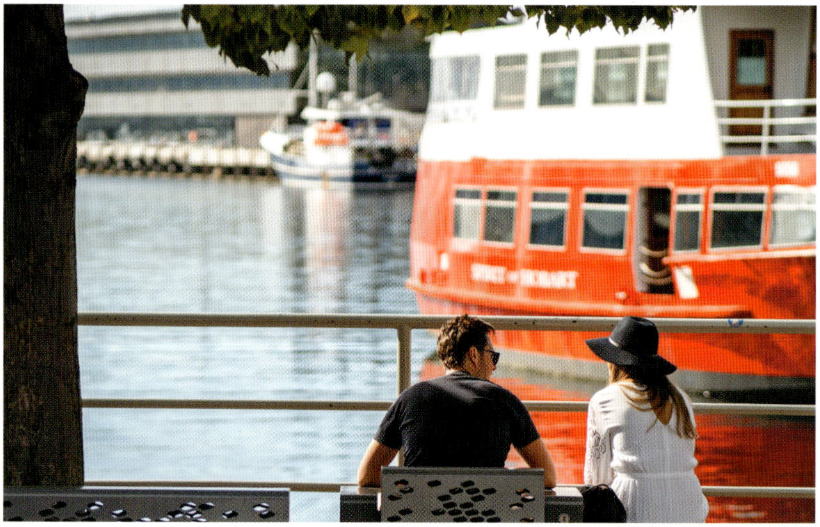

» **ABOVE** Out for a summer's day stroll along Hobart's waterfront

» **RIGHT** Romance and boating go hand in hand at the Hobart waterfront

» **OPPOSITE** Rugged coastline mixed with the brilliant blue ocean on King Island's coast

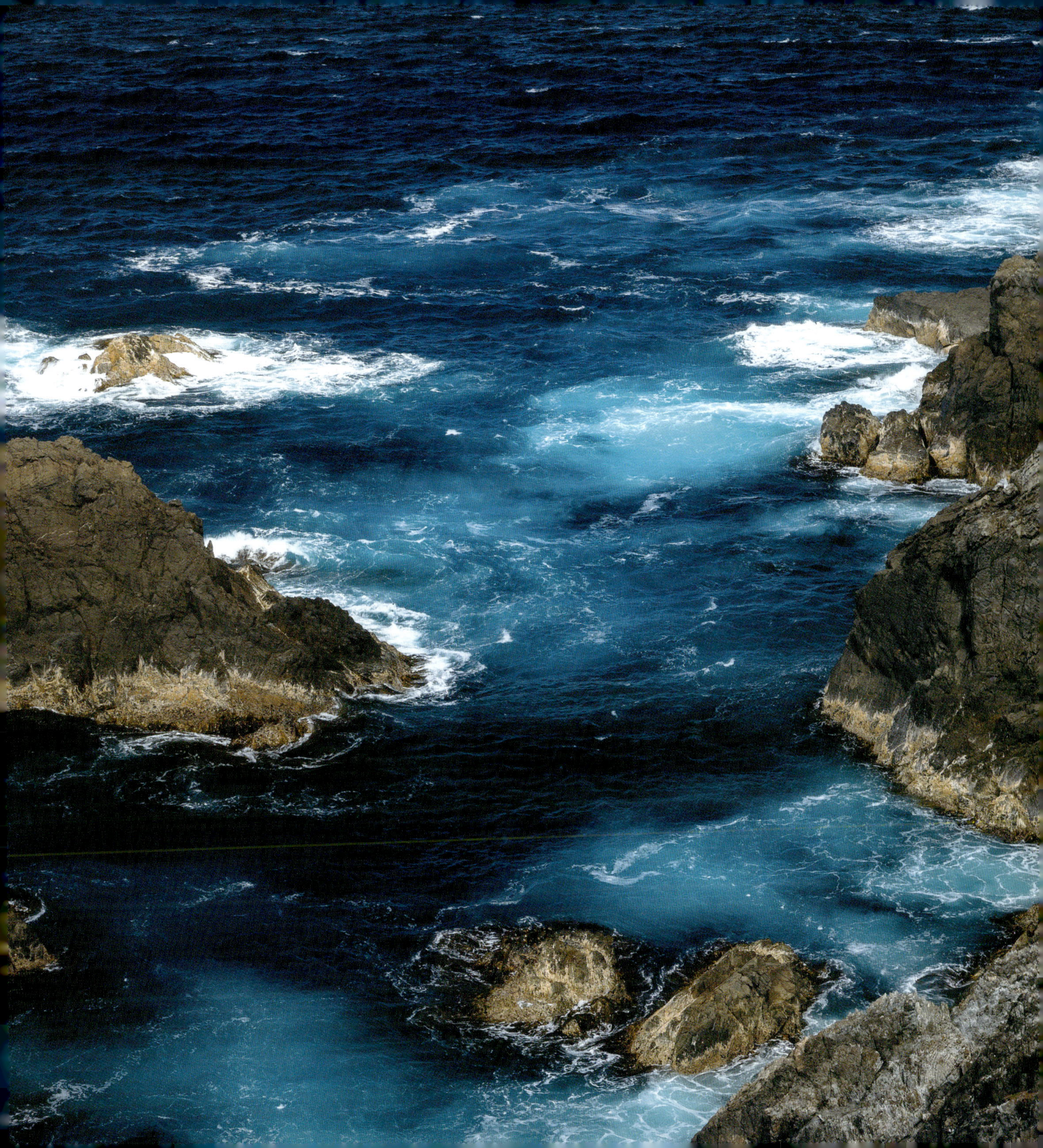

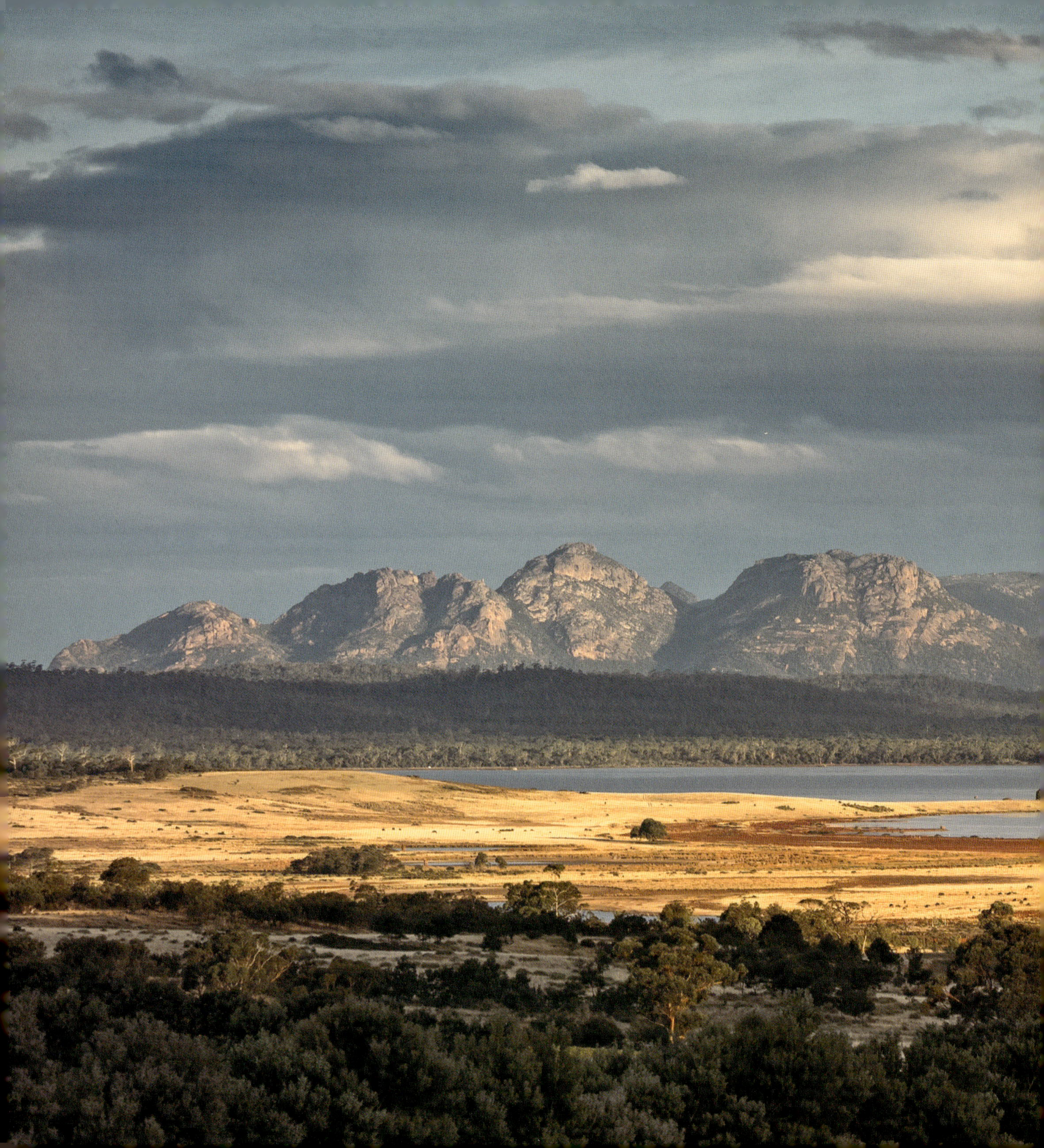

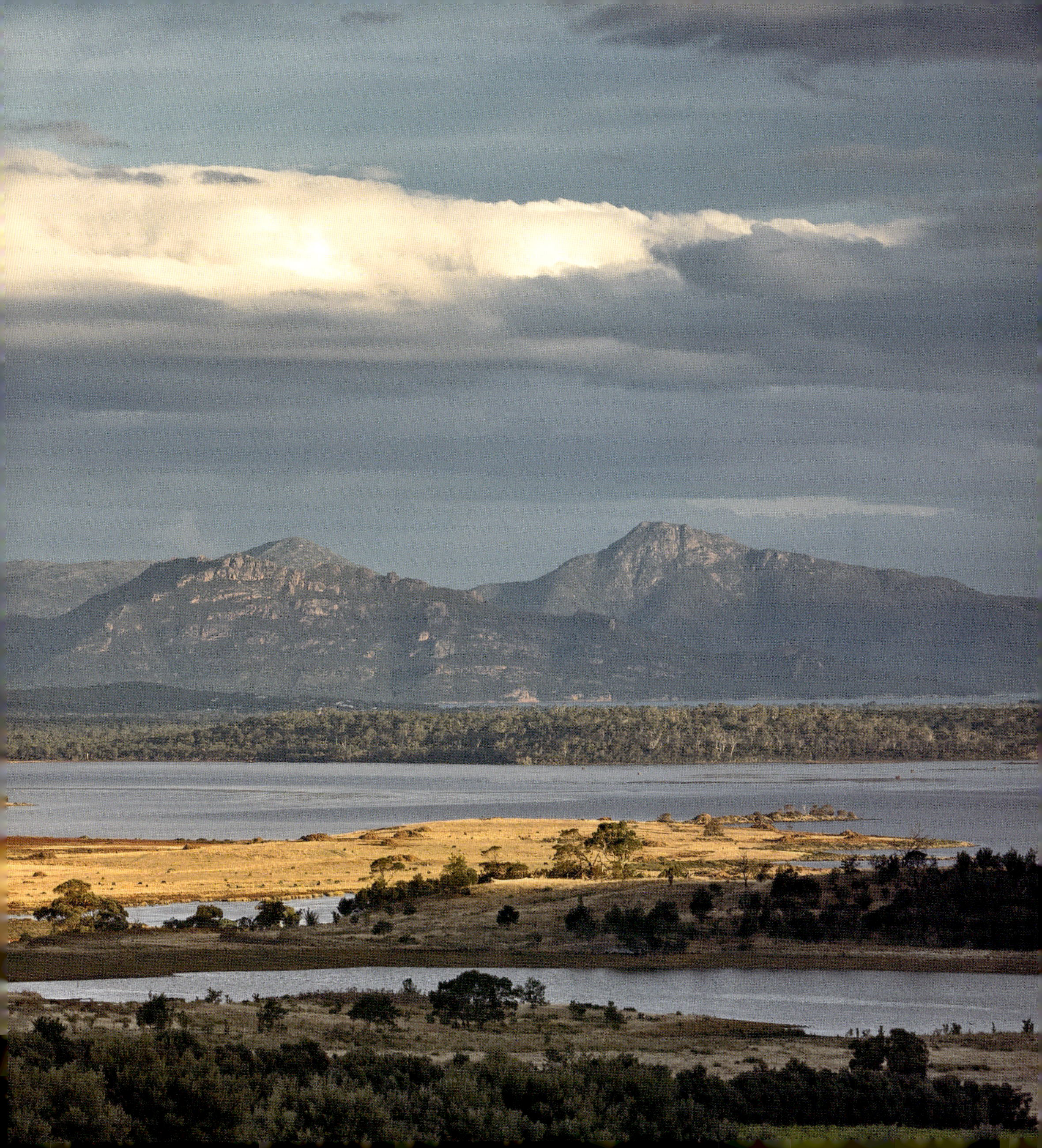

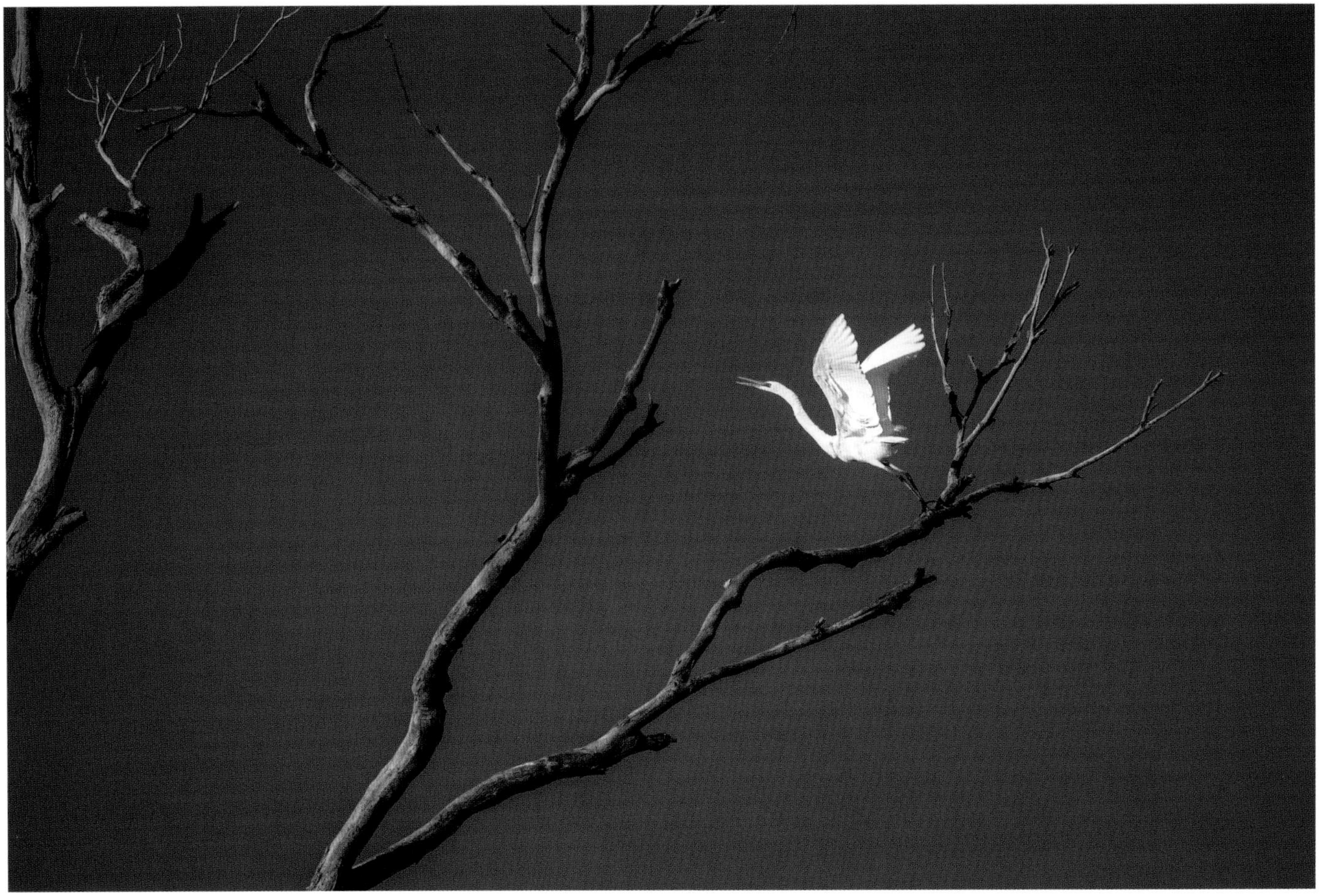

» **ABOVE** A majestic great egret soars in search of dinner around the waterways of Maria Island

» **OPPOSITE** Feeling the ghosts on a Port Arthur Historic Site Ghost Tour

» **PREVIOUS** One of Tasmania's best photo opportunities – the view of the Hazards mountain range at Devils Elbow

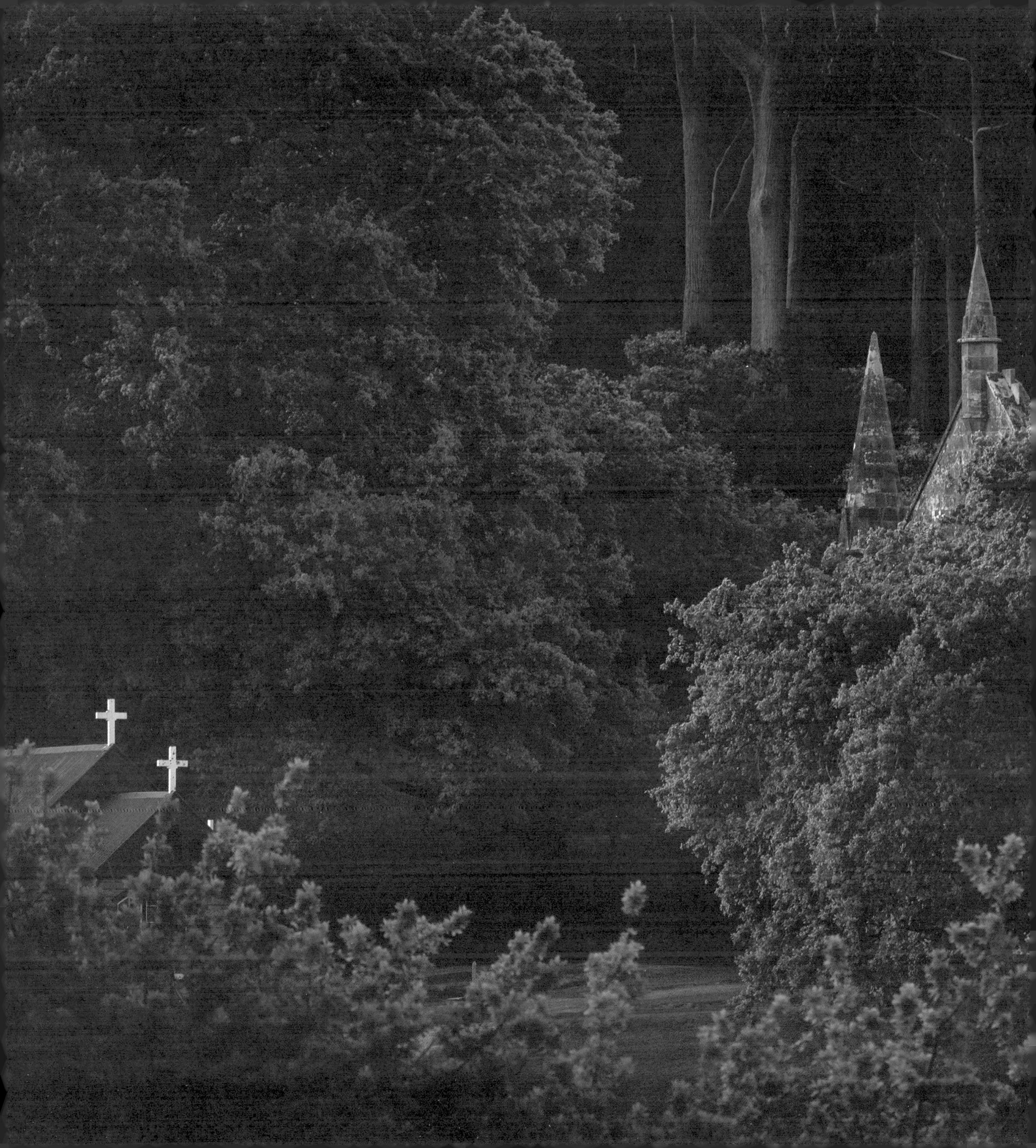

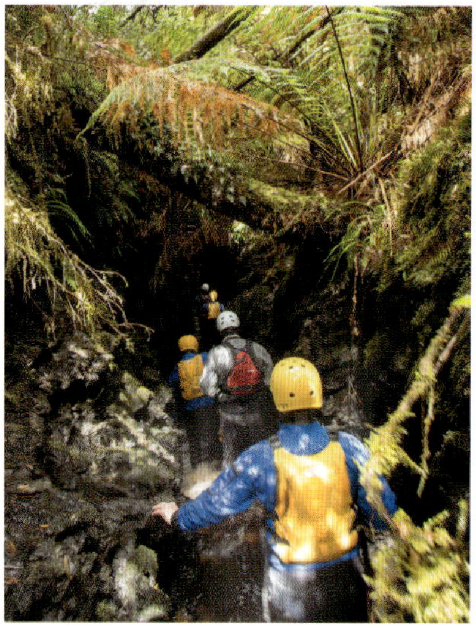

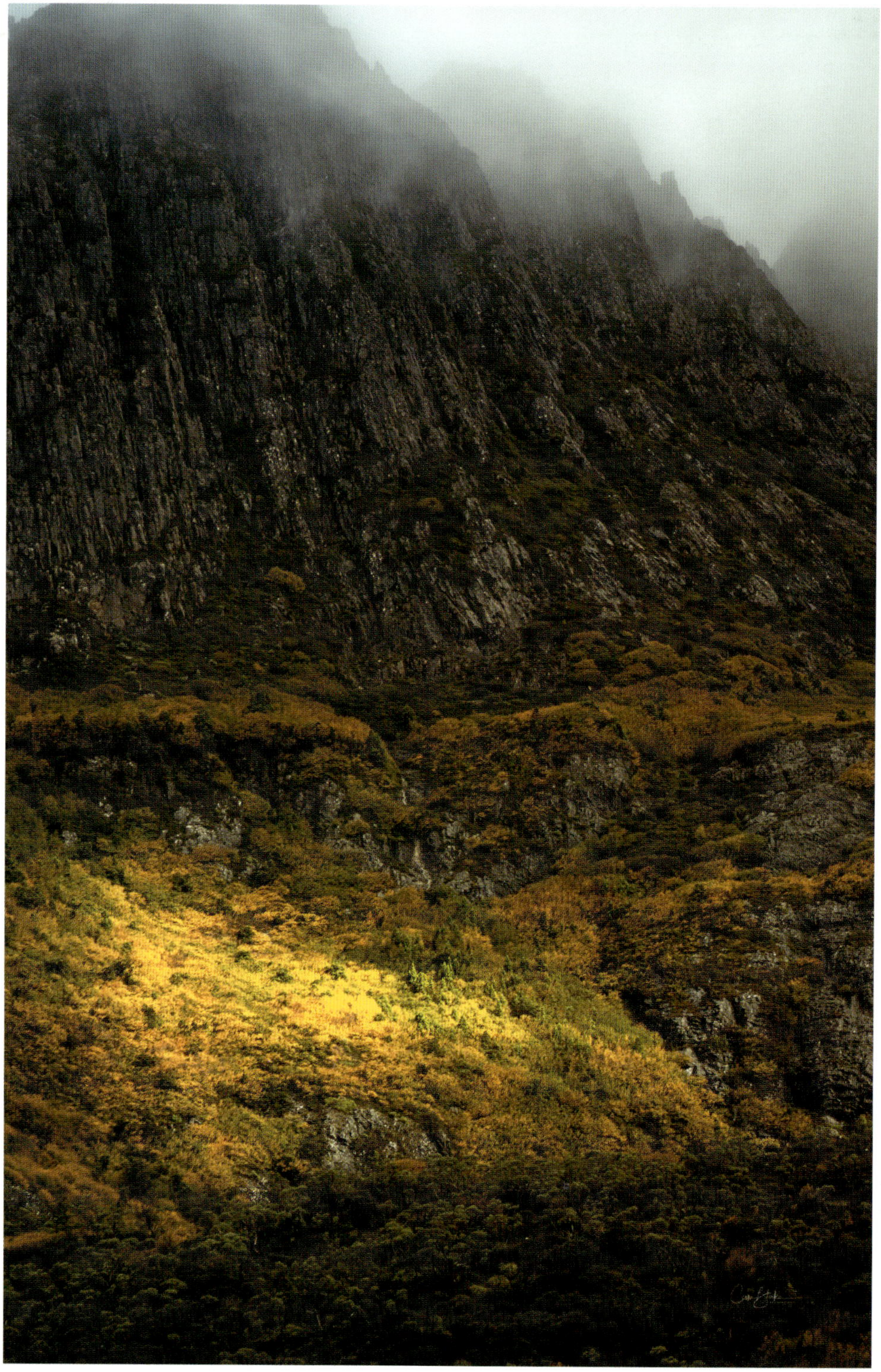

» **ABOVE** Exploring the 'Lost World' limestone caves along the Franklin River

» **RIGHT** A break in the weather reveals magical autumn colours in undergrowth at Cradle Mountain–Lake St Clair National Park.

» **OPPOSITE** Looking up at some of the world's clearest skies

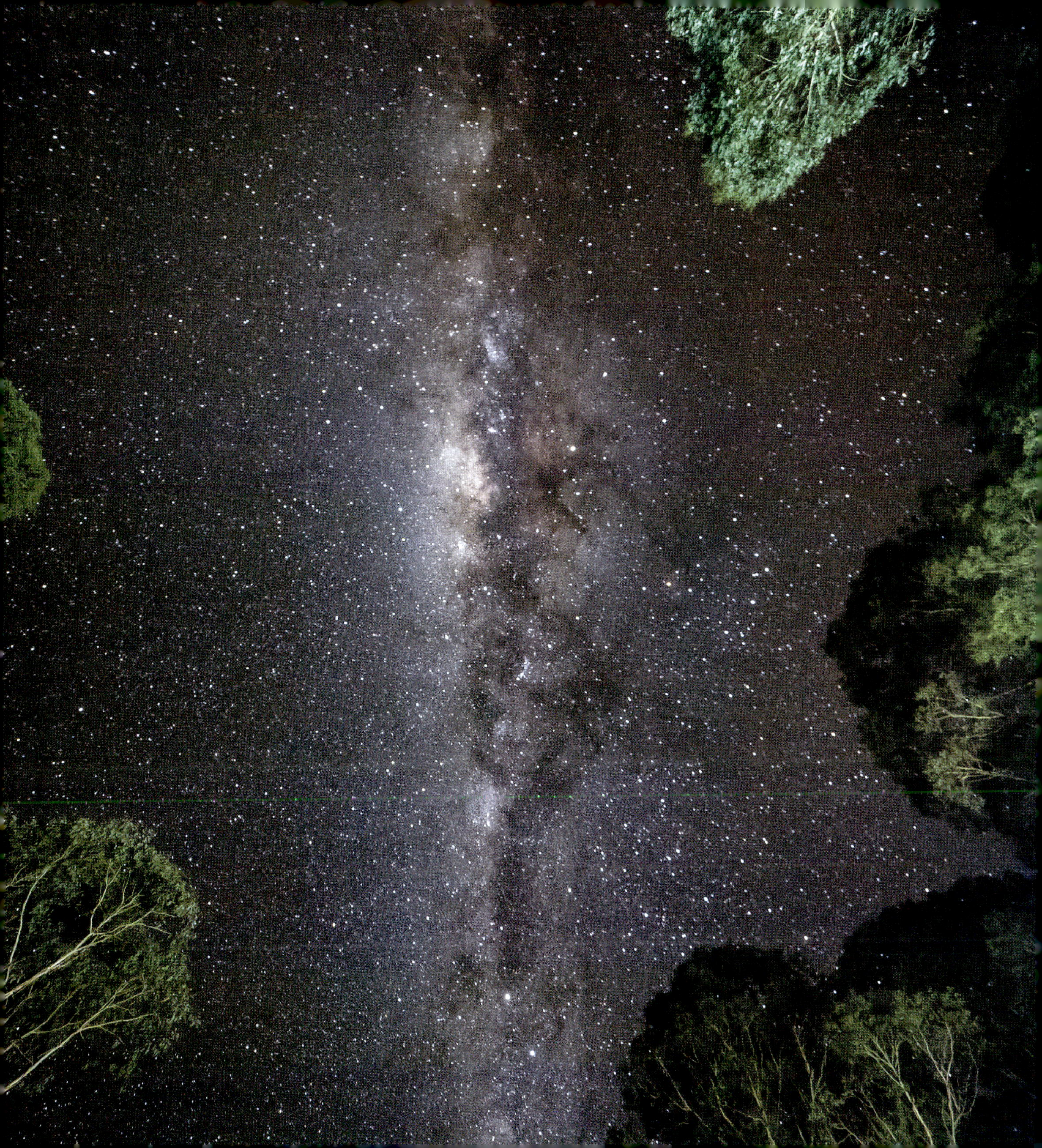

» **RIGHT** Fields of dead trees surround the road to the Great Lake region

» **OPPOSITE** Ancient ruins stand their ground as a Midlands summer storm approaches

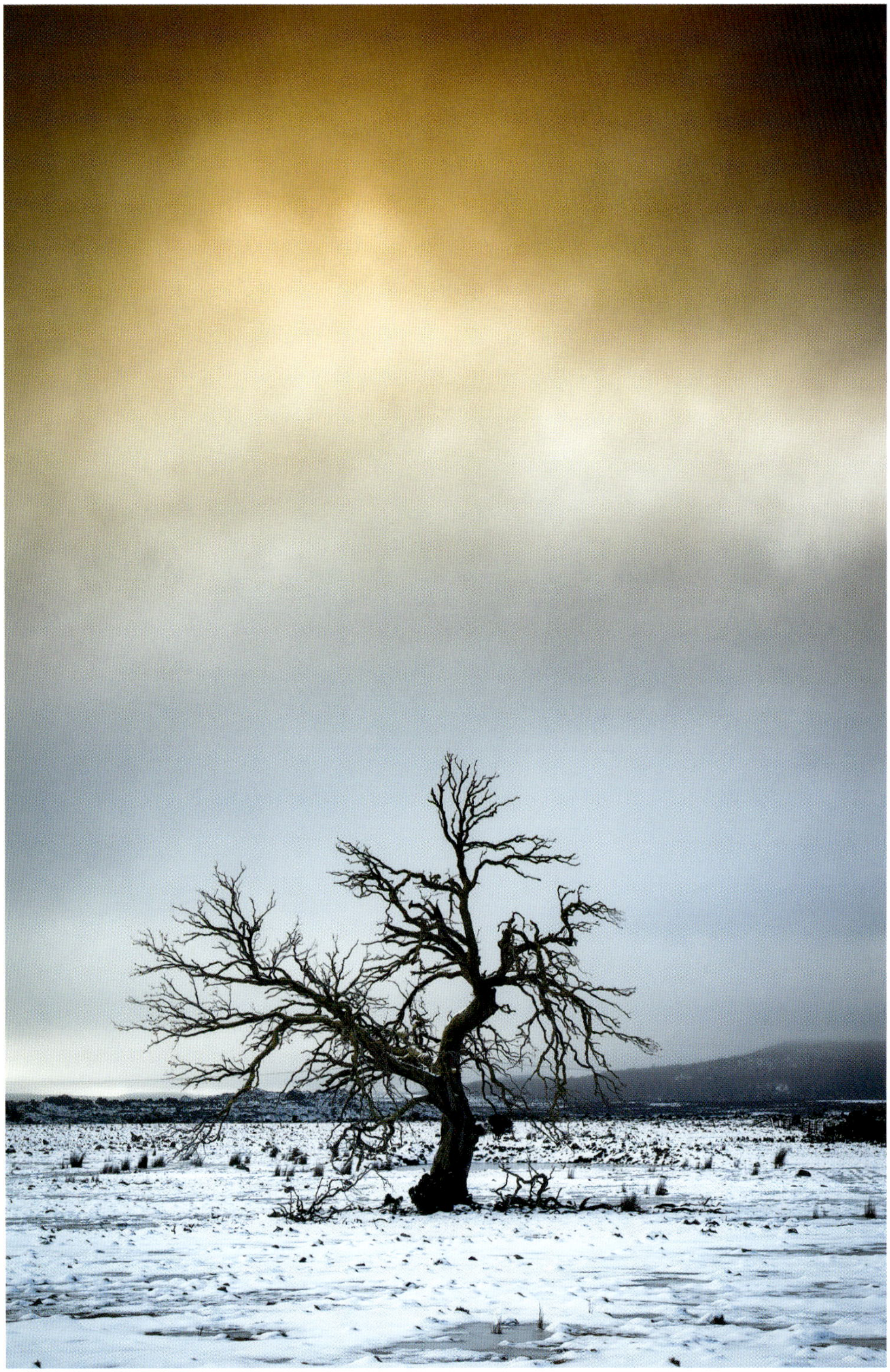

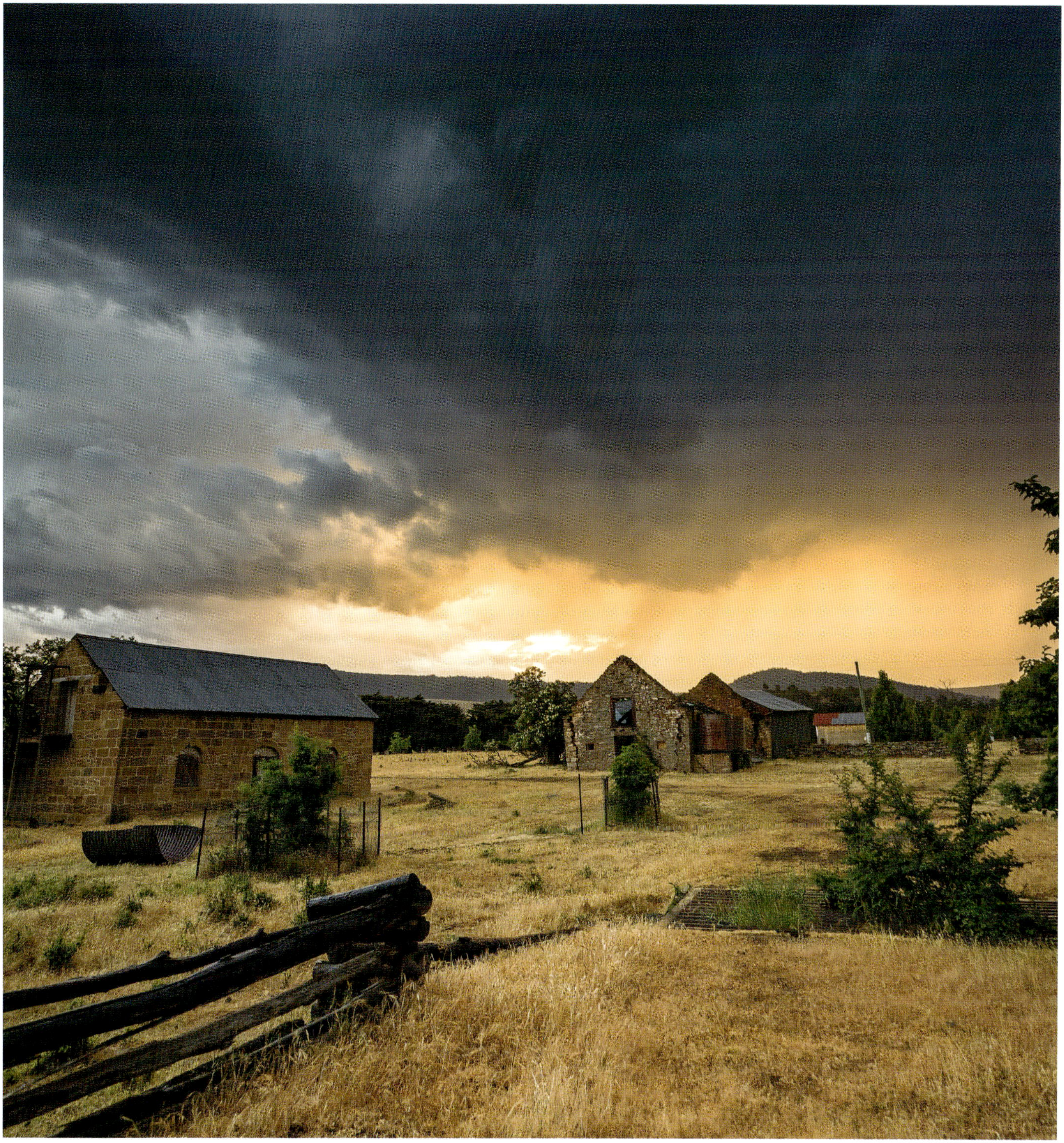

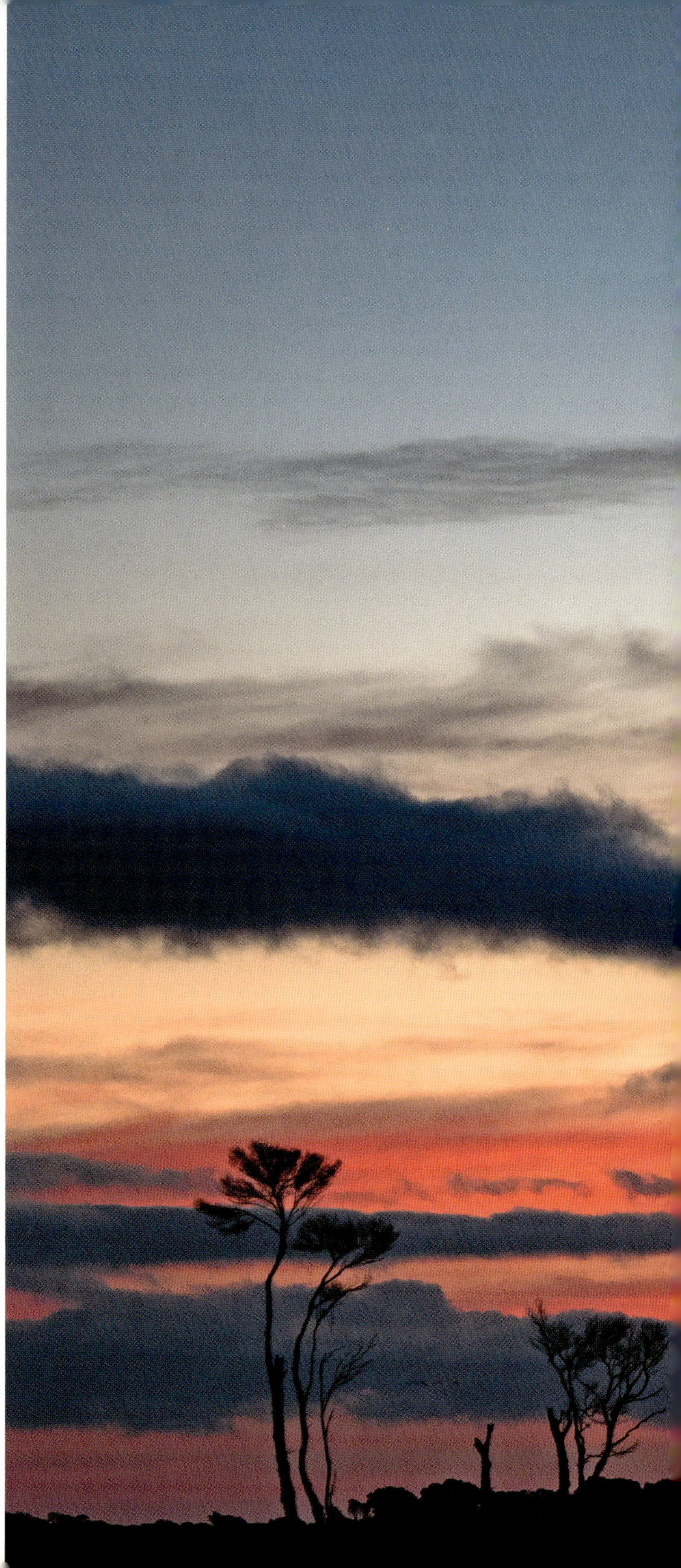

» **RIGHT** An island away from an island: Flinders Island has much to offer the intrepid traveller

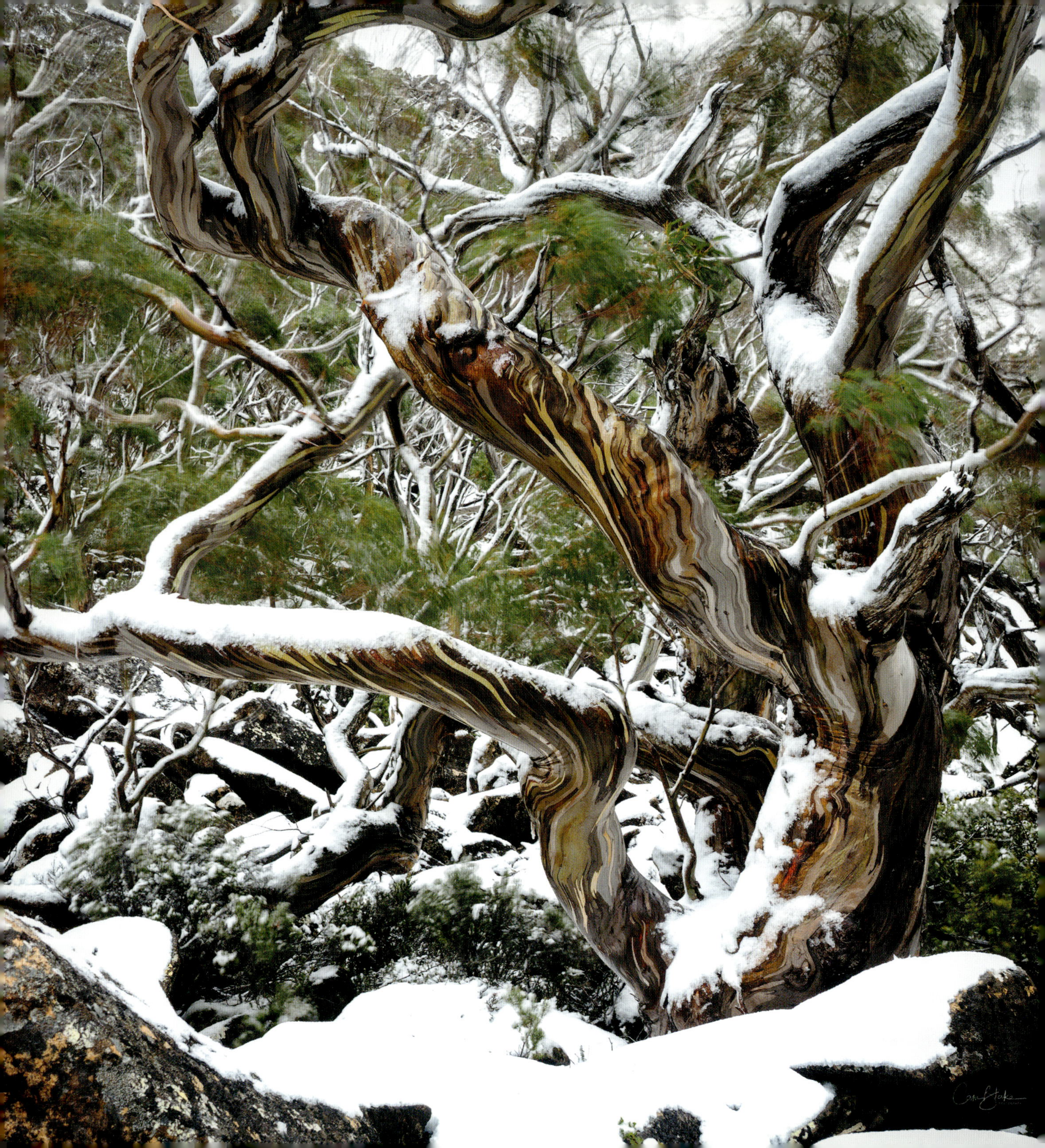

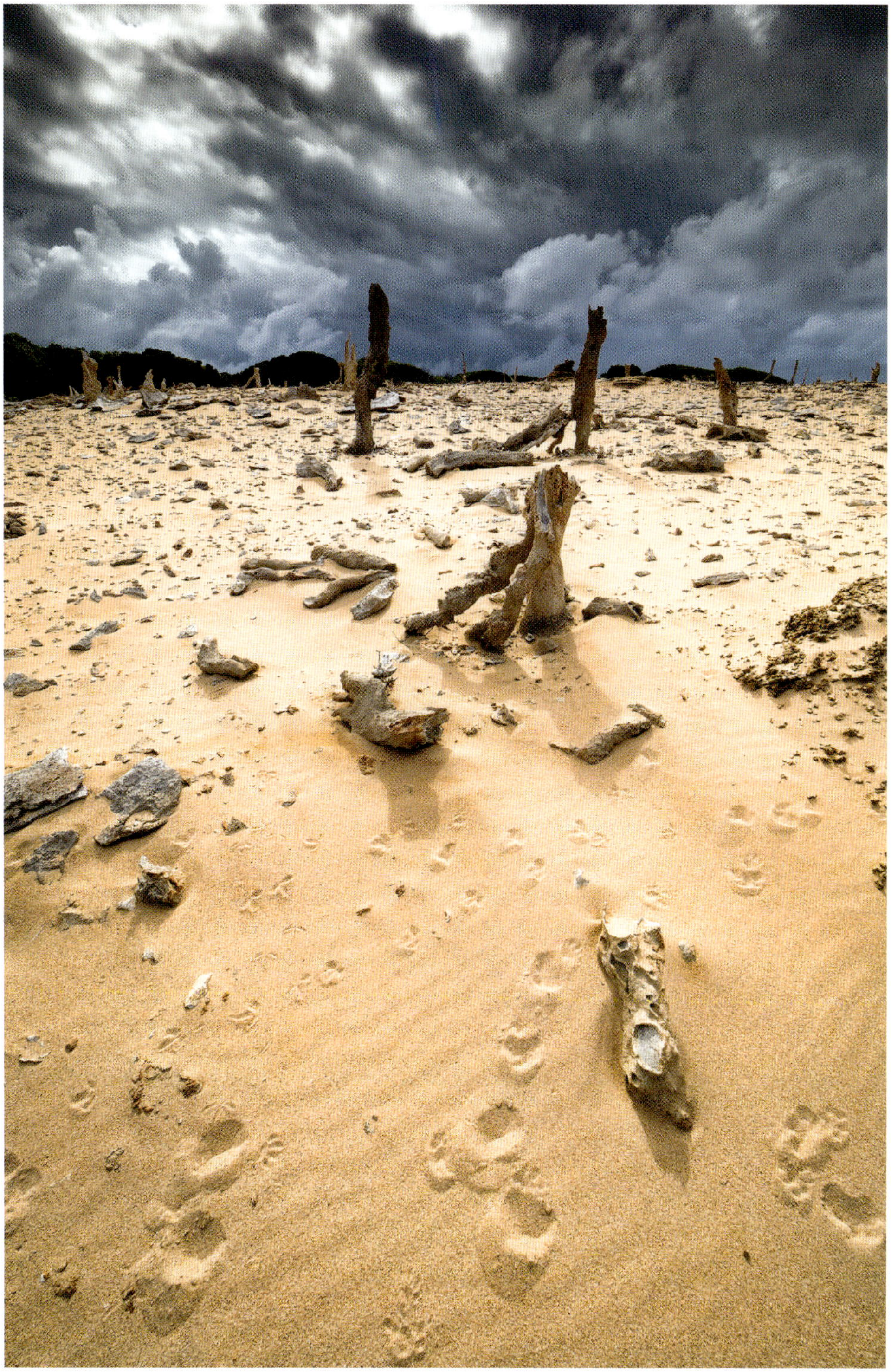

» **LEFT** King Island's 7000-year-old Calcified Forest

» **OPPOSITE** Nature doing her very best to impress with the magnificent patterns of a snow gum at Mount Field National Park

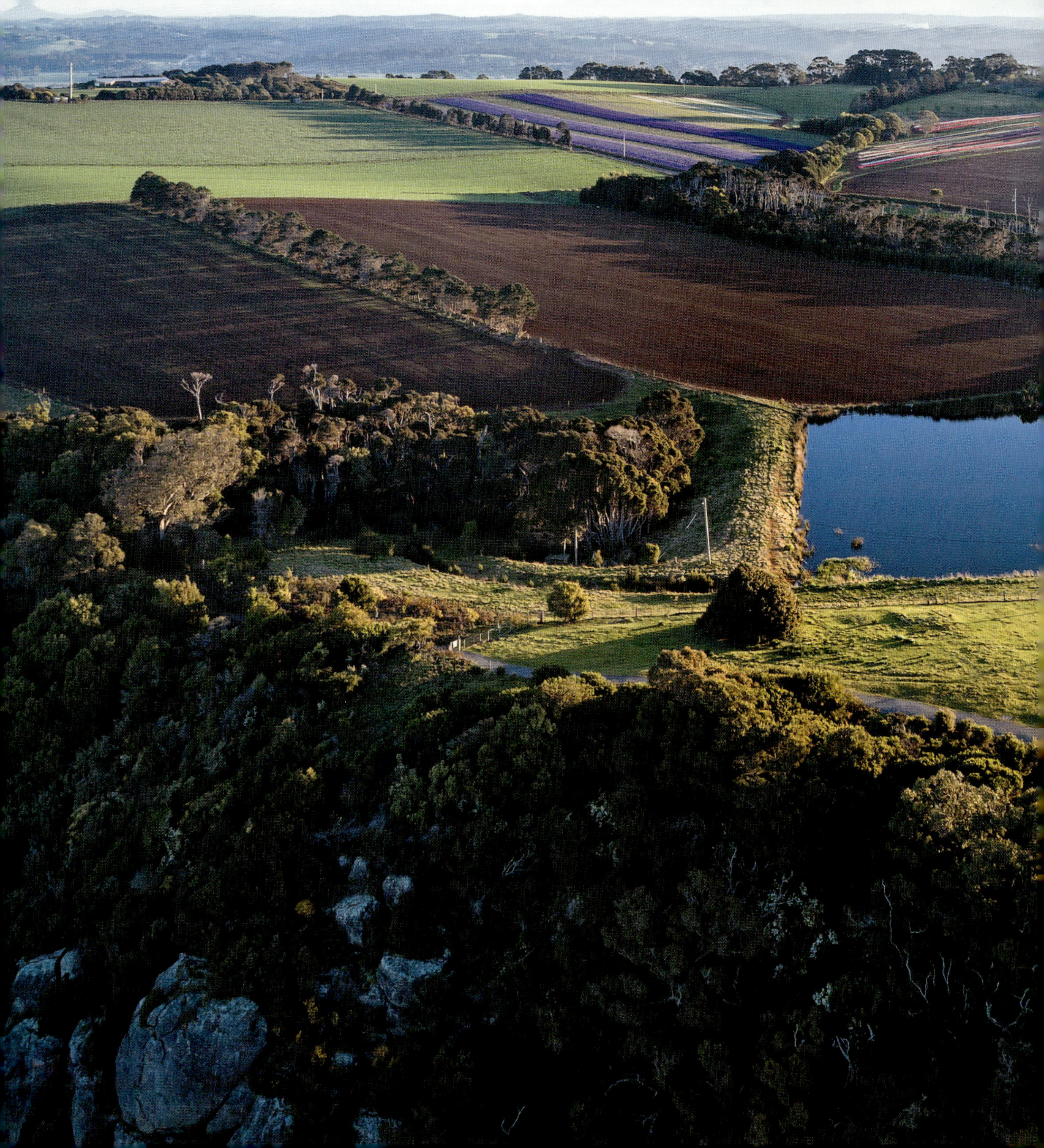

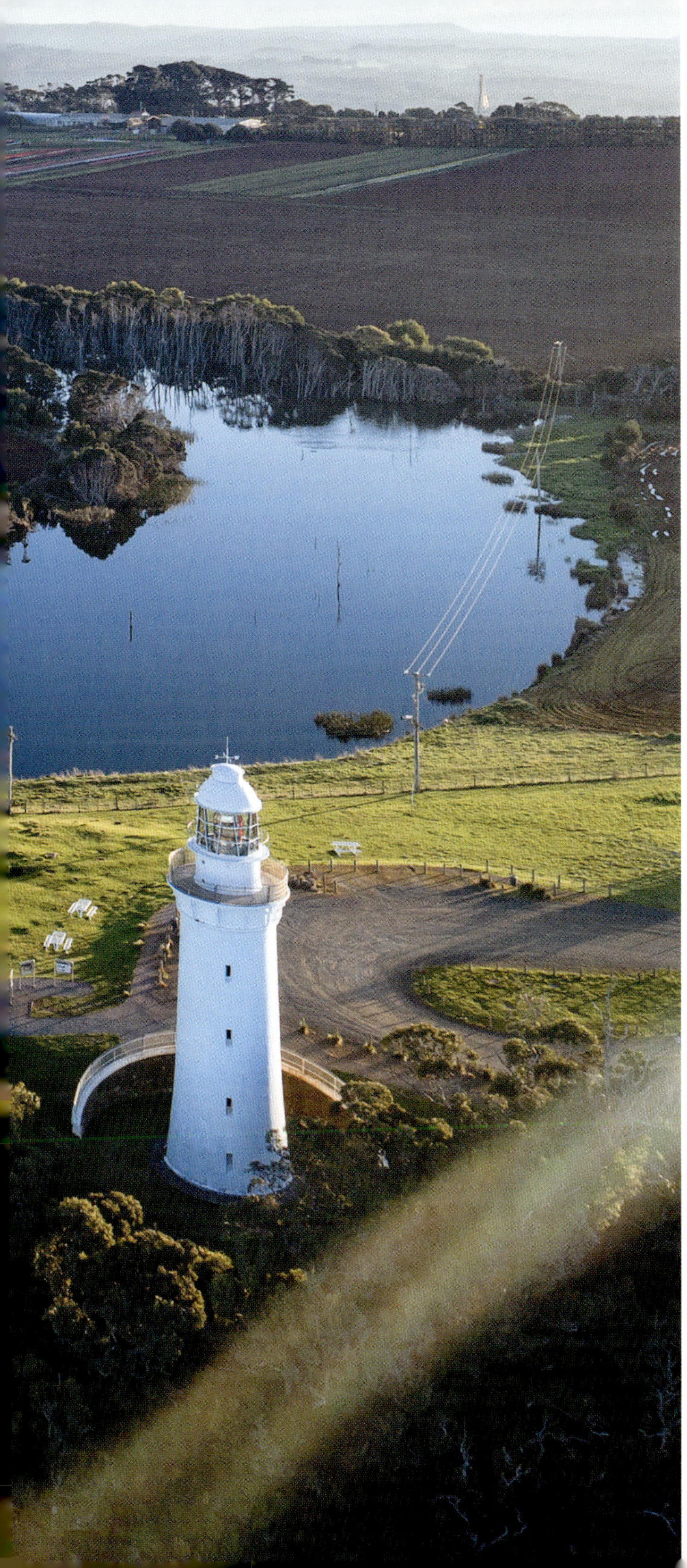

» LEFT The picturesque Table Cape Tulip farm and lighthouse bathed in afternoon sunshine

» OVERLEAF This historic pier now makes for a beautiful backdrop on King Island's east coast

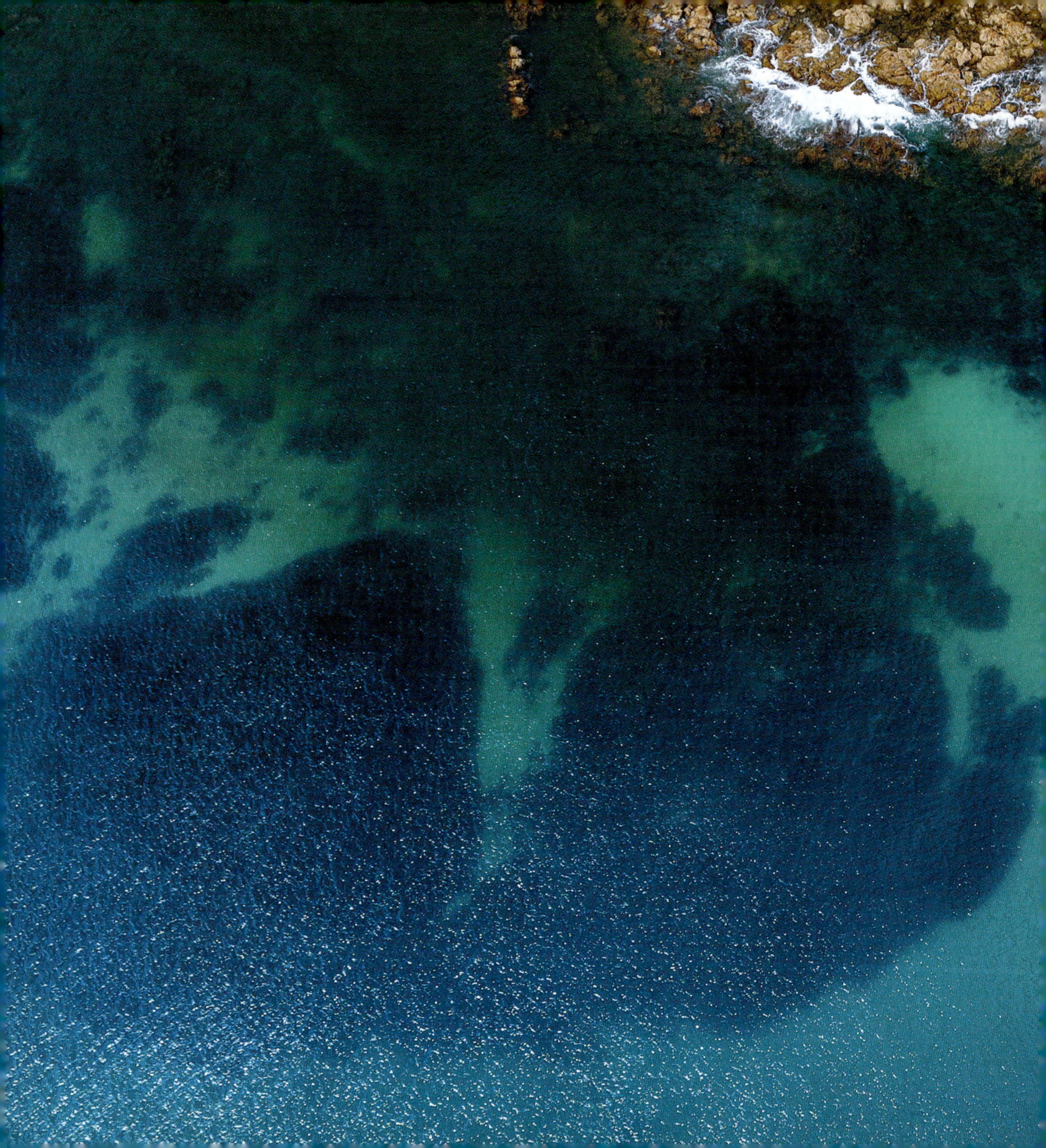

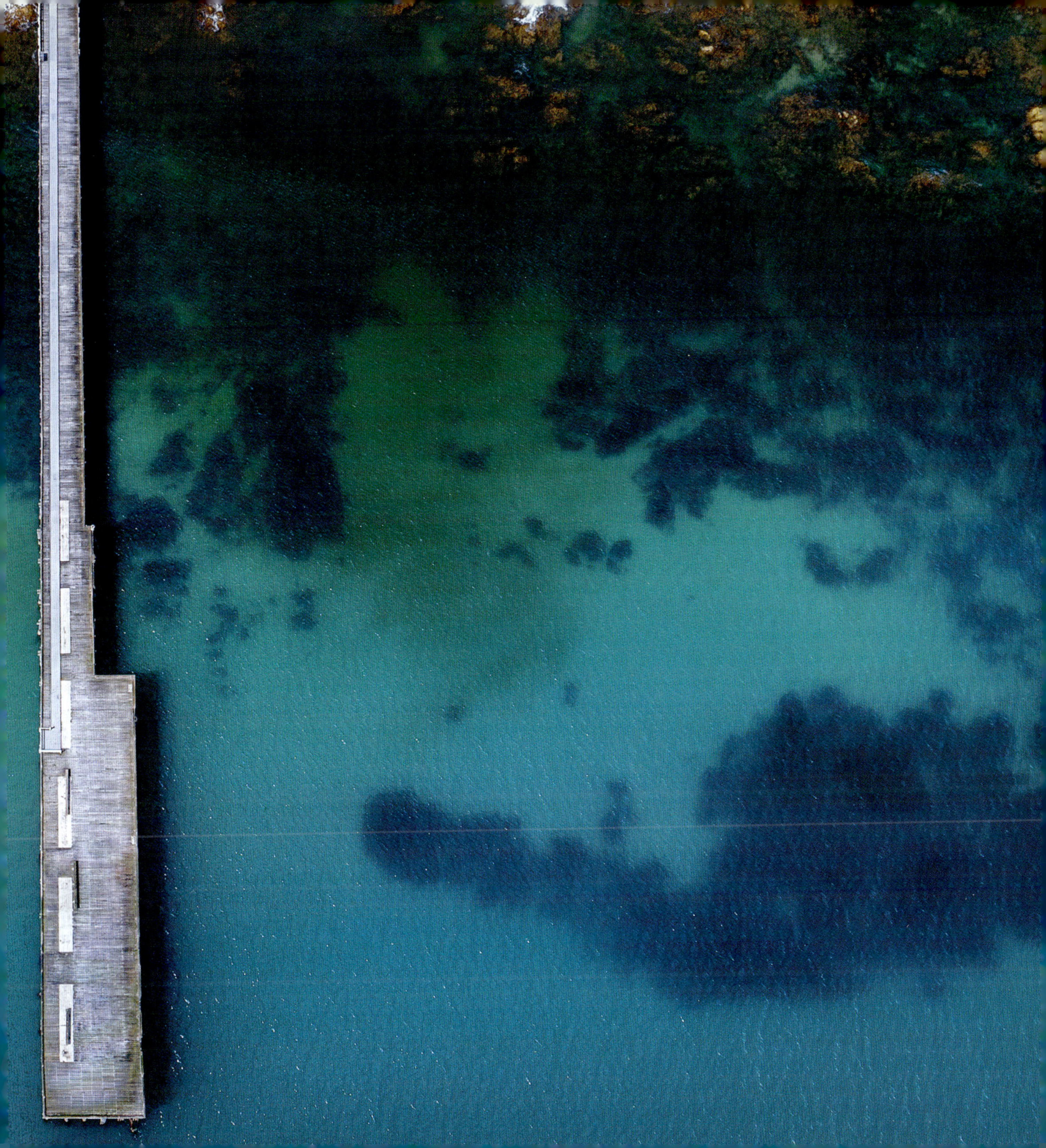

Published in 2018 by Hardie Grant Travel,
a division of Hardie Grant Publishing

Hardie Grant Travel (Melbourne)
Building 1, 658 Church Street
Richmond, Victoria 3121

Hardie Grant Travel (Sydney)
Level 7, 45 Jones Street
Ultimo, NSW 2007

www.hardiegrant.com/au/travel

Explore Australia is an imprint of Hardie Grant Travel

A catalogue record for this
book is available from the
National Library of Australia

Tasmania in Photos
ISBN 9781741175707

10 9 8 7 6 5 4 3 2 1

Publisher
Melissa Kayser

Project editor
Megan Cuthbert

Editor
Karen Tait

Editorial assistance
Aimee Barrett and Rosanna Dutson

Design
Erika Budiman

Typesetting
Megan Ellis

Prepress
Megan Ellis and Splitting Image Colour Studio

Printed in China by 1010 Printing International Limited

» **COVER TOP & BACK COVER** The tangled beauty of a Tasmanian forest floor; colours and patterns everywhere

» **COVER MIDDLE** Hobart's bustling Salamanca Market

» **COVER BOTTOM** Blue Lake is a great little stop en route to the north east region